MARKETING RESEARCH

MARKETING RESEARCH

Pallavi Bahuguna

CENTRUM PRESS
NEW DELHI-110002 (INDIA)

CENTRUM PRESS
H.O.: 4360/4, Ansari Road, Daryaganj,
New Delhi-110002 (India)
Tel: 23278000, 23261597, 23255577, 23286875
B.O.: No. 1015, Ist Main Road, BSK IIIrd Stage,
IIIrd Phase, IIIrd Block, Bangalore-560085 (INDIA)
Tel: 080-41723429
Email: centrumpress@gmail.com
Visit us at: www.centrumpress.com

Marketing Research

First Edition, 2011

ISBN 978-93-80921-19-8

PRINTED IN INDIA

Printed at Balaji Offset, Delhi.

Contents

Preface

Marketing Research concisely delivers an up-to-date review of a broad variety of marketing research topics. It takes an application-oriented approach, providing students with the tools and skills necessary to solve business problems and exploit business opportunities. The authors' years of experience in real-world marketing research is evident throughout, from their thorough treatment of qualitative research to their knowledgeable coverage of sample size rules-of-thumb, conducting a background literature review, and the importance of new market research tools and techniques.

This book broadly covers all the essential aspects related to Marketing Research, various tools and techniques of Research, Statistical techniques applied to research,changing demographics of research, relevance of Marketing research in business decision-making thus gives students a strong command of market research principles, while being short enough to use alongside your favourite cases or projects.

Author

Chapter 1

Definition, Scope, Limitations and Objectives

Market Research is a systematic, objective collection and analysis of data about a particular target market, competition, and/or environment.

It always incorporates some form of data collection whether it be secondary research or primary research which is collected direct from a respondent.

The purpose of any market research project is to achieve an increased understanding of the subject matter. With markets throughout the world becoming increasingly more competitive, market research is now on the agenda of many organisations, whether they be large or small.

MARKET RESEARCH PROCESS

To conduct market research, organisations may decide to undertake the project themselves or they might choose to commission it via a market research agency or consultancy. Whichever, before undertaking any research project, it is crucial to define the research objectives i.e. what are you trying to achieve from the research? and what do you need to know?After considering the objectives, Market Researchers can utilise many types of research techniques and methodologies to capture the data that they require.

All of the available methodologies either collect quantitative or qualitative information. The use of each very much depends on the research objectives but many believe that results are most useful when the two methods are combined.

Quantitative Research

Quantitative research is numerically oriented, requires significant attention to the measurement of market phenomena and often involves statistical analysis. For example, a bank might ask its customers to rate its overall service as either excellent, good, poor or very poor. This will provide quantitative information that can be analysed statistically. The main rule with quantitative research is that every respondent is asked the same series of questions. The approach is very structured and normally involves large numbers of interviews/ questionnaires.

Perhaps the most common quantitative technique is the 'market research survey'. These are basically projects that involve the collection of data from multiple cases – such as consumers or a set of products. Quantitative surveys can be conducted by using post, face-to-face, telephone, email or web techniques. The questionnaire is one of the more common tools for collecting data from a survey, but it is only one of a wide ranging set of data collection aids.

Qualitative Research

Qualitative research provides an understanding of how or why things are as they are. For example, a Market Researcher may stop a consumer who has purchased a particular type of bread and ask him or her why that type of bread was chosen. Unlike quantitative research there are no fixed set of questions but, instead, a topic guide is used to explore various issues in-depth. The discussion between the interviewer and the respondent is largely determined by the respondents' own thoughts and feelings.

As with quantitative techniques, there are also various types of qualitative methodologies. Research of this sort is mostly done face-to-face. One of the best-known techniques is market research group discussions. These are usually made up of 6 to 8 targeted respondents, a research moderator whose role is to ask the required questions, draw out answers, and encourage discussion, and an observation area usually behind one way mirrors, and video and/or audio taping facilities.

In addition, qualitative research can also be conducted on a 'one on one' basis i.e. an in-depth interview with a trained executive interviewer and one respondent, a paired depth, a triad and a mini group discussion.

Using Market Research Data

After compiling the data, Market Researchers evaluate it and make ceases and recommendations to their client or employer based upon their findings. They provide an organisation's management with information needed to make decisions on the promotion, distribution, design, and pricing of products or services – information that meets the initial research objectives.

Support MRW

INRODUCTION OF RESEARCH

We understand the world by asking questions and searching for answers. Our construction of reality depends on the nature of our inquiry.

Until the sixteenth century, human inquiry was primarily based on introspection. The way to know things was to turn inward and use logic to seek the truth. This paradigm had endured for a millennium and was a well-established conceptual framework for understanding the world. The seeker of knowledge was an integral part of the inquiry process.

A profound change occurred during the sixteenth and seventeenth centuries. Copernicus, Kepler, Galileo, Descartes, Bacon, Newton, and Locke presented new ways of examining nature. Our method of understanding the world came to rely on measurement and quantification. Mathematics replaced introspection as the key to supreme truths. The *Scientific Revolution* was born.

Objectivity became a critical component of the new scientific method. The investigator was an observer, rather than a participant in the inquiry process. A mechanistic view of the universe evolved. We believed that we could understand the whole by performing an examination of the individual parts. Experimentation and deduction became the tools of the scholar. For two hundred years, the new paradigm slowly evolved to become part of the reality framework of society. The *Age of Enlightenment* had arrived.

Scientific research methodology was very successful at explaining natural phenomena. It provided a systematic way of knowing. Western philosophers embraced this new structure of inquiry. Eastern philosophy continued to stress the importance of the one seeking knowledge. By the beginning of the twentieth century, a complete schism had occurred. Western and Eastern philosophies were mutually exclusive and incompatible.

Then something remarkable happened. Einstein's proposed that the observer was not separate from the phenomena being studied. Indeed, his theory of relativity actually stressed the role of the observer. Quantum mechanics carried this a step further and stated that the act of observation could change the thing being observed. The researcher was not simply an observer, but in fact, was an integral part of the process. In physics, Western and Eastern philosophies have met. This idea has not been incorporated into the standard social science research model, and today's social science community see themselves as objective observers of the phenomena being studied. However, "it is an established principle of measurement that instruments react with the things they measure." The concept of *instrument reactivity* states that an instrument itself can disturb the thing being measured.

PROBLEM RECOGNITION AND DEFINITION

All research begins with a question. Intellectual curiosity is often the foundation for scholarly inquiry. Some questions are not testable. The classic philosophical example is to ask, "How many angels can dance on the head of a pin?" While the question might elicit profound and thoughtful revelations, it clearly cannot be tested with an empirical experiment. Prior to Descartes, this is precisely the kind of question that would engage the minds of learned men. Their answers came from within. The modern scientific method precludes asking questions that cannot be empirically tested. If the angels cannot be observed or detected, the question is considered inappropriate for scholarly research.

A paradigm is maintained as much by the process of formulating questions as it is by the answers to those questions. By excluding certain types of questions, we limit the scope of our thinking. It is interesting to note, however, that modern physicists have began to ask the same kinds of questions posed by the Eastern philosophers. "Does a tree falling in the forest make a sound if nobody is there to hear it?" This seemingly trivial question is at the heart of the observer/observed dichotomy. In fact, quantum mechanics predicts that this kind of question cannot be answered with complete certainty. It is the beginning of a new paradigm.

Defining the goals and objectives of a research project is one of the most important steps in the research process. Clearly stated goals keep a research project focused. The process of goal definition usually begins by writing down the broad and general goals of the study. As the process continues, the goals become more clearly defined and the research issues are narrowed.

Exploratory research goes hand-in-hand with the goal clarification process. The literature review is especially important because it obviates the need to *reinvent the wheel* for every new research question. More importantly, it gives researchers the opportunity to build on each others work.

The research question itself can be stated as a hypothesis. A hypothesis is simply the investigator's belief about a problem. Typically, a researcher formulates an opinion during the literature review process. The process of reviewing other scholar's work often clarifies the theoretical issues associated with the research question. It also can help to elucidate the significance of the issues to the research community.

The hypothesis is converted into a null hypothesis in order to make it testable. "The only way to test a hypothesis is to eliminate alternatives of the hypothesis." Statistical techniques will enable us to reject a null hypothesis, but they do not provide us with a way to accept a hypothesis. Therefore, all hypothesis testing is indirect

MEANING AND SCOPE OF MARKETING RESEARCH

"Marketing Research is the function that links the consumer, customer and public to the marketer through information-information used to identify and define marketing opportunities and problems, generate, refine and evaluate marketing actions; monitor marketing performance; and improve understanding of marketing as a process." Marketing Research is systematic problem analysis, model building and fact finding for the purpose of important decision making and control in the marketing of goods and services. This may all sound rather complicated at the moment but you will soon understand it all. This site is a great way to brush up on your skills or to learn new information, like you would at online colleges. With so many subjects to choose from, you will be an expert in that field in no time. It uses scientific method. It is an objective process as it attempts to provide accurate authentic information. Marketing Research is sometimes defined as the application of scientific method in the solution of marketing problems.

Marketing Research plays a very significant role in identifying the needs of customers and meeting them in best possible way. The main task of Marketing Research is systematic gathering and analysis of information.

Before we proceed further, it is essential to clarify the relationship and difference between Marketing Research and Marketing Information System (MIS).Whatever information are generated by Marketing Research from internal sources, external sources, marketing intelligence agencies-consist the part of MIS.

MIS is a set of formalized procedures for generating, analyzing, storing and distributing information to marketing decision makers on an ongoing basis.

- While Marketing Research is done with a specific

purpose in mind with information being generated when it is conducted, MIS information is generated continuously.

- MIS is continuous entity while Marketing Research is a ad-hoc system.
- While in Marketing Research information is for specific purpose, so it is not rigid; in MIS information is more rigid and structured.

Marketing Research is essential for strategic market planning and decision making. It helps a firm in identifying what are the market opportunities and constraints, in developing and implementing market strategies, and in evaluating the effectiveness of marketing plans.

Marketing Research is a growing and widely used business activity as the sellers need to know more about their final consumers but are generally widely separated from those consumers. Marketing Research is a necessary link between marketing decision makers and the markets in which they operate.

Marketing Research includes various important principles for generating information which is useful to managers. These principles relate to the timeliness and importance of data, the significance of defining objectives cautiously and clearly, and the need to avoid conducting research to support decisions already made.

MARKETING RESEARCH PROCESS

Marketing research process is a set of six steps which defines the tasks to be accomplished in conducting a marketing research study. These include problem definition, developing an approach to problem, research design formulation, field work, data preparation and analysis, and report generation and presentation.

(shStages of marketing research process

Step 1: Problem Definition

The first step in any marketing research project is to define the problem. In defining the problem, the researcher should take into account the purpose of the study, the relevant background information, what information is needed, and how it will be used in decision making. Problem definition involves discussion with the decision makers, interviews with industry experts, analysis of secondary data, and, perhaps, some qualitative research, such as focus groups. Once the problem has been precisely defined, the research can be designed and conducted properly.

Step 2: Development of an Approach to the Problem

Development of an approach to the problem includes formulating an objective or theoretical framework, analytical models, research questions, hypotheses, and identifying characteristics or factors that can influence the research design. This process is guided by discussions with management and industry experts, case studies and simulations, analysis of secondary data, qualitative research and pragmatic considerations.

'Step 3: Research Design Formulation'

A research design is a framework or blueprint for conducting the marketing research project. The procedures necessary for obtaining the required information, and its purpose is to design a study that will test the hypotheses of interest, determine possible answers to the research questions, and provide the information needed for decision making. Conducting exploratory research, precisely defining the variables, and designing appropriate scales to measure them are also a part of the research design. The issue of how the data should be obtained from the respondents (for example, by conducting a survey or an experiment) must be addressed. It is also necessary to design a questionnaire and a sampling plan to select respondents for the study.

More formally, formulating the research design involves the following steps:

- Secondary data analysis
- Qualitative research
- Methods of collecting quantitative data (survey, observation, and experimentation)
- Definition of the information needed

- Measurement and scaling procedures
- Questionnaire design
- Sampling process and sample size
- Plan of data analysis

Step 4: Field Work or Data Collection

Data collection involves a field force or staff that operates either in the field, as in the case of personal interviewing (in-home, mall intercept, or computer-assisted personal interviewing), from an office by telephone (telephone or computer-assisted telephone interviewing), or through mail (traditional mail and mail panel surveys with prerecruited households). Proper selection, training, supervision, and evaluation of the field force helps minimize data-collection errors.

Step 5: Data Preparation and Analysis

Data preparation includes the editing, coding, transcription, and verification of data. Each questionnaire or observation form is inspected, or edited, and, if necessary, corrected. Number or letter codes are assigned to represent each response to each question in the questionnaire. The data from the questionnaires are transcribed or key-punched on to magnetic tape, or disks or input directly into the computer. Verification ensures that the data from the original questionnaires have been accurately transcribed, while data analysis, guided by the plan of data analysis, gives meaning to the data that have been collected. Univariate techniques are used for analyzing data when there is a single measurement of each element or unit in the sample, or, if there are several measurements of each element, each RCH variable is analysed in isolation. On the other hand, multivariate techniques are used for analyzing data when there are two or more measurements on each element and the variables are analysed simultaneously.

Step 6: Report Preparation and Presentation

The entire project should be documented in a written report which addresses the specific research questions identified, describes the approach, the research design, data collection, and data analysis procedures adopted, and presents the results and the major findings. The findings should be presented in a comprehensible format so that they can be readily used in the decision making process. In addition, an oral presentation should be made to management using tables, figures, and graphs to enhance clarity and impact.

For these reasons, interviews with experts are more useful in conducting marketing research for industrial firms and for products of a technical nature, where it is relatively easy to identify and approach the experts. This method is also helpful in situations where little information is available from other sources, as in the case of radically new products.

Chapter 2

Research and Business Decision

ROLE OF RESEARCH IN BUSINESS DECISION MAKING

When research is used for decision-making, it means we are using the methods of science to the art of management. Every organization operates under some degree of uncertainty. This uncertainty cannot be eliminated completely, although its can be minimized with the help of research methodology. Research in particularly important in the decision making process of various business organizations.

To choose the best line of action (in the light of growing competition and increasing uncertainty). Research in common context refers to a search for knowledge. It can also be defined as a scientific and systematic search for gaining information and knowledge on a specific topic or phenomena. In management research is extensively used in various areas. For example, We all know that, Marketing is the process of Planning and Executing the concepts, pricing, promotion and distribution of ideas, goods, and services to create exchange that satisfy individual and organizational objectives.

Thus, we can say that, the Marketing Concept requires Customer Satisfaction rather than Profit Maximization to be the goal of an organization. The organization should be Consumer oriented and should try to understand consumer's requirements and satisfy them quickly and efficiently, in ways that are beneficial to both the consumer and the organization.

This means that any organization should try to obtain information on consumer needs and gather market intelligence to help satisfy these needs efficiently. This can only be done only only by research. In this lecture as suggested, be discussing the role of research in management and its key ingredients.

But first let us understand the meaning of research. It will be clear after going through some important definitions of research.

Definition

Some of the definitions of Research are:

- Redman and Mory define research as a "systematized effort to gain new knowledge".
- Some people consider research as a movement, a movement from known to unknown. It is actually a voyage to discovery.
- Clifford Woody

"Research comprises of defining and redefining problems, formulating hypothesis or suggested solutions; making deductions and reaching ceases; and at last carefully testing the ceases to determine whether they fit the formulating hypothesis".

On evaluating these definitions we can conclude that Research refers to the systematic method consisting of

- Enunciating the problem,
- Formulating a hypothesis,
- Collecting the fact or data,
- Analyzing the facts and
- Reaching certain ceases either in the form of solutions towards the concerned problem or in certain generals for some theoretical formulation.

Market Research has become an important part in management decision-making. Marketing research is a critical part of such a Market intelligence system; it helps to improve management decision making by providing relevant, accurate, and timely information.

Every decision poses unique needs for information gathered through marketing research. Thus, we can say that marketing research is the function that links the

- Consumer,
- Customer,
- The public to the marketer through information.

Information used to identify and define marketing opportunities and problems;

- Generate,
- Refine, and evaluate marketing actions;
- Monitor marketing performance; and
- Improve understanding of marketing as a process.

In the nut-shell we see that Marketing research specifies:

- The information required to address these issues,
- Designs the method for collecting information,
- Manages and implements the data collection process, analyses,
- communicates the findings and their implications .

Intelligent use of Research Tools is the Key to Business Achievement

I hope the meaning of research is clear. Research provides a base for your business sound decision - making.

There are three parts involved in any of your systematic finding:

- Implicit question posed
- Explicit answer proposed
- Collection, analysis, and interpretation of the information leading from the question to answer Illustration

Consider the Statement: "We recommend that Model X-240 of music system be priced at Rs.10, 000/-" Marketing Research Manager forwarded this recommendation to Marketing Vice-President. Implicit Question What should be the selling price of model X-240?

Explicit Answer: The explicit answer is Rs.15000/=. The third part deals with the collection, analysis, and interpretation of the information leading from the question to the answer of Rs.15000/. Research is a systematic approach to gather information required for sound management decisions. Research is not synonymous to common sense. The difference lies in the methods and procedures adopted to reach a cease.

Characteristics of Research

- *Systematic Approach*: Each step must of your investigation be so planned that it leads to the next step. Planning and organization are part of this approach. A planned and organized research saves your time and money.
- *Objectivity*: It implies that True Research should attempt to find an unbiased answer to the decision-making problem.
- *Reproducibl*: A reproducible research procedure is one, which an equally competent researcher could duplicate, and from it deduces approximately the same results. Precise information regarding samples-methods, collection etc., should be specified.
- *Relevancy*:

It furnishes three important tasks:

  - It avoids collection of irrelevant information and saves time and money
  - It compares the information to be collected with researcher's criteria for action
  - It enables to see whether the research is proceeding in the right direction

- *Control*: Research is not only affected by the factors, which one is investigating but some other extraneous factors also. It is impossible to control all the factors. All the factors that we think may affect the study have to be controlled and accounted for. For Example Suppose we are studying the relationship between incomes and shopping behaviour, without controlling for education and age, it will be a height of folly, since our findings may reflect the effect of education and age rather than income.

Control Must Consider

- All the factors, which are under control, must be varied as per the study demands
- All those variables beyond the control should be recorded Structure of Research.

Most research projects share the same general structure. You might think of this structure as following the shape of an hourglass. The research process usually starts with a broad area of interest, the initial problem that the researcher wishes to study. For instance, the researcher could be interested in how to use computers to improve the performance of students in mathematics. But this initial interest is far too broad to study in any single research project (it might not even be addressable in a lifetime of research). The researcher has to narrow the question down to one that can reasonably be studied in a research project. This might involve formulating a hypothesis or a focus question.

For instance, the researcher might hypothesize that a particular method of computer instruction in math will improve the ability of elementary school students in a specific district. At the narrowest point of the research hourglass, the researcher is engaged in direct measurement or observation of the question of interest. Once the basic data is collected, the researcher begins to try to understand it, usually by analyzing it in a variety of ways. Even for a single hypothesis there are a number of analyses a researcher might typically conduct. At this point, the researcher begins to formulate some initial ceases about what happened as a result of the computerized math programmme. Finally, the researcher often will attempt to address the original broad question of interest by generalizing from the results of this specific study to other related situations. For instance, on the basis of strong results indicating that the math programmme had a positive effect on student performance, the researcher might conclude that other school districts similar to the one in the study might expect similar results.

Importance of Research in Management Decision

The role of research has greatly increased in the field of business and economy as a whole. The study of research methods provides you with the knowledge and skills you need to solve the problems and meet the challenges of today's modern pace of development.

Three factors stimulate the interest in a scientific research to decision making:

- The manager's increased need for more and better information.
- The availability of improved techniques and tools to meet this need.
- The resulting information overload.

The usefulness and contribution of research in assisting marketing decisions is so crucial that it has given rise to the opening of a new field altogether called 'marketing research'. Market research is basically the systematic gathering, recording and analyzing of the facts about business problems with a view to investigate the structure and development of a market for the purpose of formulating efficient policies for purchasing, production and sales. Research with regard to demand and market factors has great utility in business. Market analysis has become an integral tool of business policy.

Once sales forecasting is done, the Master Production Schedule (MPS) and Material Requirement Planning (MRP) can be efficiently done within the limits of the projected capacity based on the MPS Budgetary control can be made more efficient, thus replacing subjective business decisions with more logical and scientific decisions.

Modern industry with its large-scale operations tends to create a gulf between the customer and the manufacturer. Particularly when business is too big and operations are too far-flung, one cannot depend upon casual contacts and personal impressions. Research methodology has been developed as the tool by which business executives keep in touch with their customers. If an entrepreneur has to make sound decisions, he must know who has customers are and what they want. To a certain extent he relies on his salesmen and his dealers to supply him with market information but in recent years, more and more firms/executives have turned to research methodology as a medium of communication between the customer and the company.

Marketing research is the link between the manufacturer and the consumer and the means of providing consumer-orientation in all aspects of the marketing function. It is the instrument of obtaining the knowledge about the market and consumer through objective methods, which guard against the manufacturer's subjective bias. Many Researchers define marketing research as gathering, recording and analyzing of all facts about problems relating to the transfer and sale of goods and services from producer to consumer. Research methodology is an essential prerequisite for consumeroriented marketing.

It is necessary for developing the marketing strategy where in factors under the control of the organization, viz., product distribution system, advertising, promotion and price can be utilized so as to obtain maximum results in the context of the factors outside the control of the organization viz., economic environment, competitor and laws of land. Application of Marketing Research Following are a number of examples on the applications of marketing research. They clearly bring out how marketing research has been helpful in resolving marketing problems or in identifying opportunities or the development of new products.

- A pharmaceutical company3 carried out a study on the prescription behaviour for a major brand on account of its declining sales. The study brought out interesting and even startling findings on a number of aspects such as the relationship between the sales and the age of the brand, its regular promotion, its core therapeutic emphasis and the role of retailers in servicing prescriptions. Prior to the study, all these aspects had been only a matter of conjecture all the while. On the basis of findings of the study, the company changed its marketing strategy. This enabled it to regain the lost market share of its brand.
- Malayala Manorama, which is Kerala's largest publication group, has recently launched a monthly women's magazine in Hindi, Vanita. While launching this magazine, the management observed that it was convinced through market research that there was a huge vacuum in the Hindi magazine segment. This

new magazine Vanita has been positioned as a partner and friend that the modern woman can identify with. The first print run of Vanita was one lakh copies. Indications are that within a short time it may become one of the popular Hindi magazines.

- Cadbury India Limited launched Picnic from its international portfolio in February 1998. It is wrapped in vibrant colours of red, blue and yellow in conformity with its international packaging. Earlier, Cadbury India Limited commissioned a consumer research study in Mumbai. The results of this study were encouraging and showed that the Indian youth is always interested in experimenting with new food options.
- Procter and Gamble (P&G) launched Menthol, an international vibrant of Head and Shoulders. This joins the extra-conditioning anti-dandruff shampoo of the same brand. The company conducted a market research study prior to its launch. The findings of the study indicated a distinct need for a menthol-based shampoo. The study showed that in hot and humid conditions as in India, consumers prefer a shampoo which not only removes dandruff but also provides a cool and tingling sensation to the scalp.
- Another example4 from PandG shows how marketing research is used to identify new opportunities in the marketplace. The company was getting a lot of data on Vicks- Vapourub. The analysis of such data revealed that the most common symptom of cold was a headache and that majority of adults typically take a pill to cure it. This disclosed an opportunity for a product that can treat the headache as well as the other symptoms. The company thus launched Action 500. It not only treated headache but also gave relief from blocked nose. Marketing research can therefore lead to the development of a new product.
- Pepsi Foods5 has assigned great importance to

marketing research. Through research it gets systematic information about its markets and its customers.

All its research is done by the IMRB. Broadly, research studies done for Pepsi Foods fall in the following three areas:

- Studies undertaken on a continuous basis like marketing tracking studies and retail audits.
- Studies that are commissioned for specific marketing problems faced by the company.
- Studies done from time to time as per the requirement of the company such as a study to ascertain the effectiveness of an ad campaign. All these three types of research studies have tremendously helped Pepsi Foods to strengthen its position in the market. It feels the pulse of the market and is always in touch with the latest developments in the market.

- Another multinational company Whirlpool Asia lays considerable emphasis on marketing research. In this company, every activity, strategy and decision is based on data collected through the research process. It believes in planning research in advance though it is rather difficult. It strives to have a meaningful dialogue with the consumer in order to know his real opinion about its products, what difficulties he experiences and what suggestions he has to offer. Information thus received proves to be quite useful to the company in modifying its products or in evolving new ones. Whirlpool has gained an insight into the various segments in the market. In India, it has segmented the market on the basis of the different stages of the product life cycle. We hope you have the clear picture of the functions of the manager in an organization and the role of research in decision-making.

On the basis of the functions we can state some of the general objectives of Managerial Research:

- Decision-making objectives

- Economic and business objectives
- Policy objectives
- Product development
- Profit objectives
- Human Resource Development objectives
- Market objectives
  a) Innovation objectives
  b) Customer satisfaction objectives
- Promotional objectives
- Corporate change objectives

Role of Research in Important Areas

Through research, an executive can quickly get a synopsis of the current scenario, which improves his information base for making sound decisions affecting future operations of the enterprise. The following are the major areas in which research plays a key role in making effective decisions.

Marketing

Marketing research is undertaken to assist the marketing function. Marketing research stimulates the flow of marketing data from the consumer and his environment to marketing information system of the enterprise.

Market research involves the process of:

- Systematic collection
- Compilation
- Analysis
- Interpretation of relevant data for marketing decisions

This information goes to the executive in the form of data. On the basis of this data the executive develop plans and programmers. Advertising research, packaging research, performance evaluation research, sales analysis, distribution channel, etc., may also be considered in management research.

Research tools are applied effectively for studies involving:

- Demand forecasting
- Consumer buying behaviour
- Measuring advertising effectiveness

- Media selection for advertising
- Test marketing
- Product positioning
- Product potential

Marketing Research

- *Product Research*: Assessment of suitability of goods with respect to design and price.
- *Market Characteristics Research (Qualitative)*: Who uses the product? Relationship between buyer and user, buying motive, how a product is used, analysis of consumption rates, units in which product is purchased, customs and habits affecting the use of a product, consumer attitudes, shopping habits of consumers, brand loyalty, research of special consumer groups, survey of local markets, basic economic analysis of the consumer market, etc.
- *Size of Market (Quantitative)*: Market potential, total sales quota, territorial sales quota, quota for individuals, concentration of sales and advertising efforts; appraisal of efficiency, etc.
- Competitive position and Trends Research
- *Sales Research*: Analysis of sales records.
- *Distribution Research*: Channels of distribution, distribution costs.
- *Advertising and Promotion Research*: Testing and evaluating, advertising and promotion
- New product launching and Product Positioning.

Production

Research helps you in an enterprise to decide in the field of production on:

- What to produce
- How much to produce
- When to produce
- For whom to produce

Some of the areas you can apply research are:

- Product development

- Cost reduction
- Work simplification
- Profitability improvement
- Inventory control

Materials: The materials department uses research to frame suitable policies regarding:

- Where to buy
- How much to buy
- When to buy
- At what prices to buy.

Human Resource Development You must be Aware that The Human Resource Development department uses research to study wage rates, incentive plans, cost of living, employee turnover rates, employment trends, and performance appraisal. It also uses research effectively for its most important activity namely manpower planning.

Solving Various Operational and Planning Problems of

Business and Industry Various types of researches, e.g., market research, operations research and motivational research, when combined together, help in solving various complex problems of business and industry in a number of ways. These techniques help in replacing intuitive businessdecisions by more logical and scientific decisions

Government and Economic System

Research helps a decision maker in a number of ways, e.g., it can help in examining the consequences of each alternative and help in bringing out the effect on economic conditions. Various examples can be quoted such as' problems of big and small industries due to various factors–up gradation of technology and its impact on lab our and supervisory deployment, effect of government's liberal policy, WTO and its new guidances, ISO 9000/14000 standards and their impact on our exports allocation of national resources on national priority basis, etc. Research lays the foundation for all Government Policies in our economic system. We all are aware of the fact that research is applied for brining out union finance budget and railway budget every year. Government also uses research for economic planning and optimum utilization of resources for the development of the country. For systematic collection of information on the economic and social structure of the country you need Research. Such types of information indicate what is happening to the national economy and what changes are taking place.

Social Relationships

Research in social sciences is concerned with both-knowledge for self and knowledge for helping in solving immediate problems of human relations. It is a sort of formal training, which helps a individual in a better way, e.g.

- It helps professionals to earn their livelihood
- It helps students to know how to write and report various findings.
- It helps philosophers and thinkers in their new thin kings and ideas.
- It helps in developing new styles for creative work.
- It may help researchers, in general, to generalize new theories.

Types of Research

On the basis of the fundamental objectives of the research, we can classify research into two types:

Exploratory Research

Many times a decision maker is grappling with broad and poorly defined problems. If you attempt to secure better definitions by analytic thinking, it may be the wrong approach and may even be counter productive counter productive in the sense that this approach may lead to a definitive answer to the wrong question. Exploratory research uses a less formal approach. It pursues several, possibilities simultaneously and in a sense it is not quite sure of its objective. Exploratory research is designed to provide a background, to familiarize and, as the word implies, just "explore", the general subject.

A part of exploratory research is the investigation of relationships among variables without knowing why they are studied. It borders on an, idle curiosity approach, differing from it only in that the investigator thinks there may be a payoff in the application some where in the forest of questions.

Three typical approaches in exploratory research are:

- The literature survey,
- The experience survey, and
- The analysis of "insight-stimulating" examples

The literature search is fast, economical way to develop a better understanding of a problem area in which you are investigating and have limited experience and knowledge. It also familiarizes you with past research results, data sources, and the type of data available. The experience survey concentrates on persons who are particularly knowledgeable in the particular area. In this representative samples are not desired. A covering of widely divergent views is better. Researchers are not looking for ceases; they are looking for ideas. The analysis of specific examples is a sort of case study approach, but again, researchers are looking for some fresh possible divergent views.

Conclusive Research

Exploratory research gives rise to several hypotheses, which you will have to tested for drawing definite ceases. These ceases when tested for validity lay the structure for your decision-making. Conclusive research is used for this purpose of testing the hypotheses generated by exploratory research.

Conclusive research can further be classified as:

- Descriptive
- Experimental.

Descriptive Research

Descriptive research as the name suggests is designed to describe something- for example, the characteristics of users of a given product; the degree to which product use varies with income, age, sex or other characteristics; or the number who saw a specific television commercial. To be of maximum benefit, a descriptive study must only collect, data for a definite purpose. Your objective and understanding should be clear and specific. Descriptive studies vary in the degree to which a specific hypothesis is the guide. It allows both implicit and explicit hypotheses to be tested depending on the research problem. For Example: A cereal company may find its sales declining. On the basis of market feedback the company may hypothesise that teenage children do not eat its cereal for breakfast. A descriptive study can then be designed to test this hypothesis.

Experimental Research

Experimentation will refer to that process of research in which one or more variables are manipulated under conditions, which permit the collection of data, which show the effects.

Experiments will create situation so that you as a researcher can obtain the particular data needed and can measure the data accurately. Experiments are artificial in the sense that the situations are usually created for testing purposes. This artificiality is the essence of the experimental method, since it gives you more control over the factors you are studying.

If you can control the factors, which are present in a given situation, you can obtain more conclusive evidence of cause and effect relationships between any two of them. Thus, the ability to set up a situation for the express purpose of observing and recording accurately the effect on one factor when another is deliberately changed permits you to accept or reject hypothesis beyond reasonable doubt If the objective is to validate in a resounding manner the cause and effect relationship among variables, then undoubtedly experiments are much more effective than descriptive technique Thus, we can conclude that:

- Research methodology minimizes the degree of uncertainty involved in management decisions. Research lays the structure for decision-making.
- Research is not synonymous with common sense.

- Research is characterized by - systematic, objective, reproducible, relevance, and control.
- The role of research in the important areas of management has been briefly covered. The areas include marketing, production, banking, materials, human resource development, and government.
- Research process involves the five important steps-problem definition, research design, data collection, data analysis, and interpretation of results. All these steps have been explained in detail with their key elements.
- We have dichotomized the types of research into - exploratory, and conclusive.
- While exploratory research enables the researcher to generate hypotheses, they are tested for validity by the conclusive research.
- Conclusive research could be further divided into-descriptive, and experimental.
- While the descriptive procedures merely test the hypotheses, the experimental research establishes in a more effective manner the cause and effect relationships among variables.

BASIC AND APPLIED RESEARCH

Basic research-is intended to expand the body of knowledge in a field or to provide knowledge for use of others Applied researchused for solving a particular problem or guiding a specific decision.

Basic Research

- The U.S. Bureau all of census is the world's largest fac gathering agency. All its data are for use by others including market.
- The research in an advertising agency studies the result of use of coupons versus rebate as demand stimulation tactics, but not in a specific instance or in relation to a specific client's purpose.
- A study conducted by 2 professors measuring diff

between high level and low performing sales representatives, relative to their job satisfaction and their job turnover.

Applied Marketing Research

- *Hanes, hosiery company, found how to solve a longstanding industry problem*: How to sell hosiery through super markets. Hanes conducted a series of marketing studies thank R & D with strategic insights into the required one-side product design, how to display and advertise.

Result: The 'L' Eggs brand that revolutionised marketing.

- IBM's entry into PC. (Apple had moved into it earlier). This was IBM's biggest challenge.
  - Q. 1. Which market segment was best strategically?
  - Q. 2. What is the ideal product?
  - Q. 3. What is ideal dist for target market? Marketing research guided IBM's decision to these problems and they proved, when the new PC captured major market share.

Camp bell soup-They put their world favours red and white soup labels or cans for its whole life. They had periodic studies of consumer preferences. When the first sighs of the can's waving popularity cause in, camp bell accelerated consumer testing of its replacement. Plastic containers were perfected, which may be the way your soup is package.

Chapter 3

Research Design

AN OVERVIEW

Creating the Research Design

Defining a research problem provides a format for further investigation. A well-defined problem points to a method of investigation. There is no one best method of research for all situations. Rather, there are a wide variety of techniques for the researcher to choose from. Often, the selection of a technique involves a series of trade-offs. For example, there is often a trade-off between cost and the quality of information obtained. Time constraints sometimes force a trade-off with the overall research design. Budget and time constraints must always be considered as part of the design process.

Many authors have categorized research design as either *descriptive* or *causal*. Descriptive studies are meant to answer the questions of who, what, where, when and how. Causal studies are undertaken to determine how one variable affects another. McDaniel and Gates (1991) state that the two characteristics that define causality are *temporal sequence* and *concomitant variation*.

The word *causal* may be a misnomer. The mere existence of a temporal relationship between two variables does not prove or even imply that A causes B. It is never possible to prove causality. At best, we can theorize about causality based on the relationship between two or more variables, however, this is prone to misinterpretation. Personal bias can lead to totally erroneous statements. For example, Blacks often score lower on I.Q. scores than their White counterparts. It would be irresponsible to conclude that ethnicity causes high or low I.Q. scores. In social science research, making false assumptions about causality can delude the researcher into ignoring other (more important) variables.

There are three basic methods of research:

- Survey,
- Observation, and
- Experiment. Each method has its advantages and disadvantages.

The *survey* is the most common method of gathering information in the social sciences. It can be a face-to-face interview, telephone, or mail survey. A personal interview is one of the best methods obtaining personal, detailed, or in-depth information. It usually involves a lengthy questionnaire that the interviewer fills out while asking questions. It allows for extensive probing by the interviewer and gives respondents the ability to elaborate their answers. Telephone interviews are similar to face-to-face interviews. They are more efficient in terms of time and cost, however, they are limited in the amount of in-depth probing that can be accomplished, and the amount of time that can be allocated to the interview. A mail survey is generally the most cost effective interview method. The researcher can obtain opinions, but trying to meaningfully probe opinions is very difficult.

Observation research monitors respondents' actions without directly interacting with them. It has been used for many years by A.C. Nielsen to monitor television viewing habits. Psychologists often use one-way mirrors to study behaviour. Social scientists often study societal and group behaviours by simply observing them. The fastest growing form of observation research has been made possible by the bar code scanners at cash registers, where purchasing habits of consumers can now be automatically monitored and summarized.

In an *experiment*, the investigator changes one or more variables over the course of the research. When all other variables are held constant (except the one being manipulated), changes in the dependent variable can be explained by the change in the independent variable. It is usually very difficult to control all the variables in the environment. Therefore, experiments are generally restricted to laboratory models where the investigator has more control over all the variables.

SAMPLING

It is incumbent on the researcher to clearly define the target population. There are no strict rules to follow, and the researcher must rely on logic and judgment. The population is defined in keeping with the objectives of the study.

Sometimes, the entire population will be sufficiently small, and the researcher can include the entire population in the study. This type of research is called a *census* study because data is gathered on every member of the population.

Usually, the population is too large for the researcher to attempt to survey all of its members. A small, but carefully chosen *sample* can be used to represent the population. The sample reflects the characteristics of the population from which it is drawn.

Sampling methods are classified as either *probability* or *nonprobability*. In probability samples, each member of the population has a known probability of being selected. Probability methods include random sampling, systematic sampling, and stratified sampling. In nonprobability sampling, members are selected from the population in some nonrandom manner.

These include convenience sampling, judgment sampling, quota sampling, and snowball sampling. The other common form of nonprobability sampling occurs by accident when the researcher inadvertently introduces nonrandomness into the sample selection process. The advantage of probability sampling is that *sampling error* can be calculated. Sampling error is the degree to which a sample might differ from the population. When inferring to the population, results are reported plus or minus the sampling error. In nonprobability sampling, the degree to which the sample differs from the population remains unknown.

- *Random sampling:* Is the purest form of probability sampling. Each member of the population has an equal chance of being selected. When there are very large populations, it is often difficult or impossible to identify every member of the population, so the pool of available subjects becomes biased. Random sampling is frequently used to select a specified number of records from a computer file.
- *Systematic sampling*: Is often used instead of random sampling. It is also called an *Nth name selection* technique. After the required sample size has been calculated, every Nth record is selected from a list of population members. As long as the list does not contain any hidden order, this sampling method is as good as the random sampling method. Its only advantage over the random sampling technique is simplicity.
- *Stratified sampling*: Is commonly used probability method that is superior to random sampling because it reduces sampling error. A stratum is a subset of the population that share at least one common characteristic. The researcher first identifies the relevant stratums and their actual representation in the population. Random sampling is then used to select subjects for each stratum until the number of subjects in that stratum is proportional to its frequency in the population.
- *Convenience sampling*: Is used in exploratory research where the researcher is interested in getting an inexpensive approximation of the truth. As the name implies, the sample is selected because they are convenient. This nonprobability method is often used during preliminary research efforts to get a gross estimate of the results, without incurring the cost or time required to select a random sample.
- *Judgment sampling*: Is a common nonprobability method. The researcher selects the sample based on judgment. This is usually and extension of

convenience sampling. For example, a researcher may decide to draw the entire sample from one "representative" city, even though the population includes all cities. When using this method, the researcher must be confident that the chosen sample is truly representative of the entire population.

- *Quota sampling*: Is the nonprobability equivalent of stratified sampling. Like stratified sampling, the researcher first identifies the stratums and their proportions as they are represented in the population. Then convenience or judgment sampling is used to select the required number of subjects from each stratum. This differs from stratified sampling, where the stratums are filled by random sampling.
- *Snowball sampling*: Is a special nonprobability method used when the desired sample characteristic is rare. It may be extremely difficult or cost prohibitive to locate respondents in these situations. Snowball sampling relies on referrals from initial subjects to generate additional subjects. While this technique can dramatically lower search costs, it comes at the expense of introducing bias because the technique itself reduces the likelihood that the sample will represent a good cross section from the population

Chapter 4

Data Collection and Analysis

AN OVERVIEW

There are very few hard and fast rules to define the task of data collection. Each research project uses a data collection technique appropriate to the particular research methodology. The two primary goals for both quantitative and qualitative studies are to maximize response and maximize accuracy.

When using an outside data collection service, researchers often *validate* the data collection process by contacting a percentage of the respondents to verify that they were actually interviewed. Data *editing* and *cleaning* involves the process of checking for inadvertent errors in the data. This usually entails using a computer to check for out-of-bounds data.

Quantitative

Studies employ deductive logic, where the researcher starts with a hypothesis, and then collects data to confirm or refute the hypothesis. *Qualitative* studies use inductive logic, where the researcher first designs a study and then develops a hypothesis or theory to explain the results of the analysis

Information, industry experts, and secondary data may not be sufficient to define the research problem. Sometimes qualitative research must be undertaken to gain a qualitative understanding of the problem and its underlying factors. Qualitative research is unstructured, exploratory in nature, based on small samples, and may utilize popular qualitative techniques such as focus groups (group interviews), word association (asking respondents to indicate their first responses to stimulus words), and depth interviews (one-on-one interviews which probe the respondents' thoughts in detail). Other exploratory research techniques, such as pilot surveys with small samples of respondents, may also be undertaken

Quantitative

Analysis is generally fast and inexpensive. A wide assortment of statistical techniques are available to the researcher.

Computer software is readily available to provide both basic and advanced multivariate analysis. The researcher simply follows the preplanned analysis process, without making subjective decisions about the data. For this reason, quantitative studies are usually easier to execute than qualitative studies.

Qualitative studies nearly always involve in-person interviews, and are therefore very labour intensive and costly. They rely heavily on a researcher's ability to exclude personal biases. The interpretation of qualitative data is often highly subjective, and different researchers can reach different ceases from the same data. However, the goal of qualitative research is to develop a hypothesis—not to test one. Qualitative studies have merit in that they provide broad, general theories that can be examined in future research.

DATA ANALYSIS

Modern computer software has made the analysis of quantitative data a very easy task. It is no longer incumbent on the researcher to know the formulas needed to calculate the desired statistics.

However, this does not obviate the need for the researcher to understand the theoretical and conceptual foundations of the statistical techniques. Each statistical technique has its own assumptions and limitations. Considering the ease in which computers can calculate complex statistical problems, the danger is that the researcher might be unaware of the assumptions and limitations in the use and interpretation of a statistic

Secondary Data Analysis

Secondary data are data collected for some purpose other than the problem at hand. Primary data, on the other hand, are originated by the researcher for the specific purpose of addressing the research problem. Secondary data include information made available by business and government sources, commercial marketing research firms, and computerized databases.

Secondary data are an economical and quick source of background information. Analysis of available secondary data is an essential step in the problem definition process: primary data should not be collected until the available secondary data have been fully analysed

What is Secondary Research?

By far the most widely used method for collecting data is through secondary data collection, commonly called secondary research. This process involves collecting data from either the originator or a distributor of primary research. In other words, accessing information already gathered.

In most cases this means finding information from third-party sources such as marketing research reports, company websites, and other sources. But in actuality any information gathered, whether from sources external to the marketer or from internal sources, such as accessing material from previous market research carried out by the marketer's organization, old sales reports, accounting records and many others, falls under the heading of secondary research.

DATA COLLECTION: PRIMARY RESEARCH METHODS

In this tutorial we continue our discussion of how marketers collect research data by examining the methods used for collecting primary data. Unlike secondary research, where data is initially obtained by someone other than the marketer, the responsibility for collecting data under primary research falls to the marketer. In general marketers can select from two basic approaches to data collections using primary methods:

- Qualitative Data Collection
- Quantitative Data Collection

Both methods offer advantages and disadvantages which are discussed in detail in this tutorial.

PRIMARY RESEARCH - ADVANTAGES

- *Addresses Specific Research Issues*: Carrying out their own research allows the marketing organization to address issues specific to their own situation. Primary research is designed to collect the information the marketer wants to know and report it in ways that benefit the marketer. For example, while information reported with secondary research may not fit the marketer's needs (e.g., different age groupings) no such problem exists with primary research since the marketer controls the research design.
- *Greater Control*: Not only does primary research enable the marketer to focus on specific issues, it also enables the marketer to have a higher level of control over how the information is collected. In this way the marketer can decide on such issues as size of project (e.g., how many responses), location of research (e.g., geographic area) and time frame for completing the project.
- *Efficient Spending for Information*: Unlike secondary research where the marketer may spend for information that is not needed, primary data collections' focus on issues specific to the researcher improves the chances that research funds will be spent efficiently.
- *Proprietary Information*: Information collected by the marketer using primary research is their own and is generally not shared with others. Thus, information can be kept hidden from competitors and potentially offer an "information advantage" to the company that undertook the primary research.

PRIMARY RESEARCH - DISADVANTAGES

- *Cost*: Compared to secondary research, primary data

may be very expensive since there is a great deal of marketer involvement and the expense in preparing and carrying out research can be high.

- *Time Consuming*: To be done correctly primary data collection requires the development and execution of a research plan. Going from the start-point of deciding to undertake a research project to the end-point to having results is often much longer than the time it takes to acquire secondary data.
- *Not Always Feasible*: Some research projects, while potentially offering information that could prove quite valuable, are not within the reach of a marketer. Many are just too large to be carried out by all but the largest companies and some are not feasible at all. For instance, it would not be practical for McDonalds to attempt to interview every customer who visits their stores on a certain day since doing so would require hiring a huge number of researchers, an unrealistic expense. Fortunately, as suggested, see in a later tutorial there are ways for McDonalds to use other methods (e.g., sampling) to meet their needs without the need to talk with all customers.

Qualitative Data Collection

Sometimes referred to as"touchy-feely" research, qualitative data collection requires researchers to interpret the information gathered, most often without the benefit of statistical support. If the researcher is well trained in interpreting respondents' comments and activities, this form of research can offer very good information. However, it may not hold the same level of relevancy as quantitative research due to the lack of scientific controls with this data collection method. For example, a researcher may want to know more about how customers make purchase decisions. One way to do this is to sit and talk with customers using one-on-one interviews. However, if the interview process allows the researcher to vary what questions are asked (i.e., not all respondents are asked the same questions), then this type of research may lack controls needed to follow a scientific approach.

An additional drawback of qualitative research is that it can be time consuming and expensive and, consequently, only a very small portion of the marketer's desired market can participate in qualitative research. Due to the lack of strong controls in the research design (i.e., not as well structured, fewer participants), using results to estimate characteristics of a larger group is more difficult. Thus, qualitative data collection is generally not used for hypothesis testing. This is not to say qualitative research is not useful, it is very useful if its limitations are understood. It is widely employed for marketing research especially for research for the purpose of discovery, and to a lesser extent, explanation.

Qualitative data collection options include personal interviews, focus groups and observational research which are discussed next.

Qualitative Data: Personal Interviews

Talking to someone one-on-one allows a researcher to cover more ground than may be covered if a respondent was completing a survey. The reason lies with the researcher's ability to dig deeper into a respondent's comments to find out additional that might not emerge from initial responses.

Unfortunately, individual interviewing can be quite expensive and may be intimidating to some who are not comfortable sharing with a researcher.

Qualitative Data: Focus Groups

To overcome the drawbacks associated with personal interviews, marketers can turn to focus groups. Under this research format, a group of respondents (generally numbering 8-12) are guided through discussion by a moderator. The power of focus groups as a research tool rests with the environment created by the interaction of the participants. In well-run sessions, members of the group are stimulated to respond by the comments and the support of others in the group. In this way, the depth of information offered by a respondent may be much greater than that obtained through individual interviews.

However, focus groups can be costly to conduct especially if participants must be paid. To help reduce costs, online options for focus groups have emerged. While there are many positive aspects to online focus groups, the fact that respondents are not physically present diminishes the benefits gained by group dynamics. However, as technology improves, in particular video conferencing, the online focus group could become a major research option.

Qualitative Data: Observational Research

Watching customers as they perform activities can be a very useful research method, especially when customers are observed in a natural setting (e.g., shopping in a retail store, using products at home). In fact, an emerging research technique called ethnographic research has researchers following customers as they shop, work, and relax at home in order to see how they make decisions, use products and more.

Quantitative Data Collection

In general there are two basic types of primary research - quantitative data collection and qualitative data collection. Quantitative data collection involves the use of numbers to assess information. This information can then be evaluated using statistical analysis which offers researchers the opportunity to dig deeper into the data and look for greater meaning.

Certain information is by nature numerical. For example, asking a person their actual age or yearly income will result in a number. But under the right circumstances numbers can also be used to represent certain characteristics which are not on the surface considered numerical. This most often occurs with data collected within a structured and well-controlled scientific research design. For instance, research of customers' attitude toward a company's products may include the following:

Place an"X" on the line that best indicates your impression of the overall quality of our company's products:

Poor _ _ _ _ _ _ _ Excellent

In this example each line, which represents a potential customer response, could be assigned a number. For example, checking the left-most line could result in the researcher entering a"1", the next line a"2", the next line a"3" and so on. Once research is completed this question can undergo statistical analysis.

While quantitative analysis is potentially used for all types of research purposes it is most critical for hypothesis testing. In Step 6: Analyse Data, such analysis may prove very relevant by allowing the researcher to draw ceases.

Quantitative data collection comes in many forms but the most popular forms are surveys.

Quantitative Data: Surveys

This method captures information through the input of responses to a research instrument containing questions (i.e., such as a questionnaire).. Information can be input either by the respondents themselves (e.g., complete online survey) or the researcher can input the data (e.g. phone survey, mall intercept). The main methods for distributing surveys are via postal mail, phone, website or in person. However, newer technologies are creating additional delivery options including through wireless devices, such as smart phones.

Quantitative Data: Tracking

With tracking research marketers are able to monitor the behaviour of customers as they engage in regular purchase or information gathering activities. Possibly the most well-known example of tracking research is used by websites as they track customer visits. But tracking research also has offline applications, especially when point-of-purchase scanners are employed, such as tracking product purchases at grocery stores and automated collections on toll roads.

This method of research is expected to grow significantly as more devices are introduced that provide means for tracking. However, as we discussed in the Marketing Research Tutorial, some customers may see tracking devices as intrusive and many privacy advocates have raised concerns about certain tracking methods especially if these are not disclosed to customers.

Quantitative Data: Experiments

Marketers often undertake experiments to gauge how the manipulation of one marketing variable affects another (i.e., causal research).

The use of experiments has applications for many marketing decision areas including product testing, advertising design, setting price points and creating packaging. For example, a market researcher for a retail chain may want to study the effect on sales if a product display is moved to different locations in a store.

Unfortunately, performing highly controlled experiments can be quite costly. Some researchers have found the use of computer simulations can work nearly as well as experiments and may be less expensive, though the number of simulation applications for marketing decisions is still fairly limited.

Questionnaires

Questionnaires are a popular means of collecting data, but are difficult to design and often require many rewrites before an acceptable questionnaire is produced.

Advantages:

- Can be used as a method in its own right or as a basis for interviewing or a telephone survey.
- Can be posted, e-mailed or faxed.
- Can cover a large number of people or organisations.
- Wide geographic coverage.
- Relatively cheap.
- No prior arrangements are needed.
- Avoids embarrassment on the part of the respondent.
- Respondent can consider responses.
- Possible anonymity of respondent.
- No interviewer bias.

Disadvantages:

- Design problems.
- Questions have to be relatively simple.
- Historically low response rate (although inducements may help).
- Time delay whilst waiting for responses to be returned.
- Require a return deadline.
- Several reminders may be required.
- Assumes no literacy problems.
- No control over who completes it.
- Not possible to give assistance if required.
- Problems with incomplete questionnaires.
- Replies not spontaneous and independent of each other.
- Respondent can read all questions beforehand and then decide whether to complete or not. For example, perhaps because it is too long, too complex, uninteresting, or too personal.

Design of Postal Questionnaires

Theme and Covering Letter

The general theme of the questionnaire should be made explicit in a covering letter. You should state who you are; why the data is required; give, if necessary, an assurance of confidentiality and/or anonymity; and contact number and address or telephone number. This ensures that the respondents know what they are committing themselves to, and also that they understand the context of their replies. If possible, you should offer an estimate of the completion time. Instructions for return should be included with the return date made obvious. For example:'It would be appreciated if you could return the completed questionnaire by... if at all possible'.

Instructions for Completion

You need to provide clear and unambiguous instructions for completion. Within most questionnaires these are general instructions and specific instructions for particular question structures. It is usually best to separate these, supplying the general instructions as a preamble to the questionnaire, but leaving the specific instructions until the questions to which they apply. The response method should be indicated (circle, tick, cross, etc.). Wherever possible, and certainly if a slightly unfamiliar response system is employed, you should give an example.

Appearance

Appearance is usually the first feature of the questionnaire to which the recipient reacts. A neat and professional look will encourage further consideration of your request, increasing your response rate. In addition, careful thought to layout should help your analysis.

There are a number of simple rules to help improve questionnaire appearance:

- Liberal spacing makes the reading easier.
- Photo-reduction can produce more space without reducing content.
- Consistent positioning of response boxes, usually to the right, speeds up completion and also avoids inadvertent omission of responses.
- Choose the font style to maximise legibility.
- Differentiate between instructions and questions. Either lower case and capitals can be used, or responses can be boxed.

Length

There may be a strong temptation to include any vaguely interesting questions, but you should resist this at all costs. Excessive size can only reduce response rates. If a long questionnaire is necessary, then you must give even more thought to appearance.

Order

Probably the most crucial stage in questionnaire response is the beginning. Once the respondents have started to complete the questions they will normally finish the task, unless it is very long or difficult. Consequently, you need to select the opening questions with care. Usually the best approach is to ask for biographical first, as the respondents should know all the answers without much thought. Another benefit is that an easy start provides practice in answering questions.

Once the introduction has been achieved the subsequent order will depend on many considerations. You should be aware of the varying importance of different questions. Essential information should appear early, just in case the questionnaire is not completed. For the same reasons, relatively unimportant questions can be placed towards the end. If questions are likely to provoke the respondent and remain unanswered, these too are best left until the end, in the hope of obtaining answers to everything else.

Coding

If analysis of the results is to be carried out using a statistical package or spreadsheet it is advisable to code non-numerical responses when designing the questionnaire, rather than trying to code the responses when they are returned.

An example of coding is:

Male []	Female []
1	2

The coded responses are then used for the analysis.

Respondents to questionnaires rarely benefit personally from their efforts and the least the researcher can do is to thank them. Even though the covering letter will express appreciation for the help given, it is also a nice gesture to finish the questionnaire with a further thank you.

Questions

- Keep the questions short, simple and to the point; avoid all unnecessary words.
- Use words and phrases that are unambiguous and familiar to the respondent. For example,'dinner' has

a number of different interpretations; use an alternative expression such as'evening meal'.

- Only ask questions that the respondent can answer. Hypothetical questions should be avoided. Avoid calculations and questions that require a lot of memory work, for example,'How many people stayed in your hotel last year?'
- Avoid loaded or leading questions that imply a certain answer. For example, by mentioning one particular item in the question,'Do you agree that Colgate toothpaste is the best toothpaste?'
- Vacuous words or phrases should be avoided.'Generally','usually', or'normally' are imprecise terms with various meanings. They should be replaced with quantitative statements, for example,'at least once a week'.
- Questions should only address a single issue. For example, questions like:'Do you take annual holidays to Spain?' should be broken down into two discreet stages, firstly find out if the respondent takes an annual holiday, and then secondly find out if they go to Spain.
- Do not ask two questions in one by using'and'. For example,'Did you watch television last night and read a newspaper?'
- Avoid double negatives. For example,'Is it not true that you did not read a newspaper yesterday?' Respondents may tackle a double negative by switching both negatives and then assuming that the same answer applies. This is not necessarily valid.
- State units required but do not aim for too high a degree of accuracy. For instance, use an interval rather than an exact figure:

'How much did you earn last year?'

Less than £10,000 []

£10,000 but less than £20,000 []

Avoid emotive or embarrassing words - usually connected with race, religion, politics, sex, money.

Types of questions

Closed questions: A question is asked and then a number of possible answers are provided for the respondent. The respondent selects the answer which is appropriate. Closed questions are particularly useful in obtaining factual information:

Sex: Male [] Female []

Did you watch television last night? Yes [] No []

Some'Yes/No' questions have a third category'Do not know'. Experience shows that as long as this alternative is not mentioned people will make a choice. Also the phrase'Do not know' is ambiguous:

Do you agree with the introduction of the EMU?

Yes [] No [] Do not know []

What was your main way of travelling to the hotel? Tick one box only. With such lists you should always include an'other' category, because not all possible responses might have been included in the list of answers.

Sometimes the respondent can select more than one from the list. However, this makes analysis difficult:

Why have you visited the historic house? Tick the relevant answer(s). You may tick as many as you like.

Attitude questions: Frequently questions are asked to find out the respondents' opinions or attitudes to a given situation. A Likert scale provides a battery of attitude statements. The respondent then says how much they agree or disagree with each one:

Read the following statements and then indicate by a tick whether you strongly agree, agree, disagree or strongly disagree with the statement.

	Strongly agree	Agree	Disagree	Strongly disagree
My visit has been good value for money				

There are many variations on this type of question. One

variation is to have a'middle statement', for example,'Neither agree nor disagree'. However, many respondents take this as the easy option. Only having four statements forces the respondent into making a positive or negative choice. Another variation is to rank the various attitude statements, however, this can cause analysis problems:

Which of these characteristics do you like about your job? Indicate the best three in order, with the best being number

Varied work	[]
Good salary	[]
Opportunities for promotion	[]
Good working conditions	[]
High amount of responsibility	[]
Friendly colleagues	[]

A semantic differential scale attempts to see how strongly an attitude is held by the respondent. With these scales double-ended terms are given to the respondents who are asked to indicate where their attitude lies on the scale between the terms. The response can be indicated by putting a cross in a particular position or circling a number:

Work is: (circle the appropriate number)

Difficult	1 2 3 4 5 6 7	Easy
Useless	1 2 3 4 5 6 7	Useful
Interesting	1 2 3 4 5 6 7	Boring

For summary and analysis purposes, a'score' of 1 to 7 may be allocated to the seven points of the scale, thus quantifying the various degrees of opinion expressed. This procedure has some disadvantages. It is implicitly assumed that two people with the same strength of feeling will mark the same point on the scale.

This almost certainly will not be the case. When faced with a semantic differential scale, some people will never, as a matter of principle, use the two end indicators of 1 and 7. Effectively, therefore, they are using a five-point scale. Also scoring the scale 1 to 7 assumes that they represent equidistant points on the continuous spectrum of opinion. This again is probably not true. Nevertheless, within its limitations, the semantic differential can provide a useful way of measuring and summarising subjective opinions.

Other types of questions to determine peoples' opinions or attitudes are:

- Which one/two words best describes...?
- Which of the following statements best describes...?
- How much do you agree with the following statement...?

Open Questions

An open question such as'What are the essential skills a manager should possess?' should be used as an adjunct to the main theme of the questionnaire and could allow the respondent to elaborate upon an earlier more specific question. Open questions inserted at the end of major sections, or at the end of the questionnaire, can act as safety valves, and possibly offer additional information. However, they should not be used to introduce a section since there is a high risk of influencing later responses. The main problem of open questions is that many different answers have to be summarised and possibly coded.

Testing - pilot Survey

Questionnaire design is fraught with difficulties and problems. A number of rewrites will be necessary, together with refinement and rethinks on a regular basis. Do not assume that you will write the questionnaire accurately and perfectly at the first attempt. If poorly designed, you will collect inappropriate or inaccurate data and good analysis cannot then rectify the situation.

To refine the questionnaire, you need to conduct a pilot survey. This is a small-scale trial prior to the main survey that tests all your question planning. Amendments to questions can be made.

After making some amendments, the new version would be re-tested. If this re-test produces more changes, another pilot would be undertaken and so on. For example, perhaps responses to open-ended questions become closed; questions which are all answered the same way can be omitted; difficult words replaced, etc.

It is usual to pilot the questionnaires personally so that the respondent can be observed and questioned if necessary. By timing each question, you can identify any questions that appear too difficult, and you can also obtain a reliable estimate of the anticipated completion time for inclusion in the covering letter. The result can also be use to test the coding and analytical procedures to be performed later.

Distribution and Return

It is usual to supply a prepaid addressed envelope for the return of the questionnaire. You need to explain this in the covering letter and reinforce it at the end of the questionnaire, after the'Thank you'. Finally, many organisations are approached continually for information. Many, as a matter of course, will not respond in a positive way.

Interviews: Interviewing is a technique that is primarily used to gain an understanding of the underlying reasons and motivations for people's attitudes, preferences or behaviour. Interviews can be undertaken on a personal one-to-one basis or in a group. They can be conducted at work, at home, in the street or in a shopping centre, or some other agreed location.

Personal interview Advantages:

- Serious approach by respondent resulting in accurate information.
- Good response rate.
- Completed and immediate.
- Possible in-depth questions.
- Interviewer in control and can give help if there is a problem.
- Can investigate motives and feelings.
- Can use recording equipment.
- Characteristics of respondent assessed - tone of voice, facial expression, hesitation, etc.
- Can use props.
- If one interviewer used, uniformity of approach.
- Used to pilot other methods.

Disadvantages Need to set up interviews:

- Time consuming.
- Geographic limitations.
- Can be expensive.
- Normally need a set of questions.
- Respondent bias - tendency to please or impress, create false personal image, or end interview quickly.
- Embarrassment possible if personal questions.
- Transcription and analysis can present problems - subjectivity.
- If many interviewers, training required.

Types of interview Structured:

- Based on a carefully worded interview schedule.
- Frequently require short answers with the answers being ticked off.
- Useful when there are a lot of questions which are not particularly contentious or thought provoking.
- Respondent may become irritated by having to give over-simplified answers.

Semi-structured

The interview is focused by asking certain questions but with scope for the respondent to express him or herself at length.

Unstructured

This also called an in-depth interview. The interviewer begins by asking a general question. The interviewer then encourages the respondent to talk freely.

The interviewer uses an unstructured format, the subsequent direction of the interview being determined by the respondent's initial reply. The interviewer then probes for elaboration -'Why do you say that?' or,'That's interesting, tell me more' or,'Would you like to add anything else?' being typical probes.

This is a step-by-step guide to conducting an interview. You should remember that all situations are different and therefore you may need refinements to the approach.

Planning an Interview

- List the areas in which you require information.
- Decide on type of interview.
- Transform areas into actual questions.
- Try them out on a friend or relative.
- Make an appointment with respondent(s)—discussing details of why and how long.

Conducting an Interview

- *Personally*: Arrive on time be smart smile employ good manners find a balance between friendliness and objectivity.
- *At the start*: Introduce yourself re-confirm the purpose assure confidentiality - if relevant specify what will happen to the data.
- *The questions:* Speak slowly in a soft, yet audible tone of voice control your body language know the questions and topic ask all the questions.
- *Responses*: Recorded as you go on questionnaire written verbatim, but slow and time-consuming summarised by you taped - agree beforehand - have alternative method if not acceptable consider effect on respondent's answers proper equipment in good working order sufficient tapes and batteries minimum of background noise.

Telephone Interview

This is an alternative form of interview to the personal, face-to-face interview.

Advantages:

- Relatively cheap.
- Quick.
- Can cover reasonably large numbers of people or organisations.
- Wide geographic coverage.
- High response rate - keep going till the required number.

- No waiting.
- Spontaneous response.
- Help can be given to the respondent.
- Can tape answers.

Disadvantages:

- Often connected with selling.
- Questionnaire required.
- Not everyone has a telephone.
- Repeat calls are inevitable - average 2.5 calls to get someone.
- Time is wasted.
- Straightforward questions are required.
- Respondent has little time to think.
- Cannot use visual aids.
- Can cause irritation.
- Good telephone manner is required.
- Question of authority.

Getting Started

- Locate the respondent:
  - Repeat calls may be necessary especially if you are trying to contact people in organisations where you may have to go through secretaries.
  - You may not know an individual's name or title - so there is the possibility of interviewing the wrong person.
  - You can send an advance letter informing the respondent that you will be telephoning. This can explain the purpose of the research.
- Getting them to agree to take part:
  - You need to state concisely the purpose of the call - scripted and similar to the introductory letter of a postal questionnaire.
  - Respondents will normally listen to this introduction before they decide to co-operate or refuse.
  - When contact is made respondents may have questions or raise objections about why they

could not participate. You should be prepared for these.

Ensuring Quality

- *Quality of questionnaire*: Follows the principles of questionnaire design. However, it must be easy to move through as you cannot have long silences on the telephone.
- *Ability of interviewer*: Follows the principles of face-to-face interviewing.

Smooth implementation

- *Interview schedule*: Each interview schedule should have a cover page with number, name and address. The cover sheet should make provision to record which call it is, the date and time, the interviewer, the outcome of the call and space to note down specific times at which a call-back has been arranged. Space should be provided to record the final outcome of the call - was an interview refused, contact never made, number disconnected, etc.
- *Procedure for call-backs*: A system for call-backs needs to be implemented. Interview schedules should be sorted just as to their status: weekday call-back, evening call-back, weekend call-back, specific time call-back.

Comparison of Postal, Telephone and Personal Interview Surveys

The table compares the three common methods of postal, telephone and interview surveys - it might help you to decide which one to use.

Table. Comparison of the three Common Methods of Surveys

	Postal survey	Telephone survey	Personal interview
Cost (assuming a good response rate)	Often lowest	Usually in-between	Usually highest

Ability to probe	No personal contact or observation	Some chance for gathering additional data through elaboration on questions, but no personal observation	Greatest opportunity for observation, building rapport, and additional probing
Respondent ability to complete at own convenience	Yes	Perhaps, but usually no	Perhaps, if interview time is prearranged with respondent
Interview bias	No chance	Some, perhaps due to voice inflection	Greatest chance
Ability to decide who actually responds to the questions	Least	Some	Greatest
Impersonality	Greatest	Some due to lack of face-to -face contact	Least
Complex questions	Least suitable	Somewhat suitable	More suitable
Visual aids	Little opportunity	No opportunity	Greatest opportunity
Potential negative respondent reaction	'Junk mail'	'Junk calls'	Invasion of privacy
Interviewer control over interview environment	Least	Some in selection of time to call	Greatest

Time lag between soliciting and receiving response	Greatest	Least	May be considerable if a large area involved
Suitable types of questions	Simple, mostly dichotomous (yes/no) and multiple choice	Some opportunity for open-ended questions especially if interview is recorded	Greatest opportunity for open-ended questions
Requirement for technical skills in conducting interview	Least	Medium	Greatest
Response rate	Low	Usually high	High

Focus Group Interviews

A focus group is an interview conducted by a trained moderator in a non-structured and natural manner with a small group of respondents. The moderator leads the discussion. The main purpose of focus groups is to gain insights by listening to a group of people from the appropriate target market talk about specific issues of interest.

Observation

Observation involves recording the behavioural patterns of people, objects and events in a systematic manner.

Observational methods may be:

- Structured or unstructured
- Disguised or undisguised
- Natural or contrived
- Personal
- Mechanical
- Non-participant

- Participant, with the participant taking a number of different roles.

Structured or Unstructured

In structured observation, the researcher specifies in detail what is to be observed and how the measurements are to be recorded. It is appropriate when the problem is clearly defined and the information needed is specified.

In unstructured observation, the researcher monitors all aspects of the phenomenon that seem relevant. It is appropriate when the problem has yet to be formulated precisely and flexibility is needed in observation to identify key components of the problem and to develop hypotheses. The potential for bias is high. Observation findings should be treated as hypotheses to be tested rather than as conclusive findings.

Disguised or Undisguised

In disguised observation, respondents are unaware they are being observed and thus behave naturally. Disguise is achieved, for example, by hiding, or using hidden equipment or people disguised as shoppers.

In undisguised observation, respondents are aware they are being observed. There is a danger of the Hawthorne effect - people behave differently when being observed.

Natural or Contrived

Natural observation involves observing behaviour as it takes place in the environment, for example, eating hamburgers in a fast food outlet.

In contrived observation, the respondents' behaviour is observed in an artificial environment, for example, a food tasting session.

Personal

In personal observation, a researcher observes actual behaviour as it occurs. The observer may or may not normally attempt to control or manipulate the phenomenon being observed. The observer merely records what takes place.

Mechanical

Mechanical devices (video, closed circuit television) record what is being observed. These devices may or may not require the respondent's direct participation. They are used for continuously recording on-going behaviour.

Non-participant

The observer does not normally question or communicate with the people being observed. He or she does not participate.

Participant

In participant observation, the researcher becomes, or is, part of the group that is being investigated. Participant observation has its roots in ethnographic studies (study of man and races) where researchers would live in tribal villages, attempting to understand the customs and practices of that culture.

It has a very extensive literature, particularly in sociology (development, nature and laws of human society) and anthropology (physiological and psychological study of man). Organisations can be viewed as'tribes' with their own customs and practices.

The role of the participant observer is not simple.

There are different ways of classifying the role:

- Researcher as employee.
- Researcher as an explicit role.
- Interrupted involvement.
- Observation alone.

Researcher as Employee

The researcher works within the organisation alongside other employees, effectively as one of them. The role of the researcher may or may not be explicit and this will have implications for the extent to which he or she will be able to move around and gather information and perspectives from other sources. This role is appropriate when the researcher needs to become totally immersed and experience the work or situation at first hand.

There are a number of dilemmas. Do you tell management and the unions? Friendships may compromise the research. What are the ethics of the process? Can anonymity be maintained? Skill and competence to undertake the work may be required. The research may be over a long period of time.

Researcher as an Explicit Role

The researcher is present every day over a period of time, but entry is negotiated in advance with management and preferably with employees as well. The individual is quite clearly in the role of a researcher who can move around, observe, interview and participate in the work as appropriate. This type of role is the most favoured, as it provides many of the insights that the complete observer would gain, whilst offering much greater flexibility without the ethical problems that deception entails.

Interrupted involvement: The researcher is present sporadically over a period of time, for example, moving in and out of the organisation to deal with other work or to conduct interviews with, or observations of, different people across a number of different organisations. It rarely involves much participation in the work.

Observation alone: The observer role is often disliked by employees since it appears to be'eavesdropping'. The inevitable detachment prevents the degree of trust and friendship forming between the researcher and respondent, which is an important component in other methods.

Choice of Roles

The role adopted depends on the following:

- *Purpose of the research*: Does the research require continued longitudinal involvement (long period of time), or will in-depth interviews, for example, conducted over time give the type of insights required?
- *Cost of the research*: To what extent can the researcher afford to be committed for extended periods of time? Are there additional costs such as training?

- *The extent to which access can be gained*: Gaining access where the role of the researcher is either explicit or covert can be difficult, and may take time.
- *The extent to which the researcher would be comfortable in the role*: If the researcher intends to keep his identity concealed, will he or she also feel able to develop the type of trusting relationships that are important? What are the ethical issues?
- *The amount of time the researcher has at his disposal*: Some methods involve a considerable amount of time. If time is a problem alternate approaches will have to be sought.

Case-studies

The term case-study usually refers to a fairly intensive examination of a single unit such as a person, a small group of people, or a single company. Case-studies involve measuring what is there and how it got there. In this sense, it is historical. It can enable the researcher to explore, unravel and understand problems, issues and relationships. It cannot, however, allow the researcher to generalise, that is, to argue that from one case-study the results, findings or theory developed apply to other similar case-studies. The case looked at may be unique and, therefore not representative of other instances. It is, of course, possible to look at several case-studies to represent certain features of management that we are interested in studying. The case-study approach is often done to make practical improvements. Contributions to general knowledge are incidental.

The case-study method has four steps:

- Determine the present situation.
- Gather background information about the past and key variables.
- *Test hypotheses*: The background information collected will have been analysed for possible hypotheses. In this step, specific evidence about each hypothesis can be gathered. This step aims to eliminate possibilities which conflict with the evidence collected and to gain

confidence for the important hypotheses. The culmination of this step might be the development of an experimental design to test out more rigorously the hypotheses developed, or it might be to take action to remedy the problem.

- *Take remedial action*: The aim is to check that the hypotheses tested actually work out in practice. Some action, correction or improvement is made and a re-check carried out on the situation to see what effect the change has brought about.

The case-study enables rich information to be gathered from which potentially useful hypotheses can be generated. It can be a time-consuming process. It is also inefficient in researching situations which are already well structured and where the important variables have been identified. They lack utility when attempting to reach rigorous ceases or determining precise relationships between variables.

Diaries

A diary is a way of gathering information about the way individuals spend their time on professional activities. They are not about records of engagements or personal journals of thought! Diaries can record either quantitative or qualitative data, and in management research can provide information about work patterns and activities.

Advantages:

- Useful for collecting information from employees.
- Different writers compared and contrasted simultaneously.
- Allows the researcher freedom to move from one organisation to another.
- Researcher not personally involved.
- Diaries can be used as a preliminary or basis for intensive interviewing.
- Used as an alternative to direct observation or where resources are limited.

Disadvantages:

- Subjects need to be clear about what they are being

asked to do, why and what you plan to do with the data.

- Diarists need to be of a certain educational level.
- Some structure is necessary to give the diarist focus, for example, a list of headings.
- Encouragement and reassurance are needed as completing a diary is time-consuming and can be irritating after a while.
- Progress needs checking from time-to-time.
- Confidentiality is required as content may be critical.
- Analyses problems, so you need to consider how responses will be coded before the subjects start filling in diaries.

Critical Incidents

The critical incident technique is an attempt to identify the more'noteworthy' aspects of job behaviour and is based on the assumption that jobs are composed of critical and non-critical tasks. For example, a critical task might be defined as one that makes the difference between success and failure in carrying out important parts of the job. The idea is to collect reports about what people do that is particularly effective in contributing to good performance. The incidents are scaled in order of difficulty, frequency and importance to the job as a whole.

The technique scores over the use of diaries as it is centred on specific happenings and on what is judged as effective behaviour. However, it is laborious and does not lend itself to objective quantification.

Portfolios

A measure of a manager's ability may be expressed in terms of the number and duration of'issues' or problems being tackled at any one time. The compilation of problem portfolios is recording information about how each problem arose, methods used to solve it, difficulties encountered, etc. This analysis also raises questions about the person's use of time. What proportion of time is occupied in checking; in handling problems given by others; on self-generated problems; on'top-priority' problems; on minor issues, etc? The main problem with this method and the use of diaries is getting people to agree to record everything in sufficient detail for you to analyse. It is very time-consuming!

SECONDARY DATA COLLECTION

All methods of data collection can supply quantitative data (numbers, statistics or financial) or qualitative data (usually words or text). Quantitative data may often be presented in tabular or graphical form. Secondary data is data that has already been collected by someone else for a different purpose to yours.

For example, this could mean using:

- Data collected by a hotel on its customers through its guest history system
- Data supplied by a marketing organisation
- Annual company reports
- Government statistics.

Secondary data can be used in different ways:

- You can simply report the data in its original format. If so, then it is most likely that the place for this data will be in your main introduction or literature review as support or evidence for your argument.
- You can do something with the data. If you use it (analyse it or re-interpret it) for a different purpose to the original then the most likely place would be in the'Analysis of findings' section of your dissertation. A good example of this usage was the work on suicide carried out by Durkheim. He took the official suicide statistics of different countries (recorded by coroners or their equivalent) and analysed them to see if he could identify variables that would mean that some people are more likely to commit suicide than others. He found, for example, that Catholics were less likely to commit suicide than Protestants. In this way, he took data that had been collected for quite a different purpose and used it in

his own study - but he had to do a lot of comparisons and statistical correlations himself in order to analyse the data.

Most research requires the collection of primary data (data that you collect at first hand), and this is what students concentrate on. Unfortunately, many dissertations do not include secondary data in their findings section although it is perfectly acceptable to do so, providing you have analysed it. It is always a good idea to use data collected by someone else if it exists - it may be on a much larger scale than you could hope to collect and could contribute to your findings considerably.

As secondary data has been collected for a different purpose to yours, you should treat it with care.

The basic questions you should ask are:

- Where has the data come from?
- Does it cover the correct geographical location?
- Is it current (not too out of date)?
- If you are going to combine with other data are the data the same (for example, units, time, etc.)?
- If you are going to compare with other data are you comparing like with like?

Thus you should make a detailed examination of the following:

- Title (for example, the time period that the data refers to and the geographical coverage).
- Units of the data.
- Source (some secondary data is already secondary data).
- Column and row headings, if presented in tabular form.
- Definitions and abbreviations, for example, what does SIC stand for? For example, how is'small' defined in the phrase'small hotel'? Is'small' based on the number of rooms, value of sales, number of employees, profit, turnover, square metres of space, etc., and do different sources use the word'small' in different ways? Even if the same unit of measurement is used, there still could be problems. For example,

in Norway, firms with 200-499 employees are defined as'medium', whereas in the USA firms with less than 500 employees are defined as'small'.

There are many sources of data and most people tend to underestimate the number of sources and the amount of data within each of these sources.

Sources can be classified as:

- *Paper-based sources*: Journals, periodicals, abstracts, indexes, directories, research reports, conference papers, market reports, annual reports, internal records of organisations, newspapers and magazines
- *electronic sources*: CD-ROMs, on-line databases, Internet, videos and broadcasts.

The main sources of qualitative and quantitative secondary data include the follwing:

- Official or government sources.
- Unofficial or general business sources.

The output of all publishers of non-official sources is included in the most comprehensive directory available:

Mort D. (1997) Sources of Unofficial UK Statistics 3rd Edition Aldershot: Gower

The guide lists 1,059 statistical titles and series published by 635 different organisations. It excludes one-off surveys or market reports.

It lists references to the following types of sources:

- Trade associations
- Trade and other journals
- Private research publishers
- Stockbroking firms
- Large company market reports
- Llocal authorities
- Professional bodies
- Academic institutions.
- European Union (Community) sources.
- International sources.
  - Organisation for Economic Co-operation and Development (OECD)
  - United Nations and related organisations.

Sources for the last two categories are many and varied. If your dissertation requires these sources you need to conduct a more thorough search of your library and perhaps seek the assistance of the librarian.

Summary of Descriptive Statistics: So far you have collated the data and made some counts and determined percentages. The next step is to summarise the data, if possible, with one or two summary statistics. Summary or descriptive statistics describe the original data set (the set of responses for each question) by using just one or two numbers - typically an average and a measure of dispersion.

- Mode is the most frequently occurring value, although it is not often used.
- Median is the middle value.
- Mean is found by adding the values and dividing by the number of values.
- Quartiles (Q1 and Q3) are the 25% and 75% values respectively and are measures of dispersion about the median.
- Standard deviation is a measure of the dispersion about the mean; a small standard deviation implies the data are tightly bunched about the mean, whereas a large standard deviation implies the data are widely scattered about the mean.

Different types of data (scales of measurement) can be summarised by different summary statistics. The table shows the types of averages and measures of dispersion for each type.

Data	Average	Dispersion
Nominal	Mode	
Ordinal	Mode	
	Median	
	Mean	
Numerical	Mode	
	Median	Quartiles
	Mean	Standard deviation

Note that as the level gets higher more statistics can be determined.

With nominal data it is only possible to show the number or percentage of people or items falling within each category. It is also possible to state which category includes the highest number of counts - the most popular category or modal category.

Care is needed when comparing such a mean with another mean, because the data are ordinal and not numerical. One question may give a weighted mean score of 2.1 and another question a weighted mean score of 4.2. It would be incorrect to say the result for the first question is twice as good as the result for the second question. Remember the weights are purely arbitrary. The data are not numerical and therefore the principle of ratios cannot be applied.

For numerical data, all three averages and their associated measures of dispersion can be determined. However, the mode tends to be of little interest with this type of data and may be ignored in most situations. It may be necessary to use a graphical technique such as a cumulative frequency curve (ogive) to determine the median and quartiles.

We can determine the mean and standard deviation using the formula:

$$\text{St Dev} = \sqrt{\frac{\sum fx^2}{\sum f} - \left[\frac{\sum fx}{\sum f}\right]^2}$$

The term in square brackets is the arithmetic mean. The approach to the calculation is to find the variance and then take the square root to obtain the standard deviation.

For the data in question 4 in the summary questionnaire we have:

Annual salary	Number of respondents
Less than £8,000	6
£8,000 but less than £12,000	12
£12,000 but less than £16,000	10
£16,000 but less than £20,000	6
£20,000 but less than £24,000	4
£24,000 and above	2

This can be re-written with closed classes and the units in

£000s to eliminate the zeroes. Three columns of calculations are required as shown.

	Freq.	Mid Pt.		
	f	x	fx	fx^2
4 but less than 8	6	6	36	216
8 but less than 12	12	10	20	200
12 but less than 16	10	14	140	1,960
16 but less than 20	6	18	108	1,944
20 but less than 24	4	22	88	1,936
24 but less than 28	2	26	52	1,352
Total	40		544	8,608

$$\text{Variance} = \frac{8,608}{40} - \left[\frac{544}{40}\right]^2$$

= 215.2 – (13.6)2

= 215.2 – 184.96

= 30.24

St. dev. = ÷30.24

= 5.5

The mean salary of respondents is £13,6000 per annum with a standard deviation of £5,500. (The results have been multiplied by 1,000 to get the correct units for the data.)

To find the median and quartiles first determine the percentage cumulative frequencies and then draw an ogive (cumulative frequency curve) and read off:

- 25% value to get the lower quartile Q1
- 50% value to get the median
- 75% value to get the upper quartile Q3.

	f	cf	%cf
4 but less than 8	6	6	15
8 but less than 12	12	18	45
12 but less than 16	10	28	70
16 but less than 20	6	34	85
20 but less than 24	4	38	95
24 but less than 28	2	40	100
Total	40		

The percentage cumulative frequencies are then plotted to correspond with the upper class limits. From the graph (not drawn here) the following approximate results are obtained:

Q1	=	£8,700
Median	=	£12,800
Q3	=	£17,300

All the summary statistics determined so far have used the results as presented on the summary sheet. An alternative approach is to use the raw data as presented on the data sheet. However, if you are going to use this approach the data ideally should be on a spreadsheet where the in-built statistical functions can be used.

These functions are:

Summary statistic	Excel function
Arithmetic mean	=AVERAGE(cell range of data)
Median	=MEDIAN(cell range of data)
Mode	=MODE(cell range of data)
Standard deviation	=STDEVP(cell range of data)
Q1	=QUARTILE(cell range of data,1)
Q3	=QUARTILE(cell range of data,3)

So far the analysis has been concerned with determining some summary statistics. Analysis, however, consists of more than this. In particular, analysis is concerned with establishing relationships between variables. There are two common approaches to this, namely, cross-tabulations and correlation analysis.

Cross-tabulations

A cross tabulation is a matrix in which all categories representing one variable are presented in rows, and all categories representing another variable are presented in columns. Although cross-tabulations can be constructed for any type of data they are particularly useful for analysing nominal and ordinal data.

For instance, consider the questionnaire on the attitudes of restaurant staff, you may believe that a worker's opinion of their manager is dependent upon the gender of the respondent.

This hypothesis may be investigated by constructing a cross-tabulation for the two variables gender and opinion of manager. The blank table would look something like the following:

Gender (Q1)	Opinion of manager (Q2)			
	Good	Average	Poor	Total
	(1)	(2)	(3)	
Male	(1)			
Female		(2)		
Total				

You would then count how many responses fall into each cell - this is called the cell frequency. Row totals, column totals and a grand total are inserted as well. This is a time-consuming process and requires care, but invariably leads to valuable information about the relationship between the two variables.

For this example and by referring to the data sheet, we can obtain the following completed cross-tabulation:

Gender (Q1)	Opinion of manager (Q2)			Total
	Good	Average	Poor	
	(1)	(2)	(3)	
Male (1)	8	8	3	19
Female (2)	3	6	12	21
Total	11	14	15	40

Cross-tabulations can be analysed on two levels:

- Inspect the table to see if there are any patterns or cells with small and/or large cell frequencies. If there is, make a statement to reflect this pattern or possible relationship. If there is no obvious pattern, with frequencies being fairly even spread across the cells, then there is probably no relationship between the two variables.
- Test the independence of the two variables using a chi-square test. This is a sophisticated method and we do not cover it here because of the required theoretical underpinning and complexity of the technique.

If we consider the table, it would appear that most males (16 out of 19) have a reasonable opinion of their manager, whilst most females (12 out of 21) appear to have a poor opinion of their manager. This seems to indicate that the opinion of manager is dependent on the gender of respondent (for this sample!), or, there is a relationship between the two variables - gender and opinion of manager.

A possible pattern is less obvious but it would appear that males have a high rating of their work (13 out of 19 rating 1, 2 or 3), whereas females do not (16 out of 21 rating 3, 4 or 5). It would appear that the respondents' rating of their work is dependent on the gender of the respondent (for this sample).

The analysis could be continued by investigating the following hypotheses:

- Is'rating of the manager' dependent on'salary'?
- Is'rating of the manager' dependent on'age'?
- Is'opinion of work' dependent on salary'?
- Is'opinion of work' dependent on'age'?
- Is'salary' dependent on'age'?

It is possible to cross tabulate every question with every other question. This produces so much information that the result is'information overload' and you simply get very confused! You have to be selective about what you cross-tabulate.

With cross-tabulations do not use percentages, only use the actual frequencies. This is because the calculation of a percentage can be based on either row totals, or column totals, or the grand total. In other words, three percentages are possible for each cell.

Correlation Coefficient

This is another sophisticated technique that is commonly used to see if there is a linear relationship between two variables.

Diagrammatic Representation of data

Secondary data and the response counts or percentages associated with a question can be displayed in diagrammatic forms such as a line graph, bar chart or pie chart. These can greatly enhance your findings and subsequent discussion. If at all possible you should include some in your dissertation.

Whatever diagram you use, an associated commentary is essential. Do not leave it to the reader to work out what the diagram shows.

The commentary may:

- State the obvious, such as the largest and/or the smallest, or the trend
- Highlight something that is not so obvious. This is preferable.

Whenever a diagram is used you should position the diagram as close as possible to the associated commentary. Remember, the objective of using a diagram is to present something that is fairly complicated in an easy-to-understand manner as the dissertation is read. Putting it in the back of the dissertation disrupts the flow of reading and understanding.

Two common and popular mistakes made by students when presenting data or findings are as follows:

- The belief that every question or piece of data needs to have a diagram. This is not so. Be selective in the type and number of diagrams used.
- The use of a chart for simple data. For instance, a pie chart is often drawn for a question when there are just two responses, such as a gender breakdown of respondents. This is simplistic and unnecessary.
- Graphs and charts can be produced either within Word directly or by using ChartWizard in Excel and then importing the chart into the document. These require substantial, but important, technical skills. Give yourself time to re-learn them if you have forgotten them

Why we Analysis Data

The purpose of analysing data is to obtain usable and useful information.

The analysis, irrespective of whether the data is qualitative or quantitative, may:

- Describe and summarise the data
- Identify relationships between variables
- Compare variables
- Identify the difference between variables
- Forecast outcomes.

Before we look at the various ways of analysing, presenting and discussing data, we need to clarify the differences between qualitative research, quantitative research, qualitative data and quantitative data. Earlier, we distinguished between qualitative research and quantitative research. It is highly unlikely that your research will be purely one or the other - it will probably be a mixture of the two approaches. For instance, you may have taken a small sample (normally associated with qualitative research) but then conducted a structured interview or used a questionnaire (normally associated with quantitative research) to determine people's attitudes to a particular phenomenon (qualitative research). It is therefore likely that your'mixed' approach will take a qualitative approach some of the time and a quantitative approach at others. It depends on where you are in the research process.

A misconception, and source of confusion for many people, is the belief that qualitative research generates just qualitative data (text, words, opinions, etc) and that quantitative research generates just quantitative data (numbers). Sometimes this is the case, but both types of data can be generated by each approach. For instance, a postal questionnaire or structured'interview (quantitative research) will often gather factual information, for example, age, salary, length of service (quantitative data) - but may also seek opinions and attitudes (qualitative data).

A second misconception is that statistical techniques are only applicable for quantitative data. Once again, this is not so. There are many statistical techniques that can be applied to qualitative data, such as ratings scales, that has been generated by a quantitative research approach.

Unfortunately, many people are worried about numbers, and in particular about statistics, and everything that word implies. Quantitative research and the analysis of quantitative data is consequently something to be avoided. This is rarely possible because qualitative data can also be analysed using statistics. An understanding of basic statistical terms and ideas and the ability to carry out some statistical analysis (elementary or otherwise) is essential for most researchers. Also competence in these techniques, even at a basic level, is a useful skill in its own right.

A third misconception is that qualitative data analysis is easy. There are many ways of conducting qualitative research and thus many ways of analysing the resulting (qualitative) data. For example, having conducted an interview, transcription and organisation of data are the first stages of analysis. This would then be continued by systematically analysing the transcripts, grouping together comments on similar themes and attempting to interpret them and draw ceases.

We deal with data that can be analysed statistically (quantitative data and some types of qualitative data) in the section called quantitative data analysis. We cover data that cannot, or is very difficult, to analyse statistically in the section called qualitative data analysis.

purpose of analysing data is to obtain usable and useful information.

The analysis, irrespective of whether the data is qualitative or quantitative, may:

- Describe and summarise the data
- Identify relationships between variables
- Compare variables
- Identify the difference between variables
- Forecast outcomes.

Qualitative data is subjective, rich, and in-depth information normally presented in the form of words. In undergraduate dissertations, the most common form of qualitative data is derived from semi-structured or unstructured interviews, although other sources can include observations, life histories and journals and documents of all kinds including newspapers.

Qualitative data from interviews can be analysed for content (content analysis) or for the language used (discourse analysis). Qualitative data is difficult to analyse and often opportunities to achieve high marks are lost because the data is treated casually and without rigour. Here we concentrate on the content analysis of data from interviews.

Theory

When using a quantitative methodology, you are normally testing theory through the testing of a hypothesis. In qualitative research, you are either exploring the application of a theory or model in a different context or are hoping for a theory or a model to emerge from the data. In other words, although you may have some ideas about your topic, you are also looking for ideas, concepts and attitudes often from experts or practitioners in the field.

Collecting and Organising Data

The means of collecting and recording data through interviews and the possible pitfalls are well documented elsewhere but in terms of subsequent analysis, it is essential that you have a complete and accurate record of what was said. Do not rely on your memory (it can be very selective!) and either tape record the conversation (preferably) or take copious notes. If you are taking notes, write them up straight after the interview so that you can elaborate and clarify. If you are using a tape recorder, transcribe the exact words onto paper.

However you record the data, you should end up with a hard copy of either exactly what was said (transcript of tape recording) or nearly exactly what was said (comprehensive notes). It may be that parts of the interview are irrelevant or are more in the nature of background material, in which case you need not put these into your transcript but do make sure that they are indeed unnecessary. You should indicate omissions in the text with short statements.

You should transcribe exactly what is said, with grammatical errors and so on. It does not look very authentic if all your respondents speak with perfect grammar and BBC

English! You may also want to indicate other things that happen such as laughter.

Each transcript or set of notes should be clearly marked with the name of the interviewee, the date and place and any other relevant details and, where appropriate, cross-referenced to clearly labelled tapes. These transcripts and notes are not normally required to be included in your dissertation but they should be available to show your supervisor and the second marker if required.

You may wonder why you should go to all the bother of transcribing your audiotapes. It is certainly a time-consuming business, although much easier if you can get access to a transcription machine that enables you to start and stop the tape with your feet while carrying on typing. It is even easier if you have access to an audio-typist who will do this labour intensive part for you.

The advantage of having the interviews etc in hard copy is that you can refer to them very quickly, make notes in the margins, re-organise them for analysis, make coding notations in the margins and so on. It is much slower in the long run to have to continually listen to the tapes. You can read much faster than the tape will play! It also has the advantage, especially if you do the transcription yourself, of ensuring that you are very familiar with the material.

Content Analysis

Analysis of qualitative data is not simple, and although it does not require complicated statistical techniques of quantitative analysis, it is nonetheless difficult to handle the usually large amounts of data in a thorough, systematic and relevant manner. Marshall and Rossman offer this graphic description:

"Data analysis is the process of bringing order, structure and meaning to the mass of collected data. It is a messy, ambiguous, time-consuming, creative, and fascinating process. It does not proceed in a linear fashion; it is not neat. Qualitative data analysis is a search for general statements about relationships among categories of data."

Marshall and Rossman, 1990:111: Hitchcock and Hughes take this one step further: "...the ways in which the researcher moves from a description of what is the case to an explanation of why what is the case is the case."

Hitchcock and Hughes 1995:295: Content analysis consists of reading and re-reading the transcripts looking for similarities and differences in order to find themes and to develop categories.

Having the full transcript is essential to make sure that you do not leave out anything of importance by only selecting material that fits your own ideas. There are various ways that you can mark the text:

Coding paragraphs: This is where you mark each paragraph with a topic/theme/category with an appropriate word in the margin.

Highlighting paragraphs/sentences/phrases: This is where you use highlighter pens of different colours or different coloured pens to mark bits about the different themes. You could mark the bits relating to childcare and those relating to pay in a different colour, and so on. The use of coloured pens will help you find the relevant bits you need when you are writing up.

With both the methods you may find that your categories change and develop as you do the analysis. What is important is that you can see that by analysing the text in such a way, you pick up all the references to a given topic and don't leave anything out. This increases the objectivity and reduces the risk of you only selecting bits that conform to your own preconceptions.

You then need to arrange the data so that all the pieces on one theme are together.

There are several ways of doing this:

- *Cut and put in folders approach*: Make several copies of each transcript (keeping the master safe) and cut up each one just as to what is being discussed (your themes or categories). Then sort them into folders, one for each category, so that you have all together what each interviewee said about a given theme. You can then compare and look for similarities/

differences/ceases etc. Do not forget to mark each slip of paper with the respondent's name, initials or some sort of code or you won't be able to remember who said what. Several copies may be needed in case one paragraph contains more than one theme or category. This is time consuming and messy at first, but easier in the long run especially if you have a lot of data and categories.

- *Card index system*: Each transcript must be marked with line numbers for cross-referencing purposes. You have a card for each theme or category and cross-reference each card with each transcript so that you can find what everyone has said about a certain topic. This is quicker initially but involves a lot of referring back to the original transcripts when you write up your results and is usually only suitable for small amounts of data.
- *Computer analysis*: If you have access to a computer package that analyses qualitative data (e.g. NUDIST) then you can use this. These vary in the way they work but these are some of the basic common principles. You can upload your transcripts created in a compatible word-processing package and then the software allows you to mark different sections with various headings/themes. It will then sort all those sections marked with a particular heading and print them off together. This is the electronic version of the folders approach! It is also possible to use a word-processing package to cut and paste comments and to search for particular words.

There is a great danger of subjective interpretation. You must accurately reflect the views of the interviewees and be thorough and methodical. You need to become familiar with your data.

You may find this a daunting and stressful task or you may really enjoy it - sometimes so much that you can delay getting down to the next stage which is interpreting and writing up!

Presenting Qualitative Data in your Dissertation

This would normally follow the topics, themes and categories that you have developed in the analysis and these, in turn, are likely to have been themes that came out in the literature and may have formed the basis for your interview questions. It is usually a mistake to go through each interviewee in turn and what they said on each topic. This is cumbersome and does not give the scope to compare and contrast their ideas with the ideas of others.

Do not analyse the data on a question-by-question basis. You should summarise the key themes that emerge from the data and may give selected quotes if these are particularly appropriate.

Note how a point is made and then emphasized with an appropriate quote. The quotes make the whole text much more interesting and enjoyable to read but be wary of including too many. You should evaluate your own findings in this way and refer to the literature where appropriate. Remember the two concepts of presenting and discussing your findings. By presenting we mean a factual description/summary of what you found. The discussion element is your interpretation of what these findings mean and how they confirm or contradict what you wrote about in your literature section.

If you are trying to test a model then this will have been explored in your literature review and your methodology section will explain how you intend to test it. Your methodology should include who was interviewed with a clear rationale for your choices to explain how this fits into your research questions, how you ensured that the data was unbiased and as accurate as possible, and how the data was analysed. If you have been able to present an adapted model appropriate to your particular context then this should come towards the end of your findings section.

It may be desirable to put a small number of transcripts in the appendices but discuss this with your supervisor. Remember you have to present accurately what was said and what you think it means.

Analyzing survey data is an important and exciting step in the survey process. It is the time that you may reveal important facts about your customers, uncover trends that you might not otherwise have known existed, or provide irrefutable facts to support your plans. By doing in-depth data comparisons, you can begin to identify relationships between various data that will help you understand more about your respondents, and guide you towards better decisions.

It does not discusses specific usage of eSurveysPro for conducting analysis as it is intended to provide a foundation upon which you can confidently conduct your own survey analysis no matter what tool you use.

Three Common Mistakes

Before you dive into analyzing your survey results, take a look back at the big picture. What objectives were you trying to accomplish when you created your survey? Did your survey instrument meet those objectives? Is the data you collected the right data? Do you have sufficient data to properly reach a cease?

Although data analysis is the wrong time to try and rewrite your survey instrument, it is important to remember the scope of your project and stick to it. Many first time surveyors attempt to read"between the lines" while analyzing data. They attempt to answer questions that were not asked by making inferences and assumptions from those that were asked. Doing so amounts to nothing more than guesswork. To avoid this temptation, remember this simple rule:

Rule 1: If you did not ask you do not know.

Another common mistake that many first time surveyors make is to attempt to change data to compensate for poor question design. For example, if a question asked a respondent to indicate his total household income using a scale of values, a mean and median cannot be calculated. Many people try to get around this by assigning each response a value representing the range. Even if the adjustment is made consistently across all responses, the resulting calculations will be wrong. Similarly, trying to analyse a multiple-choice question as if it was a single-select question will often provide erroneous information. In order to avoid this pitfall, remember this simple rule:

Rule 2: Do not alter data to compensate for bad survey design.

A second mistake inexperienced surveyors make is to project the findings to an audience that was not either part of the survey population or not adequately represented. For example, if an HR manager conducts a benefits survey and invites all employees to participate, most people would assume that the results represent all employees since everyone had an opportunity to participate. Provided that enough employees participate, the data might be statistically valid, but is it really representative of all employees? The answer is, it depends. If the survey collected data about employee demographics that could be compared to what is known about the company, then the results do reflect the company as a whole. However, if 80% of the respondents are married and 50% of the total employee base is married, the results of the survey are skewed toward married people. If married people have different benefits needs than single people, using the survey results to make ceases about the entire employee pool would be less accurate than those ceases about the married employees or single employees independently. To avoid this temptation, remember this simple rule:

Rule 3: Do not project your data to people that did not respond.

The earlier you recognize flaws in your survey design and data collection, the more time you will save during analysis. If you questions do not provided the data you need to meet your survey objectives, you'll have to start over. If your questions are vague or ambiguous, you'll have to throw them out. If you do not have an adequate number of responses, you'll have to get more.

Survey Analysis

Analyzing any survey, web or traditional, consists of a number of interrelated processes that are intended to summarize, arrange, and transform data into information. If your survey objective was simply to collect data for your database or data warehouse, you do not have to do any analysis of the data. On the other hand, if your objective was to understand the characteristics of typical customers, then you must transform you raw results in to information that will enable you to paint a clear picture of your customers.

Assuming you need to analyse the data collected from your survey, the process begins with a quick review of the results, followed by editing, analysis, and reporting. To ensure you have accurate data before investing significant time in analysis, it is important that you do not begin analyzing results until you have completed the review and editing process.

Quick Review

Read all your results. Although, this seems like an obvious thing to do, many surveyors think that they can skip this step and dive right in to data analysis. A quick review can tell you lots about your project, including any flaws in questionnaire design or response population, before you spend hours of time in analyzing the data.

During the quick review, you should look at every question and see if the results"make sense". This"gut feel" check of the data will often uncover any issues with your survey project. Most surveyors already have an idea of how they expect their data to look.

A quick review of the data can help you quickly understand that tell you if the people that respond are the right people. For example, if you were conducting a survey of all the employees in a company and you knew that 10% were in the marketing department, 20% in sales, 45% in manufacturing, 5% in management, and 5% finance, and 15% research and development, you could reasonable expect your responses to be similarly distributed.

If your quick review disclosed 80% of your respondents were from the sales department, you know that your survey did not adequately capture a representative sample of all departments within the company.

The quick review can also highlight any problems with the survey instrument. Are most respondents answering all questions? If not, your questionnaire could be flawed in such a way that a person cannot complete the survey. A low response rate could mean your survey invitation was not compelling enough to encourage participation, or your timing was off and a follow-up reminder is needed.

Lastly, the quick review of the survey can show you what areas to focus on for detailed analysis. As stated earlier, most surveyors already know what they expect to get, so your quick review can show you the unexpected.

Editing and Cleaning

Editing and cleaning data is an important step in the survey process. Special care must be taken when editing survey data so that you do not alter or throw out responses in such a way as to bias your results. Although you can begin editing and cleaning your data as soon as results are received, caution should be used since any edits can be lost if the database is rebuilt. To be safe, wait until all data is received before you begin the editing and cleaning process.

To start, find and delete incomplete and duplicate responses. A response should be discarded if the respondent did not complete enough of the survey to be meaningful. For example, if a your survey was intended to determine future buying intentions across various demographic groups and the respondent did not answer any of the demographic questions, you should delete the response. On the other hand, if the respondent answered all the demographic questions but omitted their name or email address, then you should keep the response.

Duplicate responses are a unique issue for electronic surveys. Many tools, such as eSurveysPro, provide built in features to help minimize the risk of duplicate responses. Others, like the popular"infotainment" polls featured on many websites do nothing to eliminate duplicates. Without removing duplicates, your data will be skewed in favour of the duplicate response. Both the count and percentage of the whole will be affected by duplicate responses, and computed means and medians will also be thrown off. To find duplicate responses, carefully examine the answers to any open-ended questions. When two open-ended questions have the exact same answer, a duplicate response is likely to exist. Make sure the response is indeed a duplicate by comparing the answers to all the other questions, and then delete one of the responses if a match is found.

Data cleaning of web surveys usually involves categorizing answers to open-ended questions and multiple-choice questions that include an"other, please specify" response. Because of their nature, open-ended text response questions can provide significant value but they are nearly impossible to process without some form of summarization or tabulation. One of the easiest ways to summarize these questions is to build a list of themes and select the themes that apply as you read each response. Tools such as eSurveysPro allow you to add questions after a survey is run to do just this sort of thing.

A common problem in any survey that needs attention during the editing and cleaning process is when a respondent answers an"other, please specify" question by selecting"other" and then writing in an answer that was one of the listed response options. Without cleaning these answers, the"other" response will be overstated and the correct response will be understated. For example, a demographics question that asks for the respondent's role within the organization may have a response like"faculty, teacher, or student" and a respondent selects"other" and types"professor," you would want to clean the response by switching the other choice to the one for"faculty, teacher, or student".

Once the data preparation is complete, it is time to start analyzing the data and turning it into actionable information.

Detailed Analysis

Analysis is the most important aspect of your survey research project. At this point, you have collected a set of data that must now be turned into actionable information. The process of analysis can lead to a variety of alternative courses of action. Mistakes during analysis can lead to costly decisions down the road, so extreme caution and careful review must be followed throughout the process. Carelessness during analysis can lead to disaster. What you do during analysis will ultimately determine if your survey project is a successful or not.

Depending on what type of information you are trying to know about your audience, you will have to decide what analysis makes sense. It can be as simple as reviewing the graphs that eSurveysPro automatically creates, or conducting in-depth comparisons between questions sets to identify trends or relationships. For most surveyors, a basic analysis using charts, cross tabulations, and filters is sufficient. On the other hand, more sophisticated users may wish to do a more complex statistical analysis using high powered analytical tools such as SPSS, Excel, or any number of number crunching applications.

Graphical Analysis

Graphical analysis simply means displaying the data in a variety of visual formats that make it easy to see patterns and identify differences among the results set. There are many different graphing options available to display data, the most common are Bar, Pie, and Line charts.

Bar charts use solid bars on an X and Y-axis that extend to meet a specific data value indicated on the chart and can be shown either vertically or horizontally. These charts are flexible and are most commonly used to display data from multiple-select, rank order, single-select matrix and numerical questions. Each response option is shown as an independent bar on the chart, and the length of the bar represents the frequency the response was chosen relative to all choices.

Pie charts, or circle graphs, have colourful"slices" representing segments of your data. These charts measure values as compared to a"whole", and the total percentages of the segments always add up to 100%. Pie charts are most useful with single-select questions because the each response is represented visually as a portion of the entire pie. It is easy to interpret which answer received the most responses in a pie chart by selecting the largest potion of the pie. When comparing two sets of data using a pie chart, it is important to make sure the colours used for each response option remain consistent in each chart. If represent the same response options in each chart, this way, a side-by-side visual comparison can quickly be made. Pie charts are not appropriate for multiple-select questions because each respondent can answer choose more than one option, and the sum of the option percentages will exceed 100%.

There are other graphing options such as line charts, area charts and scatter graphs, which are useful when displaying the same data over a period of time. However these formats are not as easy to interpret for casual users, so they should be used sparingly.

Frequency Tables

Frequency tables are another form of basic analysis. These tables show the possible responses, the total number of respondents for each part, and the percentages of respondents who selected each answer. Frequency tables are useful when a large number of response options are available, or the differences between the percentages of each option are small. In most cases, pie or bar charts are easier to work with than frequency tables.

Response	Count	Per cent
Market Analysis	76	13.7%
Quantitative Analysis	150	27.0%
Strategic Planning	56	10.1%
Product Planning	33	5.9%
Promotional Communication	243	43.8%
Creating sales tools	152	27.4%
Providing channel support	157	28.3%

Cross Tabulation

Cross tabulations, or cross tabs, are a good way to compare

two subgroups of information. Cross tabs allow you to compare data from two questions to determine if there is a relationship between them. Like frequency tables, cross tabs appear as a table of data showing answers to one question as a series of rows and answers to another question as a series of columns.

Base Question	Female	Male
Product Manager	57.2%	53.4%
Director	12.6%	14.2%
Product Marketing Manager	24.7%	23.1%
Programmme Manager	2.8%	1.5%
Technical Product Manager	2.8%	7.7%
Total Counts	215	337

Cross tabs are used most frequently to look at answers to a question among various demographic groups. The intersections of the various columns and rows, commonly called cells, are the percentages of people who answered each of the responses. Females and males had relatively similar distribution among various job titles, with the exception of the tile of"Technical Product Manager", where 2.5 times as many males had the title as compared to females. For analysis purposes, cross tabs are a great way to do comparisons.

Filtering

Filtering is the most under-utilized tool used in analysis. Filters allow you select specific subsets of data to view. Unlike a cross tab, that compares two questions, a filter will allow you to examine all questions for a particular subset of the responses. By viewing only the data from the people who responded negatively, look at how they answered other questions. Find patterns or trends that help define why a person answered the way they did. You can even filter on multiple questions and criteria to do a more detailed search if necessary. For example, if you wanted to know the buying intentions of men, over the age of 40, with income of about $50,000, you would set a filter that would remove all those respondents that do not meet your criteria from the results set, thus enabling you to concentrate on the target population.

By applying filters to the date survey responses were received, you can see how the answers change from one time frame to the next. For instance, by continually running a customer satisfaction survey, you can assess changes in customer attitudes over time by filtering on the date the survey was received. You can also use a filter on date received to assess the impact of sales incentive programmmes or new product offerings by comparing survey responses before and after the change.

Filters do not permanently remove the responses of those people that do not match the specified criteria; they simply eliminate them from the current view of the data, making it much easier to perform analysis. By looking at the same question with different filters applied, differences between the various respondents represented by the filter can be quickly seen. Because filters remain in effect until cleared, don't forget to clear them before attempting to analyse your survey responses as a whole, otherwise your observations will be inaccurate, and your recommendations flawed.

Simple Regression Analysis

Determining what factors have lead to a particular outcome is called regression analysis. The regression means you're working backwards from the result to find out why a person answered the way that they did. This can be based on how they answered other questions as well.

For example, you might believe that website visitors who had trouble navigating within your website are likely not return again. If 30% of the respondents said they had trouble navigating through the website and 40% said they would not return, you could look at only those that would not return to determine if poor navigation might be the case. After filtering to only those who would not return, if 30% or less said they had trouble navigating, then this is clearly not the"reason" visitors will not return. By filtering out those that would return, we expect the percentage to increase dramatically. If it does, we still cannot conclude that navigation is"the" reason, only that it might contribute to the respondents not returning. In order to know if it is"the" reason, we would need to ask a direct question.

Reporting

After analyzing your survey data, it is time to create a report of your findings. The complexity and detail need to support you ceases, along with your intended audience, will dictate the format of your report. CEO's require a different level of detail than line managers, so for maximum results consider who is going to receive your report and tailor it to meet their unique needs.

Visual reports, such as an HTML document or Microsoft PowerPoint presentation, are best suited for simple findings. These graphical reports are best when they are light on text and heavy on graphs and charts. They are reviewed quickly rather than studied at length, and most ceases are obvious, so detailed explanations are seldom required. For more complex topics, a detailed report created in Microsoft Word or Adobe Acrobat is often required. Reports created using Word often include much more detailed information, report findings that require significant explanation, are extremely text heavy, and are often studied at great length and in significant detail.

No matter which type of report you use, always remember that information can be more powerfully displayed in a graphic format verses a text or tabular representation. Often, trends and patterns are more obvious and recommendations more effective when presented visually. Ideally, when making comparisons one or more groups of respondents, it is best to show a chart of each group's responses side-by-side. This side-by-side comparison allows your audience to quickly see the differences you are highlighting and will lead to more support for your ceases.

At the beginning of your report, you should review your survey objective and sampling method. This will help your audience understand what the survey was about, and enable you to avoid many questions that are outside of your original objectives. Your report should have a description of your sampling method, including who was invited to participate, over what time frame results were collected, and any issues that might exist relative to your respondent pool. Next, you should include your analysis and ceases in adequate detail to meet the needs of your audience. Include a table or graph for each area of interest and explain why it is noteworthy. You should make recommendations that relate back to your survey objectives. Recommendations can be as simple as conduct further studies to a major shift in company direction. In either case, your recommendation must be within the scope of your survey objective and supported by the data collected.

Cease

Survey analysis is not as easy as downloading results and printing a chart or report, yet it is not so complex that it requires a PhD. We have learned that good analysis begins with good questions, representative participation, and careful interpretation of the data, in order to produce actionable results. Techniques such as charting, filtering, cross tabulation, and regression analysis all help you spot trends and patterns within your data while helping you meet your survey objective. You now have a solid foundation upon which you can confidently conduct your own survey analysis using a tool like eSurveysPro

Chapter 5

Scaling

In the social sciences, scaling is the process of measuring or ordering entities with respect to quantitative attributes or traits. For example, a scaling technique might involve estimating individuals' levels of extraversion, or the perceived quality of products. Certain methods of scaling permit estimation of magnitudes on a continuum, while other methods provide only for relative ordering of the entities.

COMPARATIVE AND NONCOMPARATIVE SCALING

With comparative scaling, the items are directly compared with each other (*example*: Do you prefer Pepsi or Coke?). In noncomparative scaling each item is scaled independently of the others (*Example*: How do you feel about Coke?).

Composite Measures

Composite measures of variables are created by combining two or more separate empirical indicators into a single measure. Composite measures measure complex concepts more adequately than single indicators, extend the range of scores available and are more efficient at handling multiple items. In addition to scales, there are two other types of composite measures. Indexes are similar to scales except multiple indicators of a variable are combined into a single measure. The index of consumer confidence, for example, is a combination of several measures of consumer attitudes. A typology is similar to an index except the variable is measured at the nominal level.

Indexes are constructed by accumulating scores assigned to individual attributes, while scales are constructed through the assignment of scores to patterns of attributes.

While indexes and scales provide measures of a single dimension, typologies are often employed to examine the intersection of two or more dimensions. Typologies are very useful analytical tools and can be easily used as independent variables, although since they are not unidimensional it is difficult to use them as a dependent variable.

Data types

The type of information collected can influence scale construction. Different types of information are measured in different ways.

- Some data are measured at the nominal level. That is, any numbers used are mere labels: they express no mathematical properties. Examples are SKU inventory codes and UPC bar codes.
- Some data are measured at the ordinal level. Numbers indicate the relative position of items, but not the magnitude of difference. An example is a preference ranking.
- Some data are measured at the interval level. Numbers indicate the magnitude of difference between items, but there is no absolute zero point. Examples are attitude scales and opinion scales.
- Some data are measured at the ratio level. Numbers indicate magnitude of difference and there is a fixed zero point. Ratios can be calculated. Examples include: age, income, price, costs, sales revenue, sales volume, and market share.

Scale Construction Decisions

- What level of data is involved (nominal, ordinal, interval, or ratio)?
- What will the results be used for?
- Should you use a scale, index, or typology?
- What types of statistical analysis would be useful?

- Should you use a comparative scale or a noncomparative scale?
- How many scale divisions or categories should be used (1 to 10; 1 to 7; ?3 to +3)?
- Should there be an odd or even number of divisions? (Odd gives neutral centre value; even forces respondents to take a non-neutral position.)
- What should the nature and descriptiveness of the scale labels be?
- What should the physical form or layout of the scale be? (graphic, simple linear, vertical, horizontal)
- Should a response be forced or be left optional?

Comparative Scaling Techniques

- *Pairwise comparison scale*: A respondent is presented with two items at a time and asked to select one (example: Do you prefer Pepsi or Coke?). This is an ordinal level technique when a measurement model is not applied. Krus and Kennedy (1977) elaborated the paired comparison scaling within their domain-referenced model. The Bradley-Terry-Luce (BTL) model can be applied in order to derive measurements provided the data derived from paired comparisons possess an appropriate structure. Thurstone's Law of comparative judgment can also be applied in such contexts.
- *Rasch model scaling*: Respondents interact with items and comparisons are inferred between items from the responses to obtain scale values. Respondents are subsequently also scaled based on their responses to items given the item scale values. The Rasch model has a close relation to the BTL model.
- *Rank-order scale*: A respondent is presented with several items simultaneously and asked to rank them (example: Rate the following advertisements from 1 to 10.). This is an ordinal level technique.
- *Bogardus social distance scale*: Measures the degree to which a person is willing to associate with a class or

type of people. It asks how willing the respondent is to make various associations. The results are reduced to a single score on a scale. There are also non-comparative versions of this scale.

- *Q-Sort scale*: Up to 140 items are sorted into groups based a rank-order procedure.
- *Guttman scale*: This is a procedure to determine whether a set of items can be rank-ordered on a unidimensional scale. It utilizes the intensity structure among several indicators of a given variable. Statements are listed in order of importance. The rating is scaled by summing all responses until the first negative response in the list. The Guttman scale is related to Rasch measurement; specifically, Rasch models bring the Guttman approach within a probabilistic framework.
- *Constant sum scale*: A respondent is given a constant sum of money, script, credits, or points and asked to allocate these to various items (example: If you had 100 Yen to spend on food products, how much would you spend on product A, on product B, on product C, etc.). This is an ordinal level technique.
- *Magnitude estimation scale*: In a psychophysics procedure invented by S. S. Stevens people simply assign numbers to the dimension of judgment. The geometric mean of those numbers usually produces a power law with a characteristic exponent. In cross-modality matching instead of assigning numbers, people manipulate another dimension, such as loudness or brightness to match the items. Typically the exponent of the psychometric function can be predicted from the magnitude estimation exponents of each dimension.

Non-comparative Scaling Techniques

- *Continuous rating scale (also called the graphic rating scale)*: Respondents rate items by placing a mark on a line. The line is usually labeled at each end. There are sometimes a series of numbers, called scale points, under the line. Scoring and codification is difficult.

- *Likert scale*: Respondents are asked to indicate the amount of agreement or disagreement (from strongly agree to strongly disagree) on a five- to nine-point scale. The same format is used for multiple questions. This categorical scaling procedure can easily be extended to a magnitude estimation procedure that uses the full scale of numbers rather than verbal categories.
- *Phrase completion scales*: Respondents are asked to complete a phrase on an 11-point response scale in which 0 represents the absence of the theoretical construct and 10 represents the theorized maximum amount of the construct being measured. The same basic format is used for multiple questions.
- *Semantic differential scale*: Respondents are asked to rate on a 7 point scale an item on various attributes. Each attribute requires a scale with bipolar terminal labels.
- *Stapel scale*: This is a unipolar ten-point rating scale. It ranges from +5 to ?5 and has no neutral zero point.
- *Thurstone scale*: This is a scaling technique that incorporates the intensity structure among indicators.
- *Mathematically derived scale*: Researchers infer respondents' evaluations mathematically. Two examples are multi dimensional scaling and conjoint analysis.

Scale Evaluation

Scales should be tested for reliability, generalizability, and validity. Generalizability is the ability to make inferences from a sample to the population, given the scale you have selected. Reliability is the extent to which a scale will produce consistent results. Test-retest reliability checks how similar the results are if the research is repeated under similar circumstances. Alternative forms reliability checks how similar the results are if the research is repeated using different forms of the scale. Internal consistency reliability checks how well the individual measures included in the scale are converted into a composite measure.

Scales and indexes have to be validated. Internal validation checks the relation between the individual measures included in the scale, and the composite scale itself. External validation checks the relation between the composite scale and other indicators of the variable, indicators not included in the scale. Content validation (also called face validity) checks how well the scale measures what is supposed to measure. Criterion validation checks how meaningful the scale criteria are relative to other possible criteria. Construct validation checks what underlying construct is being measured. There are three variants of construct validity. They are convergent validity, discriminant validity, and nomological validity. The coefficient of reproducibility indicates how well the data from the individual measures included in the scale can be reconstructed from the composite scale.

COLLEGE AND UNIVERSITY RANKINGS

The College and university rankings are lists of universities and liberal arts colleges in higher education, an order determined by any combination of factors. Rankings can be based on subjectively perceived"quality," on some combination of empirical statistics, or on surveys of educators, scholars, students, prospective students or others. Rankings are often consulted by prospective students and their parents in the university and college admissions process.

In addition to rankings of institutions, there are also rankings of specific academic programmmes, departments, and schools. Rankings are conducted by magazines and newspapers and in some instances by academic practitioners.

Rankings may vary significantly from country to country] Colleges outside of the English speaking world are believed to have a distinct disadvantage A Cornell University study found that the rankings in the United States significantly affected colleges' applications and admissions. In the United

Kingdom, several newspapers publish league tables which rank universities.

There has been much debate since the late 1990s about both the usefulness and political correctness of college rankings in the United States. Some higher education experts, like Kevin Carey of Education Sector, have argued that such rankings as the U.S. News and World Report's college rankings system is merely a list of criteria that mirrors the superficial characteristics of elite colleges and universities. Carey,"[The] U.S. News ranking system is deeply flawed. Instead of focusing on the fundamental issues of how well colleges and universities educate their students and how well they prepare them to be successful after college, the magazine's rankings are almost entirely a function of three factors: fame, wealth, and exclusivity." He suggests that there are more important characteristics parents and students should research to select colleges, such as how well students are learning and how likely students are to earn a degree.

INTERNATIONAL RANKINGS FROM REGIONAL ORGANIZATIONS

Several regional organizations (arranged alphabetically here) provide worldwide rankings, including:

Academic Ranking of World Universities

Average positions from 3 International rankings: Newsweek, Academic Ranking of World Universities and Times Higher Education.

The Academic Ranking of World Universities compiled by the Shanghai Jiao Tong University, which was a large-scale Chinese project to provide independent rankings of universities around the world primarily to measure the gap between Chinese and"world class" universities. The results have often been cited by The Economist magazine in ranking universities of the world. The number of Nobel Prize winners (which are predominantly awarded to the physical sciences) and Fields Medalists (mathematics) Furthermore, the ranking does not take into the account whether those winners are still associated with the institutes nor consider where the award winning works were performed.

As a result, it creates a superficial phantom award counting game in favour of older and more established institutes even though these institutes may not have active winners in their faculty rosters, or the rich American institutes that attract prize winners with big financial reward even though no award winning work was done there. In Nature and Science Journals as one of the major criteria in ranking institutes appears highly superficial because many award winning works were not published in these journals. In addition to the criticisms, a 2007 paper from the peer-reviewed journal Scientometrics finds that the results from the Shanghai university rankings are irreproducible

G-Factor

A ranking of university and college web presence, the G-Factor methodology counts the number of links only from other university websites relying solely on Google's search engine. The G-Factor is an indicator of the popularity or importance of each university's website from the combined perspectives of the creators of many other university websites. It is therefore claims to be a kind of extensive and objective peer review of a university through its website - in social network theory terminology, the G-Factor measures the centrality of each university's website in the network of university websites

Global University Ranking: Global University Ranking is ranking of over 400"world-known" universities by the RatER, a Russian-based non-commercial independent rating agency supported by the academic society of Russia The methodology uses the pool of universities from what it has determined are the four main global rankings (Academic Rankings of World Universities, HEEACT, Times-QS, and Webometrics) and utilizes a pool of"experts" formed by project officials and managers to determine the rating scales for every indicator of performance of the universities in seven areas including academic performance, research performance, faculty expertise, resource availability, socially significant activities of graduates, international activities of the university, and international opinion of foreign universities. Each expert performs his own evaluation of performance indicators of all the universities. The final evaluation of each indicator is determined as the average of all the expert evaluations

HEEACT - Performance Ranking of Scientific Papers for World Universities. The Performance Ranking of Scientific Papers for World Universities is a bibliometric based ranking produced by the Higher Education Evaluation and Accreditation Council of Taiwan.

The performance measures are composed of eight indicators representing three different criteria of scientific papers performance: research productivity, research impact, and research excellence. This project employs bibliometric methods to analyse and rank the scientific papers performances of the top 500 worlds' universities and the top 300 worlds' universities among six fields.

The HEEACT performance ranking system is designed for research universities. The objective indicators used in this ranking system are designed measure both long-term and short-term research performance of each university. The 2007 ranking methodology was determined to favour universities with medical schools, and in response, HEEACT added additional fields of ranking to the ranking] The six fields based rankings are based on the subject categorization of WOS, including Agriculture and Environment Sciences (AGE)?Clinical Medicine (MED)?Engineering, Computing and Technology (ENG)?Life Sciences (LIFE)?Natural Sciences (SCI) and Social Sciences (SOC).

Newsweek

In August 2006, the American magazine Newsweek published a ranking of the Top 100 Global Universities, utilizing selected criteria from two pre-existing rankings (the Academic Ranking of World Universities by Shanghai Jiao Tong University and The Times Higher Education-QS rankings), with the additional criterion of library holdings (number of volumes). It aimed at taking into account openness and diversity, as well as distinction in research'

SCImago institutions rankings: 2009 world report

SCImago Research Group's SCImago institutions rankings: 2009 world report ranks all institutions which had more than 100 outputs indexed in the multinational publishing giant Elsevier's Scopus database in 2007. The ranking comprises 1,527 higher education institutions, 335 health organisations, 216 government organisations, 29 private bodies and 17 other organisations. SCImago derives five measures from the Scopus database: total outputs, cites per document (which are heavily influenced by field of research as well as research quality), international collaboration.

THE - QS World University Rankings

Times Higher Education, a British publication that reports specifically on issues related to higher education, in association with Quacquarelli Symonds, annually published the THE - QS World University Rankings, a list of 500 ranked universities from around the world, between 2004 and 2009 In comparison with other rankings, many more non-American universities (especially British) populate the upper tier of the THE ranking The THE - QS ranking faces criticism due to the more subjective nature of its assessment criteria, which are largely based on a'peer review' system of over 9000 scholars and academics in various fields The best-known college and university rankings in the United States-compiled by US News and World Report-bases its"World's Best Universities" rankings on data from the Times Higher Education-QS World University Rankings

On 30 October 2009, Times Higher Education broke with QS and signed an agreement with Thomson Reuters to provide the data for its annual World University Rankings, which are now called Times Higher Education World University Rankings. The magazine will develop a new rankings methodology in the coming months, in consultation with its readers, its editorial board and the firm. Thomson Reuters will collect and analyse the data used to produce the rankings on behalf of Times Higher Education. The results will be published annually from autumn 2010. QS, which has collected and analysed the rankings data for the past six years, will no longer have any involvement with Times Higher Education's World University Rankings

The connection between any unfavourable image/ reputation universities may develop (and/or their association, by country, to those universities linked to the wrongdoing) to a halt in their climb or even to a drop in their Times Higher Education - QS World University Rankings. This is because 40% and 10% of THE - QS World Methodology is based on Academic Peer Review and Employer Review respectively. In essence, any unfavourable image developed by a group of universities, associated by country, tends to harm their collective rankings. For this reason, universities worldwide should seriously consider adhering to internationally accepted standards so that they don not run the risk of sliding in the ranks on the international front.

However, the Times Higher Education-QS World University Rankings have been criticised by many more for placing too much emphasis on peer review, which receives 40 per cent of the overall score. Some people have expressed concern about the manner in which the peer review has been carried out In a report, Peter Wills from the University of Auckland, New Zealand wrote of the Times Higher Education-QS World University Rankings:

"But we note also that this survey establishes its rankings by appealing to university staff, even offering financial enticements to participate. Staff are likely to feel it is in their greatest interest to rank their own institution more highly than others. This means the results of the survey and any apparent change in ranking are highly questionable, and that a high ranking has no real intrinsic value in any case. We are vehemently opposed to the evaluation of the University to the outcome of such PR competitions."

Some errors have also been reported in the faculty-student ratio used in the ranking. At the 16th Annual New Zealand

International Education Conference held at Christchurch, New Zealand in August 2007, Simon Marginson presented a paper that outlines the fundamental flaws underlying the Times Higher Education-QS World University Rankings.

Some of the points mentioned include:

- Half of the THES index is comprised by existing reputation: 40 per cent by a reputational survey of academics ('peer review'), and another 10 per cent determined by a survey of'global employers'. The THES index is too easily open to manipulation as it is not specified who is surveyed or what questions are asked. By changing the recipients of the surveys, or the way the survey results are factored in, the results can be shifted markedly.
  - The pool of responses is heavily weighted in favour of academic'peers' from nations where The Times (sic) is well-known, such as the UK, Australia, New Zealand, Malaysia and so on.
  - It's good when people say nice things about you, but if it is better when those things are true. It is hard to resist the temptation to use the THES rankings in institutional marketing, but it would be a serious strategic error to assume that they are soundly based.
  - Results have been highly volatile. There have been many sharp rises and falls, especially in the second half of the THES top 200 where small differences in metrics can generate large rankings effects. Fudan in China has oscillated between 72 and 195, RMIT in Australia between 55 and 146. In the US, Emory has risen from 173 to 56 and Purdue fell from 59 to 127."

WEBOMETRICS

Webometrics Ranking of World Universities The Webometrics Ranking of World Universities is produced by the Cybermetrics Lab (CCHS), a unit of the National Research Council (CSIC), the main public research body in Spain. It offers information about more than 6,000 universities just as to their web-presence (a computerised assessment of the scholarly contents and visibility and impact of the whole university webdomain). The Webometrics Ranking is built from a database of over 16,000 universities. The Top 6,000 universities are shown in the main rank, but even more are covered in the regional lists. Institutions from developing countries benefit from this policy as they obtain knowledge of their current position even if they are not World-Class Universities. The ranking started in 2004 and is based on a combined indicator that takes into account both the volume of the Web contents and the visibility and impact of this web publications according to the number of external inlinks they received. The ranking is updated every January and July, providing Web indicators for universities worldwide.

This approach takes into account the wide range of scientific activities represented in the academic websites, frequently overlooked by the bibliometric indicators.

Webometric indicators are provided to show the commitment of the institutions to Web publication. Thus, Universities of high academic quality may be ranked lower than expected due to a restrained web publication policy.

The results show a high correlation with others Rankings but also a larger than expected presence of US and Canada universities in the Top 200, delayed positions of small and medium size biomedical institutions as well as many French, Italian and Japanese universities not in top ranks

WUHAN UNIVERSITY

Another ranking is by the Research Centre for Chinese Science Evaluation at Wuhan University. The ranking is based on Essential Science Indicators (ESI).

Regional and National Rankings

Regional and national rankings are carried out in Africa, Asia, Europe, North America, South America and Oceania.

- *Egypt*: Cairo University is ranked between 401 to 500 in the QS World University Ranking for 2009

- *South Africa*: Academic League tables of South African universities are largely based on international university rankings, because there have not as yet been published any specifically South African rankings.
- *China*: The Chinese Academy of Management Science produces the Chinese university rankings.
- *Iran*: Fakhre Mazi magazine states the most significant universities of Iran and worldwide.
- *Pakistan*: Higher Education Commission in Pakistan releases annual ranking of universities in Pakistan, based on strict standards
- *India*: Magazines like India Today, Outlook, Mint, Dataquest and EFY conduct annual surveys with listed rankings in the major disciplines.
- *Philippines*: Higher education in the Philippines Academic rankings in the Philippines are conducted by the Professional Regulation Commission and the Commission on Higher Education, and this is based on the average passing rates in all courses of all Philippine colleges and universities in the board tests
- *European Union*: The European Commission also weighed in on the issue, when it compiled a list of the 22 universities in the EU with the highest scientific impact, measuring universities in terms of the impact of their scientific output. This ranking was compiled as part of the Third European Report on Science and Technology Indicators, prepared by the Directorate General for Science and Research of the European Commission in 2003.

Being an official document of the European Union (from the office of the EU commissioner for science and technology), which took several years of specialist effort to compile, it can be regarded as a highly reliable source. Unlike the other rankings, it only explicitly considers the top institutions in the EU, but ample comparison statistics with the rest of the world are provided in the full report. The report say"University College London comes out on top in both publications, however, the table lists the top scoring university as"Univ London" indicating that the authors counted the scientific output of the University of London, rather than its individual constituent colleges.

In this ranking, the top two universities in the EU are also Oxford and Cambridge, as in the Jiao Tong and Times ranking. This ranking, however, stresses more the scientific quality of the institution, as opposed to its size or perceived prestige Thus smaller, technical universities, such as Eindhoven (Netherlands) and Munich (Germany) are ranked third, behind Cambridge, and followed by University of Edinburgh in the UK. The report does not provide a direct comparison between EU and universities in the rest of the world - although it does compute complex scientific impact score, measured against a world average.

In December 2008, the European Commission has published a call for tenders, inviting bidders to design and test a new multi-dimensional university ranking system with global outreach. The first results of the envisaged pilot project will be available in the first half of 2011.

- *France*: Le Nouvel Observateu and other popular magazines occasionally offer rankings of universities,"Grandes écoles" and their preparatory schools, the"Prépas".
- *Germany*: The English version of the German CHE University Ranking is provided by the DAAD.

In December 2007, a new ranking was published in Germany from the Centre for Higher Education Development. The CHE"Ranking of Excellent European Graduate Programmes" (CHE ExcellenceRanking for short) included the disciplines of biology, chemistry, mathematics and physics. The ranking is designed to support the search for master's or doctoral programmes at higher education institutions (HEIs). Alongside this, the CHE wants to highlight the research strengths of European HEIs and provide those HEIs listed in the ranking with ideas for the further improvement of their already excellent programmes.

Every year, the CHE also publishes a ResearchRanking

showing the research strengths of German universities. The CHE ResearchRanking is based on the research-related data of the CHE UniversityRanking.

- *Ireland: The Sunday Times compiles a league of Irish universities based on a mix of criteria, for example*:
  - Average points needed in the Leaving Certificate (end-of-secondary-school examination) for entry into an undergraduate course
  - Completion rates, staff-student ratio and research efficiency
  - Quality of accommodation and sports facilities
  - Non-standard entry (usually mature students or students from deprived neighbourhoods)
  - Athletics
- *Italy*: Every year La Repubblica, in collaboration with CENSIS compiles a league of Italian universities.
- *Romania*: A ranking of Romanian universities was published in 2006 and 2007 by the Ad Astra association of Romanian scientists.
- *Switzerland*: The swissUp Ranking provided a ranking for Swiss university and polytechnic students until 2004. The swissUp Ranking is no more conducted. Switzerland has no ranking anymore or evaluation system of its universities.
- *UK*: The Research Assessment Exercises (RAE) are attempts by the UK government to evaluate the quality of research undertaken by British Universities. Each subject, called a unit of assessment is given a ranking by a peer review panel. The rankings are used in the allocation of funding each university receives from the government. The last assessment was made in 2001. The RAE provides quality ratings for research across all disciplines. Panels use a standard scale to award a rating for each submission. Ratings range from 1 to 5*, according to how much of the work is judged to reach national or international levels of excellence. Higher education institutions (HEIs) which take part receive grants

from one of the four higher education funding bodies in England, Scotland, Wales and Northern Ireland.

There are several annual University and College Rankings:

- Times Good University Guide
- Independent Complete University Guide
- The Sunday Times University Guide
- The Guardian - University Guide (mainly for undergraduate studies)

Standards of undergraduate teaching are assessed by the Quality Assurance Agency for Higher Education (QAA), an independent body established by the UK's universities and other higher education institutions in 1997. The QAA was under contract to the Higher Education Funding Council for England to assess quality for universities in England in a system of subject review. This replaced a system of Teaching Quality Assessments (TQAs) which aimed to assess the administrative, policy and procedural framework within which teaching took place did directly assess teaching quality. As this system of universal inspection was hugely burdensome, it was replaced by a system of information provision, one part of which is a national student survey which has been run three times, and publishes scores which have been used by the league table industry. The rankings have had to create artificial differences, however, as students are generally very satisfied.

- *Ukraine*: Ministry of Education and Science of Ukraine performs official yearly university evaluations Zerkalo Nedeli newspaper ranked the top 200 Ukrainian universities in 2007.Kyiv Student Council ranks universities on criteria of students` satisfaction.
- *South America*: In Argentina the evaluation, accreditation, and ranking of the higher education programmmes is made by the National Commission for University Evaluation and Accreditation
- *Brazil*: Maclean's, a Canadian news magazine, publishes an annual ranking of Canadian Universities, called the Maclean's University Rankings The criteria used by the magazine include

characteristics of the student body, classes, faculty, finances, the library, and reputation. The rankings are split into three categories: primarily undergraduate (schools that focus on undergraduate studies with few to no graduate programmmes), comprehensive (schools that have both extensive undergraduate studies and an extensive selection of graduate programmmes), and medical doctoral (schools that have a professional medical programmme and a selection of graduate programmmes)

These rankings have received scrutiny and criticism from universities. For example, the University of Calgary produced a formal study examining the methodology of the ranking, illuminating the factors that determined the university's rank, and criticizing certain aspects of the methodology. In addition, the University of Alberta and the University of Toronto have both expressed displeasure over Maclean's ranking system. A notable difference between rankings in the United States and Maclean's rankings, however, is that Maclean's does not include privately-funded universities in its rankings. However, the vast majority and the best-known universities in Canada are publicly funded.

Beginning in September 2006, a number (over 20) of Canadian universities, including several of the most prestigious and largest universities such as the University of Toronto, University of British Columbia, University of Alberta and McMaster University, jointly refused to participate in Maclean's survey The president of the University of Alberta, Indira Samarasekera, wrote of this protest that Maclean's initially filed a"Freedom of Information" request but that"it was too late" for the universities to respond.

New York Times reported that, given the U.S. News weighting methodology,"it's easy to guess who's going to end up on top: Harvard, Yale and Princeton round out the first three essentially every year. In fact, when asked how he knew his system was sound, Mel Elfin, the rankings' founder, often answered that he knew it because those three schools always landed on top. When a new lead statistician, Amy Graham, changed the formula in 1999 to one she considered more statistically valid, the California Institute of Technology jumped to first place.

United States National Research Council Rankings

The National Research Council ranks the doctoral research programmes of universities across the US but the last time it produced a report was in 1995. There is no announced date for the next report but data collection for it began in 2006

The Top American Research Universities

A research ranking of American universities is researched and published in the Top American Research Universities by The Centre for Measuring University Performance. The information used can be found in public-accessible materials, reducing the possibility of manipulation. The research method is consistent from year to year and any changes are explained in the publication itself. References from other studies are cited

Washington Monthly College rankings

The Washington Monthly's"College Rankings", last published in 2009, began as a research report in 2005 and introduced its first official rankings in the September 2006 issue.

It offers American university and college rankings based upon the following criteria:

- "How well it performs as an engine of social mobility (ideally helping the poor to get rich rather than the very rich to get very, very rich)"
- "How well it does in fostering scientific and humanistic research"
- "How well it promotes an ethic of service to country".

Forbes College rankings

In 2008, Forbes.com published a list of"America's Best Colleges." Forbes updated the list in 2009 The Forbes rankings use the listing of alumni published in Who's Who in America, student evaluations of professors from ratemyprofessors.com, self-reported salaries of alumni from payscale.com, four-year graduation rates, numbers of students and faculty receiving"nationally competitive awards", and four-year accumulated student debt to calculate the rankings. The 2009 rankings were praised for inclusion of less commonly recognized colleges in their rankings, as well as their higher rankings of US military academies; however, they were also criticized for their heavy emphasis on liberal arts colleges, heavy reliance on highly subjective sources, and the significantly lower rankings given to many nationally recognized colleges and research institutions, including members of the Ivy League The validity of rankings in which the federal service academies which are completely funded with taxpayer money are compared to institutions that must find their own funds are open to question

Forbes also published"Top Colleges For Getting Rich." These rankings are considered questionable because they were partly based upon anonymous readers' votes] For example, it ranks College of the Holy Cross higher than it does Johns Hopkins University based on figures obtained by payscale.com which ranks colleges by self-reported earnings of graduates.

Other Rankings of US Universities

Other organizations which compile general US annual college and university rankings include the Fiske Guide to Colleges, Princeton Review, and College Prowler.

One commercial ranking service is Top Tier Educational Services Student centred criteria are used and despite the two-year completely updated study, the rankings are updated every quarter from new input data. The criteria include subjective data, such as peer assessment, desirability, and objective data, such as ACT and SAT scores, and the high school GPA of admitted students.

Such new rankings plans measures what decision makers think as opposed to why. They may or may not augment these statistics for reputation with hard, qualitative information. The authors discuss their rankings system and methodology with students but do not share their specific research tools or formulas. Again, the problem with such a ranking that uses subjective opinions is that it is very prone to personal bias, prejudice and bounded rationality. Also, public universities will be penalized because besides an academic mission, they have a social mission. They simply cannot charge as much money, or be as selective, as private universities. Also, the fact that the ranking service is a commercial company raises the question whether there are any hidden business motives behind its rankings.

Among the rankings dealing with individual fields of study is the Philosophical Gourmet Report or"Leiter Report" (after its founding author, Brian Leiter, then of the University of Texas at Austin, now University of Chicago), a ranking of philosophy departments. This report has been at least as controversial within its field as the general U.S. News rankings, attracting criticism from many different viewpoints. Notably, practitioners of continental philosophy, who perceive the Leiter report as unfair to their field, have compiled alternative rankings.

Avery et al. recently published a working paper for the National Bureau of Economic Research titled"A Revealed Preference Ranking of U.S. Colleges and Universities." Rather than ranking programmmes by traditional criteria, their analysis uses a statistical model based on applicant preferences. They based their data on the applications and outcome of 3,240 high school students. The authors feel that their ranking is less subject to manipulation compared to conventional rankings.

The Gourman Report, which was last published in 1996, ranked the quality of undergraduate majors and graduate programmmes.

There also exist Gallup polls that ask American adults,"All in all, what would you say is the best college or university in the United States?" Global Language Monitor produces a"TrendTopper MediaBuzz" rankings of the Top 225 US colleges and universities twice a year, according to their appearances on the internet, in blogs, social media, and global electronic and print media It publishes overall results for both University and College categories using the Carnegie Foundation for the Advancement of Teaching's classifications as the basis to distinguish between Universities and Liberal Arts Colleges. The rankings include 125 top universities, the 100 top colleges, the change in the rankings over time, a"Predictive Quantities Indicator" (PQI) Index number (for relative rankings), as well as rankings by Momentum (yearly and 90-day snapshots), and rankings by State. Most recently, the schools were ranked on November 1, 2009, with the last day of 2008 as the base, with two interim snapshots in 2009. The PQI index is produced by Global Language Monitor's proprietary PQI algorithm, which has been criticized by some linguists for its use in a highly publicized counting of the total number of English words.The Global Language Monitor also sells the TrendTopper MediaBuzz Reputation Management solution for higher education for which"colleges and universities can enhance their standings among peers" The Global Language Monitor states that it"does not influence the Higher Education rankings in any way"

- *Mexico*: Estudio Comparativo de Universidades Mexicanas (ECUM). Mexican colleges, universities and other research institutions have been compared in the Estudio Comparativo de Universidades Mexicanas (ECUM) produced within the Universidad Nacional Autónoma de México(UNAM) ECUM provides data on intitutional participation on ISI Web of Knowledge indexed journals; faculty participation in each of the three levels of Mexico's National Researchers System (SNI); graduate degrees within CONACYT's (National Council of Science and Technology) register of quality graduate programmmes (PNPC).

ECUM provides online access to data for 2007 and 2008 through the Explorador de datos del ECUM (ExECUM). Institutional data can be visualized through three options:

- A selection of the most prominent 58 universities (43

publics and 13 privates). This selection accounts for more than 60 per cent of undergraduate and graduate enrollments. It includes public federal universities (UNAM, Instituto Politécnico Nacional, Universidad Autónoma Metropolitana, Universidad Pedagógica Nacional, Universidad del Ejercito y la Fuerza Aérea, Colegio de México, Universidad Autónoma de Chapingo, Universidad Autónoma Agraria Antonio Narro); 35 public state universities (UPES), and a group of private institutions that feature within ECUM's selected classification data.

- Result tables for the top 20 institutions in each of the data labels in this study. These include some of the selected universities in addition to the rest of Mexico's higher education institutions, as well as institutes, centres and other research producing organizations.
- A personalized selection option from more that 600 institutions. These are classified by institutional type, institutional gatherings, by activity sector or in alphabetical order.

ExECUM has been designed in order to allow users to establish comparison types and levels which they consider relevant. For this purpose data is presented in its raw form and virtually no indicators or ponderations are built within this system. Users can establish relationships between variables and build their own indicators according to their own need and analythical perspectives.

Based on this comparative study project, the Dirección General de Evaluación Institucional at UNAM, creators of ECUM, have published a first report called Desempeño de Universidades Mexicanas en la Función de Investigación: Estudio Comparativo providing an analysis of the data for 2007.

- *Criticism (North America)*: American college and university ranking systems have drawn criticism from within and outside higher education in Canada and the United States. Some institutions critical of the ranking systems include Reed College, Alma College, Mount Holyoke College, St. John's College, Earlham College, MIT, and Stanford University.

2007 Movement

On 19 June 2007, during the annual meeting of the Annapolis Group, members discussed the letter to college presidents asking them not to participate in the"reputation survey" of the U.S. News and World Report survey. As a result,"a majority of the approximately 80 presidents at the meeting said that they did not intend to participate in the U.S. News reputational rankings in the future." However, the decision to fill out the reputational survey or not will be left up to each individual college as:"the Annapolis Group is not a legislative body and any decision about participating in the US News rankings rests with the individual institutions. The statement also said that its members"have agreed to participate in the development of an alternative common format that presents information about their colleges for students and their families to use in the college search process. This database will be web based and developed in conjunction with higher education organizations including the National Association of Independent Colleges and Universities and the Council of Independent Colleges.

U.S. News and World Report editor Robert Morse issued a response on 22 June 2007, in which he argued: "In terms of the peer assessment survey, we at U.S. News firmly believe the survey has significant value because it allows us to measure the"intangibles" of a college that we can't measure through statistical data. Plus, the reputation of a school can help get that all-important first job and plays a key part in which grad school someone will be able to get into. The peer survey is by nature subjective, but the technique of asking industry leaders to rate their competitors is a commonly accepted practice. The results from the peer survey also can act to level the playing field between private and public colleges."

In reference to the alternative database discussed by the Annapolis Group, Morse also argued:

"It's important to point out that the Annapolis Group's stated goal of presenting college data in a common format has been tried before [...] U.S. News has been supplying this exact college information for many years already. And it appears that NAICU will be doing it with significantly less comparability and functionality. U.S. News first collects all these data (using an agreed-upon set of definitions from the Common Data Set). Then we post the data on our website in easily accessible, comparable tables. In other words, the Annapolis Group and the others in the NAICU initiative actually are following the lead of U.S. News."

In 1996, Gerhard Casper, then-president of Stanford University, US News and World Report simply changes the formulas used to calculated financial resources:

Knowing that universities - and, in most cases, the statistics they submit - change little from one year to the next, we can only conclude that what are changing are the formulas the magazine's number massagers employ. And, indeed, there is marked evidence of that this year. In the category"Faculty resources," even though few of us had significant changes in our faculty or student numbers, our class sizes, or our finances, the rankings' producers created a mad scramble in rank order [...data...]. Then there is"Financial resources," where Stanford dropped from #6 to #9, Harvard from #5 to #7. Our resources did not fall; did other institutions' rise so sharply? we infer that, in each case, the formulas were simply changed, with notification to no one, not even your readers, who are left to assume that some schools have suddenly soared, others precipitously plummeted

QUESTIONNAIRE DESIGN

Questionnaires are an inexpensive way to gather data from a potentially large number of respondents. Often they are the only feasible way to reach a number of reviewers large enough to allow statistically analysis of the results. A well-designed questionnaire that is used effectively can gather information on both the overall performance of the test system as well as information on specific components of the system.

If the questionnaire includes demographic questions on the participants, they can be used to correlate performance and satisfaction with the test system among different groups of users.

It is important to remember that a questionnaire should be viewed as a multi-stage process beginning with definition of the aspects to be examined and ending with interpretation of the results. Every step needs to be designed carefully because the final results are only as good as the weakest link in the questionnaire process. Although questionnaires may be cheap to administer compared to other data collection methods, they are every bit as expensive in terms of design time and interpretation.

The steps required to design and administer a questionnaire include:

- Defining the Objectives of the survey
- Determining the Sampling Group
- Writing the Questionnaire
- Administering the Questionnaire
- Interpretation of the Results

This document will concentrate on how to formulate objectives and write the questionnaire. Before these steps are examined in detail, it is good to consider what questionnaires are good at measuring and when it is appropriate to use questionnaires.

WHAT CAN QUESTIONNAIRES MEASURE?

Questionnaires are quite flexible in what they can measure, however they are not equally suited to measuring all types of data. We can classify data in two ways, Subjective vs. Objective and Quantitative vs. Qualitative.

When a questionnaire is administered, the researchers control over the environment will be somewhat limited. This is why questionnaires are inexpensive to administer. This loss of control means the validity of the results are more reliant on the honesty of the respondent. Consequently, it is more difficult to claim complete objectivity with questionnaire data then with results of a tightly controlled lab test. For example, if a group of participants are asked on a questionnaire how long it took them to learn a particular function on a piece of software, it is likely that they will be biased towards themselves and answer, on average, with a lower than actual time. A more objective usability test of the same function with a similar group of participants may return a significantly higher learning time. More elaborate questionnaire design or administration may provide slightly better objective data, but the cost of such a questionnaire can be much higher and offset their economic advantage. In general, questionnaires are better suited to gathering reliable subjective measures, such as user satisfaction, of the system or interface in question.

Questions may be designed to gather either qualitative or quantitative data. By their very nature, quantitative questions are more exact then qualitative. For example, the word"easy" and"difficult" can mean radically different things to different people.

Any question must be carefully crafted, but in particular questions that assess a qualitative measure must be phrased to avoid ambiguity. Qualitative questions may also require more thought on the part of the participant and may cause them to become bored with the questionnaire sooner. In general, we can say that questionnaires can measure both qualitative and quantitative data well, but that qualitative questions require more care in design, administration, and interpretation.

WHEN TO USE A QUESTIONNAIRE?

There is no all encompassing rule for when to use a questionnaire. The choice will be made based on a variety of factors including the type of information to be gathered and the available resources for the experiment.

A questionnaire should be considered in the following circumstances:

- *When resources and money are limited*: A Questionnaire can be quite inexpensive to administer. Although preparation may be costly, any data collection plans will have similar preparation expenses. The administration cost per person of a questionnaire can be as low as postage and a few photocopies. Time is also an important resource that questionnaires can maximize. If a questionnaire is self-administering, such as a e-mail questionnaire, potentially several thousand people could respond in a few days. It would be impossible to get a similar number of usability tests completed in the same short time.

- *When it is necessary to protect the privacy of the participants*: Questionnaires are easy to administer confidentially. Often confidentiality is the necessary to ensure participants will respond honestly if at all. Examples of such cases would include studies that need to ask embarrassing questions about private or personal behaviour.
- *When corroborating other findings*: In studies that have resources to pursue other data collection strategies, questionnaires can be a useful confirmation tools. More costly planss may turn up interesting trends, but occasionally there will not be resources to run these other tests on large enough participant groups to make the results statistically significant. A follow-up large scale questionnaire may be necessary to corroborate these earlier results.

Defining the Objectives of the Survey

The importance of well-defined objectives can not be over emphasized. A questionnaire that is written without a clear goal and purpose is inevitably going to overlook important issues and waste participants' time by asking useless questions. The questionnaire may lack a logical flow and thereby cause the participant to lose interest.

Consequential, what useful data you may have collected could be further compromised. The problems of a poorly defined questionnaire do not end here, but continue on to the analysis stage. It is difficult to imagine identifying a problem and its cause, let alone its solution, from responses to broad and generalizing questions. In other words, how would it be possible to reach insightful ceases if one didn't actually know what they had been looking for or planning to observe.

A objective such as"to identify points of user dissatisfaction with the interface and how these negatively affect the software's performance" may sound clear and to the point, but it is not. The questionnaire designer must clarify what is meant by user dissatisfaction. Is this dissatisfaction with the learning of the software, the power of the software, of the ease of learning the software? Is it important for the users to learn the software quickly if they learn it well? What is meant by the software's performance? How accurate must the measurements be? All of these issues must be narrowed and focused before a single question is formulated. A good rule of thumb is that if you are finding it difficult to write the questions, then you haven't spent enough time defining the objectives of the questionnaire. The questions should follow quite naturally from the objectives.

Writing the Questionnaire

At this point, we assume that we have already decided what kind of data we are to measure, formulated the objectives of the investigation, and decided on a participant group. Now we must compose our questions.

If the preceding steps have been faithfully executed, most of the questions will be on obvious topics. Most questionnaires, however, also gather demographic data on the participants. This is used to correlate response sets between different groups of people. It is important to see whether responses are consistent across groups. For example, if one group of participants is noticeably less satisfied with the test interface, it is likely that the interface was designed without fair consideration of this group's specific needs. This may signify the need for fundamental redesign of the interface. In addition, certain questions simply may only be applicable to certain kinds of users. For example, if one is asking the participants whether they find the new tutorial helpful, we do not want to include in our final tally the responses of experienced users who learned the system with an older tutorial. There is no accurate way to filter out these responses without simply asking the users when they learned the interface.

Typically, demographic data is collected at the beginning of the questionnaire, but such questions could be located anywhere or even scattered throughout the questionnaire. One obvious argument in favour of the beginning of the questionnaire is that normally background questions are easier to answer and can ease the respondent into the questionnaire. One does not want to put off the participant by jumping in to the most difficult questions. We are all familiar with such kinds of questions.

It is important to ask only those background questions that are necessary. Do not ask income of the respondent unless there is at least some rational for suspecting a variance across income levels.

There is often only a fine line between background and personal information. You do not want to cross over in to the personal realm unless absolutely necessary. If you need to solicit personal information, phrase your questions as unobtrusively as possible to avoid ruffling your participants and causing them to answer less than truthfully.

What Kind of Questions do we Ask?

In general, there are two types of questions one will ask, open format or closed format.

Open format questions are those that ask for unprompted opinions. In other words, there are no predetermined set of responses, and the participant is free to answer however he chooses. Open format questions are good for soliciting subjective data or when the range of responses is not tightly defined. An obvious advantage is that the variety of responses should be wider and more truly reflect the opinions of the respondents. This increases the likelihood of you receiving unexpected and insightful suggestions, for it is impossible to predict the full range of opinion. It is common for a questionnaire to end with and open format question asking the respondent for her unabashed ideas for changes or improvements.

Open format questions have several disadvantages. First, their very nature requires them to be read individually. There is no way to automatically tabulate or perform statistical analysis on them. This is obviously more costly in both time and money, and may not be practical for lower budget or time sensitive evaluations. They are also open to the influence of the reader, for no two people will interpret an answer in precisely the same way. This conflict can be eliminated by using a single reader, but a large number of responses can make this impossible. Finally, open format questions require more thought and time on the part of the respondent. Whenever more is asked of the respondent, the chance of tiring or boring the respondent increases.

Closed format questions usually take the form of a multiple-choice question. They are easy for the respondent, give. There is no clear consensus on the number of options that should be given in an closed format question. Obviously, there needs to be sufficient choices to fully cover the range of answers but not so many that the distinction between them becomes blurred. Usually this translates into five to ten possible answers per questions. For questions that measure a single variable or opinion, such as ease of use or liability, over a complete range (easy to difficult, like to dislike), conventional wisdom says that there should be an odd number of alternatives. This allows a neutral or no opinion response. Other schools of thought contend that an even number of choices is best because it forces the respondent to get off the fence. This may induce the some inaccuracies for often the respondent may actually have no opinion. However, it is equally arguable that the neutral answer is over utilized, especially by bored questionnaire takers. For larger questionnaires that test opinions on a very large number of items, such as a music test, it may be best to use an even number of choices to prevent large numbers of no-thought neutral answers.

Closed format questions offer many advantages in time and money. By restricting the answer set, it is easy to calculate percentages and other hard statistical data over the whole group or over any subgroup of participants. Modern scanners and computers make it possible to administer, tabulate, and perform preliminary analysis in a matter of days. Closed format questions also make it easier to track opinion over time by administering the same questionnaire to different but similar participant groups at regular intervals. Finally closed format questions allow the researcher to filter out useless or extreme answers that might occur in an open format question.

Whether your questions are open or closed format, there are several points that must by considered when writing and interpreting questionnaires:

- *Clarity*: This is probably the area that causes the greatest source of mistakes in questionnaires. Questions must be clear, succinct, and unambiguous. The goal is to eliminate the chance that the question will mean different things to different people. If the designers fails to do this, then essentially participants will be answering different questions.

To this end, it is best to phrase your questions empirically if possible and to avoid the use of necessary adjectives. For example, it asking a question about frequency, rather than supplying choices that are open to interpretation such as:

- Very Often
- Often
- Sometimes
- Rarely
- Never

It is better to quantify the choices, such as:

- Every Day or More
- 2-6 Times a Week
- About Once a Week
- About Once a Month
- Never

There are other more subtle aspects to consider such as language and culture. Avoid the use of colloquial or ethnic expressions that might not be equally used by all participants. Technical terms that assume a certain background should also be avoided.

- *Leading Questions*: A leading question is one that forces or implies a certain type of answer. It is easy to make this mistake not in the question, but in the choice of answers. A closed format question must supply answers that not only cover the whole range of responses, but that are also equally distributed throughout the range. All answers should be equally likely. An obvious, nearly comical, example would be a question that supplied these answer choices:
  - Superb
  - Excellent
  - Great
  - Good
  - Fair
  - Not so Great

  A less blatant example would be a Yes/No question that asked:
  - Is this the best CAD interface you have every used?

In this case, even if the participant loved the interface, but had an favourite that was preferred, she would be forced to answer No. Clearly, the negative response covers too wide a range of opinions.

A better way would be to ask the same question but supply the following choices:

- Totally Agree
- Partially Agree
- Neither Agree or Disagree
- Partially Disagree
- Totally Agree

This example is also poor in the way it asks the question. It's choice of words makes it a leading question and a good example on phrasing.

- *Phrasing*: Most adjectives, verbs, and nouns in English have either a positive or negative connotation. Two words may have equivalent meaning, yet one may be a compliment and the other an insult. Consider the two words"child-like" and"childish", which have virtually identical meaning. Child-like is an affectionate term that can be applied to both men and women, and young and old, yet no one wishes to be thought of as childish.

In the example of"Is this the best CAD interface you have every used?" clearly"best" has strong overtones that deny the participant an objective environment to consider the interface. The signal sent the reader is that the designers surely think it is the best interface, and so should everyone else. Though this may seem like an extreme example, this kind of superlative question is common practice.

A more subtle, but no less troublesome, example can be made with verbs that have neither strong negative or positive overtones.

Consider the following two questions:

- Do you agree with the Governor's plan to oppose increased development of wetlands?
- Do you agree with the Governor's plan to support curtailed development of wetlands?

They both ask the same thing, but will likely produce different data. One asks in a positive way, and the other in a negative. It is impossible to predict how the outcomes will vary, so one method to counter this is to be aware of different ways to word questions and provide a mix in your questionnaire. If the participant pool is very large, several versions may be prepared and distributed to cancel out these effects.

- *Embarrassing Questions*: Embarrassing questions dealing with personal or private matters should be avoided. Your data is only as good as the trust and care that your respondents give you. If you make them feel uncomfortable, you will lose their trust. Do not ask embarrassing questions.
- Hypothetical Questions Hypothetical are based, at best, on conjecture and, at worst, on fantasy.

  I simple question such as:

  - If you were governor, what would you do to stop crime?

This forces the respondent to give thought to something he may have never considered. This does not produce clear and consistent data representing real opinion. Do not ask hypothetical questions.

- *Prestige Bias*: Prestige bias is the tendency for respondents to answer in a way that make them feel better. People may not lie directly, but may try to put a better light on themselves. For example, it is not uncommon for people to respond to a political opinion poll by saying they support Samaritan social programmmes, such as food stamps, but then go on to vote for candidates who oppose those very programmmes. Data from other questions, such as those that ask how long it takes to learn an interface, must be viewed with a little skepticism. People tend to say they are faster learners than they are.

There is little that can be done to prevent prestige bias. Sometimes there just is no way to phrase a question so that all the answers are noble. The best means to deal with prestige bias is to make the questionnaire as private as possible. Telephone interviews are better than person-to-person interviews, and written questionnaires mailed to participants are even better still. The farther away the critical eye of the researcher is, the more honest the answers.

Now What?

Now that you've completed you questionnaire, you are still not ready to send it out. Just like any manufactured product, your questionnaire needs to go through quality testing. The major hurdle in questionnaire design is making it clear and understandable to all. Though you have taken great care to be clear and concise, it is still unreasonable to think that any one person can anticipate all the potential problems. Just as a usability test observes a test user with the actual interface, you must observe a few test questionnaire takers. You will then review the questionnaire with the test takers and discuss all points that were in any way confusing and work together to solve the problems. You will then produce a new questionnaire. It is possible that this step may need to be repeated more than once depending on resources and the need for accuracy.

Ceases

Questionnaire design is a long process that demands careful attention. A questionnaire is a powerful evaluation tool and should not be taken lightly. Design begins with an understanding of the capabilities of a questionnaire and how they can help your research. If it is determined that a questionnaire is to be used, the greatest care goes into the planning of the objectives. Questionnaires are like any scientific experiment. One does not collect data and then see if they found something interesting. One forms a hypothesis and an experiment that will help prove or disprove the hypothesis.

Questionnaires are versatile, allowing the collection of both subjective and objective data through the use of open or closed format questions. Modern computers have only made the task of collecting and extracting valuable material more efficient. However, a questionnaire is only as good as the questions it contains. There are many guidelines that must be met before you questionnaire can be considered a sound research tool. The majority deal with making the questionnaire understandable and free of bias. Mindful review and testing is necessary to weed out minor mistakes that can cause great changes in meaning and interpretation. When these guidelines are followed, the questionnaire becomes a powerful and economic evaluation tool

Chapter 6

Statistics in Research

The word'Statistics' refers to some numerical facts relating to any phenomena in social sciences or exact sciences. Facts and figures pertaining to population, production, national income, profits, sales, bank rates, family patterns, dowry system, animal kingdom, plant life, bacteria; will all constitute statistics. The word'statistics' seems to have derived from either the Latin word'status' or the Italian word'Statitsta' both meaning'a political state'.

The word'statistics' is presently referred to in two distinct senses. In its first reference as a plural noun, it means an aggregate or collection of numerical or quantitative expressions of facts i.e.'numerical data' or simply'data'. In its second reference as a singular noun, it means a body of principles and methods used in the collection, presentation, analysis and interpretation of numerical data.

Bowley defines statistics as the science of counting in one context. The emphasis made here is only on the collection of data. At another place he says: statistics may rightly be called the science of averages.Boddington defines statistics as the science of estimates and probabilities. Lovitt, the science of statistics deals with the collection. Classification and tabulation of numerical facts as the basis for explanation, description and comparison of phenomena. Seligman defines statistics as the science which deals with the methods of collecting classifying, presenting, comparing and interpreting numerical data collected to throw some light on any sphere of enquiry. Croxton and Cowden define statistics as the collection, presentation analysis and interpretation of numerical data.

CHARACTERISTICS OF STATISTICS

- Statistics should be numerically expressed. For example the statement Rajan is of height 6' 1" makes the fact clear and easily understandable.
- Statistics are aggregates of facts. Statistics means the facts pertaining to a group of individuals or individual item.
- Statistics are affected to a market extent by a multiplicity of causes. There are a variety of forces or factors operating on the facts and figures in an aggregate. The influence of any particular factor cannot be isolated.
- Statistics must be collected in a systematic manner for a predetermined purpose. Determination of the main purpose or objectives of any scientific study is the first and the most important step which in turn paves way for other operations to follow.
- Statistics are enumerated or estimated according to reasonable standards of accuracy.
- Statistics should be placed in relation to each other.

APPLICATIONS OF STATISTICS

Sociology is one of the social sciences aiming to discover the basic structure of human society, to identify the main forces that hold groups together or weaken them and to learn the conditions that transform social life. It highlights and illuminates aspects of social life that otherwise might be only obscurely recognized and understood. The sociologist may be called upon for help with a special problem such as social conflict, urban plight or the war on poverty or crimes. His contribution lies in the ability to clarify the underlaying nature of social problems to estimate more exactly their dimensions and to identify aspects that seem most amenable to remedy with the knowledge and skills at hand. He naturally lands in sociological research which is the purposeful effort to learn more about society than one can in the ordinary course of living. Keeping in view of the problem he sets forth his objectives collects materials or data and uses statistical techniques and the knowledge and theory already established on similar topics to achieve his objectives. So statistical data and statistical methods are quite indispensable for sociological research studies. There is a growing emphasis recently on social survey methods or research methodology in all faculties of arts.

Sociologists seek the help of statistical tools to study cultural change in the society, family pattern, prostitution, crime,marriage system etc.They also study statistically the relation between prostitution and poverty, crime and poverty,drunkness and crime, illiteracy and crime etc.Thus statistics is of immense use in various sociological studies.

Statistics and Government

The functions of a government are more varied and complex. Various depts in the state are required to collect and record statistical data in a systematic manner for an effective administration. Data pertaining to various fields namely population, natural resources, production both agricultural and industrial,finance,trade,exports and imports, prices, labour, transport and communication, health, education, defence,crimes etc are the most fundamental requirements of the state for its administration. It is only on this basis of such data; the government decides on the priority areas, gives more attention to them through target oriented programmes and studies the impact of the programmes for its future guidelines.

Statistics and Planning

Modern age is an age of planning and statistics are indispensable for planning. Tippett planning greater or lesser degree according to the government in power is the order of the day and without statistics, planning is inconceivable. Based only on a correct assessment of various resources both human and material of the country proper planning can be made. A study of data relating to population, agriculture, industry, prices, employment, health, education enables the planners to fix up time-bound targets on the social and economic fronts evaluation of such economic and social programmes at different stages by means of related data gathered continuously and systematically is also done to decide whether the programmes are on towards the goal or targets set.

Statistics and Economics

In the fields of economics it is almost impossible to think of a problem which does not require an extensive use of statistical data. Most of the laws in economics are based on a study of a large number of units and their analysis is enabled by statistical data and the statistical methods. The important economic aspects like production, consumption, exchange and distribution are described, compared and correlated with the aid of statistical tools. By a statistical study of time series on prices, sales, production one can study their trends, fluctuations and the underlaying causes. Thus statistics is indispensable in economic analysis.

Methods of Central Tendency of Averages

Condensation of data is necessary for a proper statistical analysis. A large number of big numbers are not only confusing to mind but also difficult to analyse.After a thorough scrutiny of collected data, classification which is a process of arranging data into different homogenous classes according to resemblances and similarities is carried out first.Then of course tabulation of data is resorted to. The classification and tabulation of the collected data besides removing the complexity render condensation and comparison.

An average is defined as a value which should represent the whole mass of data. It is a typical or central value summarizing the whole data. It is also called a measure of central tendency for the reason that the individual values in the data show some tendency to centre about this average. It will be located in between the minimum and the maximum of the values in the data.

There are five types of average which are:

- Arithmatic Mean
- Median
- Mode

- Geometric Mean and
- Harmonic Mean

Arithmetic Mean: The Arithmetic mean or simply the mean is the best known easily understood and most frequently used average in any statistical analysis. It is defined as the sum of all the values in the data.

Median: Median is another widely known and frequently used average.It is defined as the most central or the middle most value of the data given in the form of an array. By an array, we mean an arrangement of the data either in ascending order or descending order of magnitude. In the case of ungrouped data one has to form an array first and then locate the middle most value which is the median. For ungrouped data the median is fixed by using,

Median = [n+1/2] the value in the array.

Mode: The word mode seems to have been derived French'a la mode' which means'that which is in fashion'. It is defined as the value in the data which occurs most frequently. In other words, it is the most frequently occurring value in the data. For ungrouped data we form the array and then fix the mode as the value which occurs most frequently. If all the values are distinct from each other, mode cannot be fixed. For a frequency distribution with just one highest frequency such data are called unimodal or two highest frequencies [such data are called bimodal],mode is found by using the formula,

Mode = l + cf2/f1+f2

Where l is the lower limit of the model class, c is its class interval f1 is the frequency preceding the highest frequency and f2 is the frequency succeeding the highest frequency.

Relative merits and demerits of Mean, Median and Mode

Mean: The mean is the most commonly and frequently used average. It is a simple average, understandable even to a layman. It is based on all the values in a given data. It is easy to calculate and is basic to the calculation of further statistical measures of dispersion, correlation etc. Of all the averages, it is the most stable one. However it has some demerits. It gives undue weightages to extreme value. In other words it is greatly influenced by extreme values.Moreover; it cannot be calculated for data with open - ended classes at the extreme. It cannot be fixed graphically unlike the median or the mode. It is the most useful average of analysis when the analysis is made with full reference to the nature of individual values of the data.Inspite of a few shortcomings; it is the most satisfactory average.

Median: The median is another well-known and widely used average. It is well-defined formula and is easily understood. It is advantageously used as a representative value of such factors or qualities which cannot be measured. Unlike the mean, median can be located graphically. It is also possible to find the median for data with open ended classes at the extreme. It is amenable for further algebraic processes.However,it is an average, not based on all the values of the given data. It is not as stable as the mean. It has only a limited use in practice.

Mode: It is a useful measure of central tendency, as a representative of the majority of values in the data. It is an average, easily understood by even laymen. Its calculations are not difficult. It can be ascertained even for data with open-ended classes at the extreme. It can be located by graphical means using a frequency curve. The mode is not based on all the values in the data. It become less useful when the data distribution is not uni-model.Of all the averages, it is the most unstable average.

Measures Of Dispersion

When a mass of quantitative data is collected for a statistical purpose, it is tabulated to a form with in view that its characteristics as a whole may be readily determined. A single significant and representative expression or a measure called average is then computed to summarize or explain as a whole the entire data. This form of a comparing two or more groups or series but an average along is not a satisfactory criterion for such a purpose. Dispersion means the extent of values around some average.

There are four measures of dispersion, namely:

- Range
- Quartile Deviation or semi interquartile range

- Mean Deviation
- Standard Deviation

Range

Range is the simplest measure of dispersion. It is defined as the positive difference between the largest and the smallest values in the given data. It is easily understood and computed but depends exclusively on the two extreme values while it is desirable to have a measure dependent on all the values. The range is a very useful measure in statistical quality control of products in industries wherein the interest lies in getting a quick rather than an accurate measure of variability.

Quartile Deviation or Semi-interquartile Range

This measure is based on two measures called the lower or first quartile and the upper or third quartile. The lower quartile denoted as Q1 is defined as the value which leaves ¼ of the values below it when the data forms an array and the third quartile denoted as Q3 is the value which leaves 3/4s of values below it when the data forms an array. Once Q1 and Q3 are known, the quartile deviation Q-D is given by

Q-D= Q3 – Q1/2 and

Q3- Q1 is called the interquartile range

Mean Deviation

The mean deviation of a data is defined as the means of the absolute deviation of values from some average especially the arithmetic mean or median. It is a better measure of dispersion than range and Q D as it takes into account, all the values in the given data for ungrouped data.

M.D about median M can also be defined by considering median instead of mean.

Standard Deviation

The standard deviation abbreviated as S.D and symbolically represents as sigma is the most important and wide used measure of dispersion. It is defined as the root mean square deviation of values from their mean i.e. it is the square root of the means of square deviation of values from their mean. The square of the s.d. is called the variance.

Coefficient of Dispersion

For any data, it is always desirable that the measure of dispersion is less. A small value for the measure means that the values in the data are more or less consistent, centreing on their average. Suppose it is required to compare the dispersion between two or more data. For this purpose any measure of dispersion cannot be used as such for two reasons 1.the two data under study may certain to different variables such as heights and weights of the individual.

Number of marriages and ages of persons who have committed suicides etc and 2.even if the variables in the two data are the same, their averages may be different. Such a measure is the coefficient of dispersion which is defined as the ratio between measure dispersion and an average. This coefficient is a constant, rendering ready comparison of dispersion between data.

There are four coefficients which are commonly referred, namely:

- Quartile coefficient of dispersion = Quartile Deviation/Mean
- Coefficient of variation (C.V) = Standard Deviation/ Mean × 100
- Mean Deviation/Mean
- Mean Deviation/Median of which the first two are the most frequently used coefficients.

Association of Attributes

In social sciences, we come across certain phenomena which are incapable of quantitative measurement.Blindness, deafness, religion; juvenile delinquency, marital status etc are some phenomena which are not measurable. Such characteristics are called attributes. In these cases, one can make only counting of individuals who possess or do not possess these attributes. In other words what can do is to state so many individuals are blind or so many non-blind. While dealing with one attribute the classification of data is done on the basis of presence or absence of the attribute. It is also absolutely essential that a clear-cut definition of the attribute under study is made because only such a definition paves way for the counting of the individuals possessing or not possessing the attribute.

Two attributes are said to be associated only if they appear together in a great number of cades than is to be expected if they are independent. On the other hand, if the number of observed cases is less than the expected, under assumption of independence, attributes are associated. In order to ascertain whether the attributes are associated or not the following methods can be used.

- Comparison of observed and expected frequencies.
- Proportion method
- Yule's coefficient of Association
- Coefficient of colligation
- Coefficient of contingency

Association of Attributes

In social sciences, we come across certain phenomena which are incapable of quantitative measurement.Blindness, deafness, religion; juvenile delinquency, marital status etc are some phenomena which are not measurable. Such characteristics are called attributes. In these cases, one can make only counting of individuals who possess or do not possess these attributes.

In other words what can do is to state so many individuals are blind or so many non-blind. While dealing with one attribute the classification of data is done on the basis of presence or absence of the attribute. It is also absolutely essential that a clear-cut definition of the attribute under study is made because only such a definition paves way for the counting of the individuals possessing or not possessing the attribute. Two attributes are said to be associated only if they appear together in a great number of cades than is to be expected if they are independent. On the other hand, if the number of observed cases is less than the expected, under assumption of independence, attributes are associated. In order to ascertain whether the attributes are associated or not the following methods can be used.

- Comparison of observed and expected frequencies.
- Proportion method
- Yule's coefficient of Association
- Coefficient of colligation
- Coefficient of contingency

Scientific Study of Social Phenomena

The need to have sociology as a new branch of knowledge was realised quite late and many branches of knowledge had already taken shape and gained respectability before sociology was conceived. These branches of knowledge have been termed as Sciences. Sociology grew under the shadow of illustrious predecessors like Physics and Biology tended to emulate their patterns.

The basic assumption that is central to these sciences that distinguish them from medieval learning is that: Truth about the world can be known through sensory observation. Thus the scientist seeks his truth by observing the world rather than by waiting for revelations. Sociology also inherited this premise. An illustration of knowledge based upon sensory observation is if one sees a bird that is called by the people a crow and finds its black, then one arrives at the ceases that crow is black. The veracity of this knowledge lies in the fact that it is supported by sensory observation. But our senses can sometimes deceive us.Scientists adopt certain procedural steps that seek to reduce such a possibility. These acts of procedural steps constitute the Scientific Method.

Elements of Scientific Methods Perspective

Knowledge based on sensory observation has a paradoxical character. The following statement seeks to convey this paradox in a simple way. In order to gain knowledge about anything we should know something about it. If we know nothing at all about the object of our enquiry we shall never be able to know anything about it. In case we are totally ignorant about something and yet want to acquire knowledge about it through sensory observation, we make certain assumptions about it, and start our enquiry with the belief that these assumptions are true. Of course if these assumptions are not supported by facts gathered through sensory observations, we should be ready to abandon them. The significance of these assumptions is that they tell us what to look for or where to direct our sensory observation. If a Doctor trained in modern medicine wants to find out the reasons for the symptoms like headache, giddiness, and general weakness, he might examine the digestive systems, the food taken by his patient or he might monitor the heart beats and blood pressure or enquire about his sleeping patterns and also take in to account the weather conditions. He may find his answer from these conditions.

A shaman in a tribal village also tries to cure a patient with similar symptoms. He may explore the possibility of a spell caused by a witch or disenchantment of the super natural power with the person concerned due to some act of omission or commission on his part. In the case of the doctor trained in modern medicine his search for the cause is governed by a set of assumptions namely: human body is unified whole though it has specialized parts.

These parts tend to be interdependent and malfunctioning of one lead to malfunctioning of the other. Basing himself on such assumption he is likely to see interrelationship between headache and digestion failure etc.On the other hand the shaman by means of assumption that world is governed by super natural forces that need to be propitiated. Failure to do so might invite divine retribution. Thus one can see how underlying assumptions shape one's enquiry. A set of mutually consistent assumptions which underlie our approach to things we want to explore is called a perspective. All systematized enquiries need perspective. So it is required for sociology as well.

Concepts

Language is a system of symbols that forms the medium through which we comprehend the world around and inside us and it is the basis of our thought processes. It also acts as a means of communication with others without which social life would be impossible.

Language has been termed as a system of symbols because linguistic terms are abstractions i.e they are mentally created and to them certain meanings are imputed by which they come to stand for the real phenomena.

All languages are made up of concepts. Only difference being that concept in scientific language is more precisely and unambiguously defined. Concepts help in comprehending the reality that a science is engaged in studying. They act as mediums of short cut communication among those associated with the enquiry. In sociology most of the concepts are terms taken from day to day language which is given precise meaning.

Theory and Facts

There is an intricate relation between theory and fact. The popular understanding of this relationship obscures more than it illuminates. They are generally conceived as direct opposites. Theory is confused with speculation and theory remains speculation until it is proved. When this proof is made, theory becomes fact. Facts are thought to be definite, certain, without question and their meaning to be self-evident. Science is thought to be concerned with facts alone. Theory is supposed to be realm of philosophers. Scientific theory is therefore thought to be merely summation of facts that have been accumulated upon a given subject. However if we observe the way scientists actually do research, it becomes clear 1. Theory and fact are not diametrically opposed but inextricably intertwined.2. Theory is not speculation.3.Scientists are very much concerned with both theory and facts.

A fact is regarded as an empirically verifiable observation. A theory refers to the relationship between facts or to the ordering of them in some meaningful way. Facts of science are the product of observations that are not random but meaningful, i.e., theoretically relevant. Therefore we cannot think of facts and theory as being opposed rather they are interrelated in many complex ways. The development of science can be considered as a constant interplay between theory and fact.

Theory is a tool of science in these ways:

- It defines the major orientation of a science, by defining the kinds of data that are to be abstracted.
- It offers a conceptual plans by which the relevant phenomena are systematized, classified and interrelated.
- It summarizes facts into empirical generalizations and systems of generalizations.
- It predicts facts and
- It points to gaps in our knowledge.

On the other hand facts are also productive of theory in these ways:

- Facts help to initiate theories.
- They lead to the reformulation of existing theory.
- They cause rejection of theories that do not fit the facts.
- They change the focus and orientation of theory and
- They clarify and redefine theory.

There is interplay between theory and fact. Although popular opinion thinks of theory as being opposed to fact since theory is mere speculation, observation of what scientists actually do suggests that fact and theory stimulate each other. The growth of science is seen is seen in new facts and new theory. Facts take their ultimate meaning from the theories which summarize them, classify them, predict them, point them out and define them. However theory may direct the scientific process, facts in turn play a significant role in the development of theory.

New and anomalous facts may initiate new theories. New observations lead to the rejection and reformulation of existing theory or may demand that we redefine our theories. Concepts which had seemed definite in meaning are clarified by the specific facts relating to them. The sociologist must accept the responsibilities of the scientists who must see fact in theory and theory in fact. This is more difficult than philosophic speculation about reality or the collection of superficial certainties but it leads more surely to the achievement of scientific truth about social behaviour.

GATHERING INFORMATION AND CONSTRUCTING EXPLANATIONS

The basic procedural steps involved in gathering information and construction of explanation are:

- Observation
- Comparison and Classification
- Generalization

Observation

Scientific knowledge is based on sensory observation of reality. Those aspects of reality that are definite certain self-evident and have independent existence are called"Facts". Since they have an independent existence of their own so they are amendable to sensory observation. However scientific investigation is not a search for isolated and random facts rather it is a guided enquiry to test the authenticity of definite propositions that form the starting point of gathering information. They are called"hypothesis".

A hypothesis states what we are looking for. It formulates the logical relationship between different aspects of reality expressed in terms of scientific concepts. A good hypothesis should be scientific, simple and presented in a testable form. Sociology also makes use of hypothesis in carrying our sociological research but this practice is not always strictly adhered to. Especially when a sociologist is trying to explore society, about which he knows very little, it would not be possible to begin the research with hypothesis. Some example of hypothesis which may be used in sociological enquiry can be.

- Crime rates are higher in urban areas than in rural areas.
- Pace of urbanization increases with that of industrialization.

Sometimes hypothesis may be tested under experimental conditions. Most of the established sciences do use experimental method quite successfully. However, in

Sociology, experimental method is only rarely possible due to both practical and ethical reason: so observation is carried out mostly under non-experimental conditions. Sources of data include social survey, observational and interview methods etc.

Comparison and Classification

Next step in research is to process the information collected so as to make it intelligible. Comparison and classification are the steps involved in processing the data. Sometimes sociologists also try to build typologies by using comparative method.

Typologies are models consisting of a set of traits which tend to occur in conjunction with each other. When the typology is rooted in empirical data and the traits included are such that they tend to be most commonly distributed, it is called the average type. Building an average type helps in categorizing the whole class of phenomenal under one category.

Otherwise the researcher would be left to deal with such phenomena as isolated cases. Mechanical solidarity and Organic solidarity are examples of such average types. They are the mental creations of the social scientists and in their pure form they could not be found to be replicated anywhere in reality. Such typologies are called ideal types.

Generalization

A generalization is a form of propositional knowledge that holds true for the whole class of phenomena. It postulates the existence of a determinate relationship between a set of variables (variable is an aspect of reality that can assume different values) in terms of which empirically ascertainable regularities can be explained.

However in Sociology perfect casual relationship is not possible. At best we can establish statistical correlations. The generalizations can be arrived at if a hypothesis is repeatedly supported by empirical data. If generalization is found to be almost universally true, it may be called a law. Other terms for generalization having different degrees of generality are a theory a thesis or a tendency statement.

Generalisation serve two major functions:

- They make knowledge manageable.
- Generalizations also help in predicting the phenomena.

Prediction becomes possible.Nature behaves in an ordered manner and science aims at discovering this order that is expressed through generalization. Thus generalizations are possible only so long as reality itself displays a regular pattern. Sociology also approaches its subject matter on the premise that social reality is an ordered and patterned reality. However sociologists have not been able to discover laws similar to those in physical and natural sciences, the reason being that their assumption about the nature of social reality is only partly true and therefore only limited generalization indicating broad trends could be discovered. The social phenomena are extremely complex and changeable and do not conform to any definite pattern.

Hypothesis

Facts are dependent upon a theoretical framework for their meaning. They are also statements of relationships between concepts. Theory can give direction to the search for facts. A hypothesis states what we are looking for. When facts are assembled, ordered and seen in a relationship they constitute a theory. The theory is not speculation but is built upon fact. Now the various facts in a theory may be logically analysed and relationships other than those stated in the theory can be deduced. At this point there is no knowledge as to whether such deductions are correct. The formulation of the deduction however constitutes a hypothesis; if verified it becomes part of a future theoretical construction. The relation between the hypothesis and theory is very close indeed. A theory states a logical relationship between facts. From this theory other propositions can be deduced that should be true, if the first relationship holds. These deduced propositions are hypotheses.

A hypothesis looks forward. It is a proposition which can be put to a test to determine its validity. It may seem contrary to or in accord with common sense. It may prove to be correct or incorrect. In any event however, it leads to an empirical test. Whatever the outcome, the hypothesis is a question put in such a way that an answer of some kind can be forthcoming. It is an example of the organized skepticism of science. The refusal to accept any statement without empirical verification. Every worthwhile theory then permits the formulation of additional hypotheses. These when tested are either proved or disapproved and in turn constitute further tests of the original theory.

Design of Proof: Testing the Hypothesis

The function of the hypothesis is to state a specific relationship between phenomena in such a way that this relationship can be empirically tested. The basic method of this demonstration is to design the research so that logic will require the acceptance or rejection of the hypothesis on the basis of resulting data.

The basic designs of logical proof were formulated by John Stuart Mill and still remain the foundation of experimental procedure although many changes have been made. His analysis provides two methods. The first of these is called the method of agreement. When stated positively this holds that when two or more cases of a given phenomenon have one and only one condition in common then that condition may be regarded as the cause or effect of the phenomenon. The classical experimental design is a development from both the positive and negative canons and attempts to avoid the weaknesses of both of them. In the simplified form Mill called it the method of difference. To develop the classical design of proof by the method of difference it is necessary only to make two series of observations and situations.

Design of Sociological Research

"Design of Sociological Research" or Research Design is a broad plan of a piece of empirical research specifying the manner in which data are to be collected and analysed in order to test Research Design derived from theory, or to develop insights into the problem being investigated. It combines relevance of the problem with economy in procedure. The design stage is most crucial phase of the research process. A particular design may specify whether experiment, social survey, participant observation, other methods, or a combination of more than one method will be used.

Nowadays it has became imperative to chart out the research design before starting any work, Modern research in sociology thus specifies the probable method to be used for date collection analysis, etc keeping in view, time money and, of course, the topic of research.

Generally, a research design includes the following steps:

- Universe of Study (whether a tribe, or a village, or an urban areas, or a particular group, etc.)
- Subject of Study (whether it focuses on the whole society, or any specific institution or a part of it).
- Tentative relationship between certain variables (Formulating a Research Design but it is not obligatory to start with a Research Design; certain research designs lack Research Design).
- Sets of selected methods (whether participant observation, Interview, Questionnaire, or some other methods of data collection would be used).
- Analytical categories (by which the empirical data is subjected to analysis and interpretation).

Although the steps for formulating a research design remain common the designs differ, depending on the research purpose. The latter may be to report an unknown tribe, or to investigate the intricacies of an institution, or to test a specific Research Design in field situation, or to test a well-designed Research Design in controlled situations. Depending on the research purpose, one delineates an appropriate research design. However, validity of the steps for forming the design will always have to be there. Every study has its own purpose, but all the research purposes can be conceptualized as falling in one of the following categories. Each category refers to a type of research design. Thus, generally, social scientists identify three types of research design on the basis of different research purposes.

These are:

- *Explanatory research Design*: When the purpose of the study is to explore a new universe, one that has not been studied earlier, the research design, is called explanatory. The research purpose in this case is to gain familiarity in unknown areas. Often explanatory research design is used to formulate a problem for precise investigation, or aims at formulating Research Design. Thus, often when the universe of study is an unknown community, explanatory design forms the first step of research, after which other types of research designs can be used.

  Two very good examples of explanatory designs are:
  - Malinowski's study of Trobriand society; and
  - Whyte's study of the Street Corner Society.

Both these studies for the collection of data have relied on the special method of participant observation. Both researchers had an explanatory objective.

Rather than aiming to test a limited set of specific Research Design, Malinowski and Whyte present in advance only the out line a conceptual model and provide a wide range of detail from which a number of other Research Design can be derived. Instead of concentrating on just unspecific areas and selecting a few aspects for consideration (as may be the case in descriptive research design), researchers gather such a great variety of data that they are able to see the actors in their total life situation. Explanatory studies are not to be confused with raw empiricism, with fact gathering that is unrelated to sociological theory. The explanatory study always carries with it a set of concepts that guide the researcher to look for the facts.

- *Descriptive research Design*: Generally, if a researcher is studying a community which is familiar and his research purpose is to depict accurately and in detail the characteristics of a particular institution, group or an event in the community, the appropriate research design is called Descriptive research Design. Sometimes, descriptive design forms a second step of research, the first step being explanatory design. Thus some times, research Research Design is formulated through explanatory design and to test the Research Design, descriptive design is formulated.

- *Experimental research Design*: The research design that is used to test a Research Design of causal relationship under controlled situation is called experimental design. The essence of the experimental design (in sociology) lies in its testing Research Design derived from a theory.

  The experimentation in sociology observes the following aspects:

  - In an experimental design, the investigator controls or manipulates an independent variable or stimulus (X),
  - And observes the effects on the dependent variable (Y), and
  - The effect of the independent variable on the dependent variable is observed by minimizing the effects of extraneous variables that might confound the result.
  - These propositions are tested off on the sample, generally called the experimental sample (E).

Experimentation in sociology raises certain important questions, viz. ethical question, difficulties in forming a control sample and retaining it over time; the difficulties encountered in controlling the extraneous environment, etc. Realizing these problems, in some of the'experiments' carried out by sociologists, the experimental sample is used as the control sample. It is debatable whether the absence of a control means a non -experimental study. This actually is a modification of the classic experimental design.

The theoretical propositions followed here are the following:

- Experimental sample is also the control sample.

- The experimental sample is measured in the given respect before introducing the independent variable,
- After it has been measured, the stimulus for independent variable is introduced.
- The experimental sample is measured after stimulus and the change is calculated.

This modification of the experimental design in generally accepted in sociology and is called before and after research. The best example of this type of research design is the Hawthorne study carried out by E. Mayo, F. Roethlisberger, W. Disckson and G. Homans.In this study, the relationship between physical conditions of world (independent variable) and the productivity of the worker (dependent variable) is examined.

CONTENT ANALYSIS

Content analysis is a research technique for the systematic, objective and quantitative description of the content of research data procured through interviews, questionnaires, schedules and other linguistic expressions, written or oral. This definition is a slight modification of the one formulated by Bernard Berelson in his famed communications researches.Familarity with social science concepts and theory greatly aids in categorizing research data. Frequently certain categories seem to flow out of the data at hand. On the whole however the use of concepts and categories requires deliberate thought.

Psychologist D.C McClelland who regards a written research record as a piece of frozen behaviour calls attention to various forms of content-analysis to which such records can be subjected; interaction process analysis; value analysis in which attempts are made to classify and conceptualize the content according to various values referred to in the behaviour units, need -sequence analysis that attempts to score the changes which occur in the data when the subjects are under the influence of induced need-states; symbolic analysis which is a technique for analyzing latent meaning behind manifest content especially in psycho-analytical materials.

Other social scientists suggest other forms of social analysis. Whatever form of analysis to which qualitative data are subjected an explicit breakdown is required of some totality into the smallest possible units if the data will be quantified. In short individual cases of human behaviour can become of scientific significance since it is possible to classify and categorize behaviour patterns, social processes, and personal traits to isolate their similarities and differences and conceptualize them appropriately.

But as George Lundberg has stressed unless the varied data are gathered according to scientific principles are systematically classified and generalized into specific types of behaviour individual cases are useless for scientific purposes.

Problems of Objectivity

Objectivity is a goal of scientific investigation. Sociology also being a science aspires for the goal objectivity. Objectivity is a frame of mind so that personal prejudices, preferences or predilections of the social scientists do not contaminate the collection of analysis of data. Thus scientific investigations should be free from prejudices of race, colour, religion, sex or ideological biases.

The need of objectivity in sociological research has been emphasized by all important sociologists. For example Durkheim in the Rules of the Sociological Method stated that social facts must be treated as things and all preconceived notions about social facts must be abandoned. Even Max Weber emphasized the need of objectivity when he said that sociology must be value free. Radcliff Brown the social scientist must abandon or transcend his ethnocentric and egocentric biases while carrying out researches. Similarly Malinowski advocated cultural relativism while anthropological field work in order to ensure objectivity.

However objectivity continues to be an elusive goal at the practical level. In fact one school of thought represented by Gunnar Myrdal states that total objectivity is an illusion which can never be achieved. Because all research is guided by certain viewpoints and view points involve subjectivity.Myrdal suggested that the basic viewpoints should be made clear. Further he felt that subjectivity creeps in at various stages in the course of sociological research. Merton believes that the very choice of topic is influenced by personal preferences and ideological biases of the researcher.

Besides personal preferences the ideological biases acquired in the course of education and training has a bearing on the choice of the topic of research. The impact of ideological biases on social-research can be very far-reaching as seen from the study of Tepostalan village in Mexico. Robert Redfield studied it with functionalist perspective and concluded that there exists total harmony between various groups in the village while Oscar Lewis studied this village at almost the same time from Marxist perspective and found that the society was conflict ridden. Subjectivity can also creep in at the time of formulation of hypotheses.

Normally hypotheses are deduced from existing body of theory. All sociological theories are produced by and limited to particular groups whose viewpoints and interests they represent. Thus formulation of hypotheses will automatically introduce a bias in the sociological research. The third stage at which subjectivity creeps in the course of research is that of collection of empirical data. No technique of data collection is perfect. Each technique may lead to subjectivity in one way or the other. In case of participant observation the observer as a result of nativisation acquires a bias in favour of the group he is studying. While in non-participant observation of the sociologist belongs to a different group than that under study he is likely to impose his values and prejudices.

In all societies there are certain prejudices which affect the research studies. In case of interview as a technique the data may be influenced by context of the interview, the interaction of the participants, and participant's definition of the situation and if adequate rapport does not extend between them there might be communication barriers. Thus according to P.V Young interview sometimes carries a subjectivity. Finally it can also affect the field limitations as reported by Andre Beteille study of Sripuram village in Tanjore where the

Brahmins did not allow him to visit the untouchable locality and ask their point of view.

Thus complete objectivity continues to be an elusive goal. The researcher should make his value preference clear in research monograph. Highly trained and skilled research workers should be employed. Various methods of data collection research should be used and the result obtained from one should be cross-checked with those from the other. Field limitations must be clearly stated in the research monograph.

Sociology as a Value-free Science

The subject matter of sociology is human behaviour in society. All social behaviour is guided by values. Thus the study of social behaviour can never be value-free if value freedom is interpreted in the sense of absence of values because values of the society under investigation form a part of the social facts to be studied by sociology. Moreover social research is in itself a type of social behaviour and is guided by the value of search for true knowledge. Then what is meant as clarified by Max Weber value-free sociology means that the sociologist while carrying social research must confine called value relevance.

Thus the values can operate at three levels:

- At the level of philological interpretation.
- At the level of ethical interpretation in assigning value to an object of enquiry.
- At the level of rational interpretation in which the sociologists seeks the meaningful relationship between phenomena in terms of causal analysis. The point of value interpretation is to establish the value towards which an activity is directed.

Sociologists should observe value neutrality while conducting social research. It means that he should exclude ideological or non -scientific assumption from research. He should not make evaluative judgment about empirical evidence. Value judgment should be restricted to sociologists' area of technical competence. He should make his own values open and clear and refrain from advocating particular values.

Value neutrality enables the social scientists to fulfill the basic value of scientific enquiry that is search for true knowledge. Thus sociology being a science cherishes the goal of value neutrality. Alvin Gouldner value-free principle did enhance the autonomy of sociology where it could steadily pursue basic problems rather than journalistically react to passing events and allowed it more freedom to pursue questions uninteresting either to the respectable or to the rebellious.

It made sociology freer as Comte had wanted it to be -to pursue all its own theoretical implications. Value free principle did contribute to the intellectual growth and emancipation of the enterprise.Value-free doctrine enhanced freedom from moral compulsiveness; it permitted a partial escape from the parochial prescriptions of the sociologists' local or native culture. Effective internalization of the value-free principle has always encouraged at least a temporary suspension of the moralizing reflexes built into the sociologist by his own society. The value-free doctrine has a paradoxical potentiality; it might enable men to make better value judgments rather than none. It could encourage a habit of mind that might help men in discriminating between their punitive drives and their ethical sentiments. However in practice it has been extremely difficult to fulfill this goal of value neutrality.

Values creep in various stages in sociological research. Gunnar Myrdal total value neutrality is impossible.'Chaos does not organize itself into cosmos. We need view points.' Thus in order to carry out social research viewpoints are needed which form the basis of hypothesis which enables the social scientists to collect empirical data. These view-points involve valuations and also while formulating the hypothesis. Thus a sociologist has to be value frank and should make the values which have got incorporated in the choice of the topic of the research of the formulation of hypothesis clear and explicit at the very outset in the research. The value-free doctrine is useful both to those who want to escape from the world and to those who want to escape into it. They think of sociology as a way of getting ahead in the world by providing them with neutral techniques that may be sold on the open market to any buyer. The belief that it is not the business of sociologist to make value judgments is taken by some to mean that the market on which they can vend their skills is unlimited.

Some sociologists have had no hesitation about doing market research designed to sell more cigarettes although well aware of the implications of recent cancer research. Gouldner the value-free doctrine from Weber's standpoint is an effort to compromise two of the deepest traditions of the western thought, reason and faith but that his arbitration seeks to safeguard the romantic residue in modern man. Like Freud, Weber never really believed in an enduring peace or in a final resolution of this conflict. What he did was to seek a truce through the segregation of the contenders by allowing each to dominate in different spheres of life.

Techniques of Data Collection

Basic requirements for scientific data are that it should be reliable and impartial. In Sociology these conditions are hard to meet. Yet numerous methods are used to minimize errors in data.

Some of the commonly used sources in collecting data are:

- Existing materials including the official statistical record and historical and contemporary documents.
- Social surveys through questionnaire and schedules
- Interviewing
- Observation- Participants and non-participant

Existing Material

Statistical Sources

Government statistics particularly census or statistics produced by large industrial or commercial firms, trade unions or other organizations provide one important account of data which sociologist can use in their analysis. An outstanding example of the imaginative use of official statistics in the positivist tradition is the study of suicide made by the famous French sociologist Emile Durkheim in the 19th century.

However official statistics are the kind of data that are not collected by sociologists themselves and so there problems while analyzing the data.

Historical Documents

Records and accounts of qualitative kind for example relating to belief, values, social relationship or social behaviour may also be contemporary or may refer to earlier periods. There are several difficulties immediately present themselves in the use of records from the past.

Few chroniclers of social relation and social action record observations in the systematic way in which the sociologists are interested. There are often intriguing and sympathetic records but the information that is vital to the sociologist is often missing.

Contemporary Records

Contemporary records relating to social relationship and social behaviour are seldom used as the sole source of information and sociological research. They are usually one source of a particular account or achievement.

Techniques of Data Collection

Social Survey

The basic procedure in survey is that people are asked a number of questions on that aspect of behaviour which the sociologist is interested in. A number of people carefully selected so that their representation of their population being studied are asked to answer exactly the same question so that the replies to different categories of respondents may be examined for differences.

One type of survey relies on contacting the respondents by letter and asking them to complete the questionnaire themselves before returning it. These are called Mail questionnaires. Sometimes questionnaires are not completed by individuals separately but by people in a group under the direct supervision of the research worker. A variation of the procedure can be that a trained interviewer asks the questions and records the responses on a schedule from each respondent.

These alternate procedures have different advantages and disadvantages. Mail questionnaires are relatively cheap and can be used to contact respondents who are scattered over a wide area. But at the same time the proportion of people who return questionnaires sent through post is usually rather small. The questions asked in main questionnaires have also to be very carefully worded in order to avoid ambiguity since the respondents cannot ask to have questions clarified for them. Using groups to complete questionnaires means that the return rate is good and that information is assembled quickly and fairly.

Administrating the interview schedules to the respondents individually is probably the most reliable method. Several trained interviewers may be employed to contact specific individuals. The questionnaires and schedules can consist of both close-ended and open-ended questions. Also a special attention needs to be paid to ensure that the questionnaires are filled in logical order.

Where aptitude questions are included great care must be exercised to ensure the proper words are used. In case of schedules emphasis and interactions may also be standardized between different individuals and from respondents to respondents.

Finally proper sampling techniques must be used to ensure that the sample under study represents the universe of study. In order to enhance the reliability of data collected through questionnaires and schedules, these questionnaires and schedules must be pretested through pilot studies.

Techniques of Data Collection

Interviewing

Social surveys may depend either on questionnaires that are self-administered or on schedules completed by trained research workers personally interviewing then is not a method of data collection distinct from social surveying but rather a technique which may vary from the brief formal contact as when the interviewer is working for the firms public opinion consultants or a market research organization and simply asks a housewife a few highly specific questions on limited range of topics to a long interview in which the research worker allows the respondents to develop points at leisure and take up others as he chooses.

The brief formal interview in which the working of the questions and the order in which they are asked is fixed is called structured interview while the freer discursive interview is called unstructured interview.

The object of using structured interview is to standardize the interview as much as possible and thus to reduce the effect that the interviewer's personal approach or biases may have upon the result and even when structured interviews are used, proper training can do a lot to ensure further the reliability and validity of research.

The personality of the interviewer and the social characteristics that the respondents attribute to him can be having influence on the result. The effort of interviewer's bias can be estimated by comparing one interviewer's result with other.

The problem of interviewer's bias in an unstructured interview is much greater. Here the interviewer is left to his common devices as far as the way he approaches a respondent is concerned. There is no fixed list of questions to work through. Instead the interviewer may work from a guide that will remind him of the topics he wishes to cover.

The training of the interviewer is crucial here not simply training in the social skills of keeping the conversation going on a topic that the respondent may not be very interested in but also in acquiring sensitivity to those things his respondents tells him which are specially relevant to the theoretical topics he is pursuing.

This means that unstructured interviews can be carried out by people trained in sociological theory. They are then able to size upon stray comments made by the respondents which can be developed and lead on to important theoretical insight.

Techniques of Data Collection

Observation: Participant and Non Participant

The rationale behind the use of observation in sociological research is that the sociologist should become party to a set of social actions sufficiently able to be able to assess directly the social relationship involved.

The degree of involvement may vary considerable from being merely a watcher on the sidelines to be deeply involved in and being a part of what is going on. The former type of observation techniques are called non-participant while the latter is called participant observation. Sometimes one way observations screen have been used to watch groups in actions that they are unaware that they are being watched and the observer cannot affect their actions by his presence. The sociologist is visibly present and is a part of the situation either as a sociologist or in another guise. Where the sociologist is merely an observer it is usually assumed that he knows enough about what the actors are doing to be able to understand their behaviour.

Any sociological observer has then to some extent be a participant observer he must at least share sufficient cultural background with the actors to be able to construe their behaviour meaningfully but the degree of participation and of sharing of meaning may vary considerably. Examples of such studies are Nel Anderson's study of Hobo-Indians and William White study of Street Corner Society.

Techniques of Data Collection

It is often impossible to collect information about the entire population of people or things in which social researchers are interested. In these cases, a sample of the total is selected for study. Most statistical studies are based on samples and not on complete enumerations of all the relevant data. The main criteria when sampling are to ensure that a sample provides a faithful representation of the totality from which it is selected, and to know as precisely as possible the probability that a sample is reliable in this way. Randomization meets these criteria, because it protects against bias in the selection process and also provides a basis on which to apply statistical distribution theory that allows an estimate to be made of the probability that ceases drawn from the sample are correct. A statistical sample is a miniature picture or cross-section of the entire group or aggregate from which the sample is taken. The entire group from which a sample is chosen is known as the population, universe or supply.

Simple Random Sampling

The basic type of random sample is known as a simple random sample, one in which each person or item has an equal chance of being chosen. Often a population contains various distinct groups or strata that differ on the attribute that is being researched.

Stratified Random Sampling

Stratified random sampling involves sampling of each stratum separately. This increases precision, or reduces time, effort and cost of allowing smaller sample sizes for a given level of precision. For example, poverty is known to be most common among the elderly, the unemployed and single parent families, so research on the effect of poverty might will sample separately each of these three strata as part of a survey of poverty in the population as a whole which would permit the total sample size to be reduced because the investigator would know that the groups most affected by poverty were guaranteed inclusion.

Cluster Sampling

Cluster sampling is sometimes used when the population naturally congregates into clusters. For example, managers are clustered in organizations, so a sample of managers could be obtained by taking a random sample of organizations and investigating the managers in each of these. Interviewing or observing managers on this basis would be cheaper and easier than using a simple random sample of managers scattered across all organizations in the country. This is usually less precise than a simple random sample of the same size, but in practice the reduction in cost per element more than compensated for the decrease in precision.

Multi-stage Sampling

Sampling may be done as one process or in stages, known as multi-stage sampling.Multi-stage designs are common when populations are widely dispersed. Thus a survey of business managers might proceed by selecting a sample of corporations as first stage units, perhaps choosing these corporations with a probability proportionate to their size, and then selecting a sample of managers within these corporations at the second stage.

Alternatively, a sample of individual factories or office buildings within each corporation could be chosen as the second stage units, followed by sample of managers in each of these as a third stage. Stratification can also be used in the design, if for example occupational sub-groups are known to differ from each other, by selecting state such as personnel, production, and finance management and sampling within each of these.

For sampling to be representative, one needs a complete and accurate list of the first stage units that make up the relevant population, a basic requirement that is not always easily met.

This forms the sampling frame. Selection from the frame is best done by numbering the items and using a table of random numbers to identify which items form the sample, though a quasi-random method of simply taking every item from the list is often appropriate. The reliability of a sample taken from a population can be assessed by the spread of the sampling distribution, measured by the standard deviation of this distribution, called the standard error. As a general rule, the larger is the size of the sample the smaller the standard error.

Area Sampling

In sampling of this kind small areas are designated as

sampling units and the households interviewed include all or a specified fraction of those found in a canvass of these designated small areas.

The basic sampling units or segments chosen may be relatively large or relatively small depending on such factors as the type of area being studied, population distribution, the availability of suitable maps and other information and the nature and desired accuracy of the data being collected.

Measurement of Attitude

Attitudinal behaviour is a certain set of observable behaviour which is preparatory to and indicative of the subsequent actual behaviour. For the purpose of measuring attitudes only the overt symbolic type of acts are taken into account because such acts alone can be observed. Examples of such acts are speaking; writing and gesturing etc.Attitude indicate a tendency which can be helpful in predicting the subsequent behaviour.Herein lies the importance of measuring attitudes.

Measurement of attitudes is useful in various aspects of day to day life. For example it helps in predicting consumer behaviour in making demand forecasts in providing an insight into the public response to various welfare measured indicated by the Government in maintaining peace and social order and in social research.

The sources of information regarding the attitude of a person are:

- Life history documents including biographies, autobiographies, diaries, letters and memories.
- *Oral interviews*: Opinions of the respondent may be elicited by personally asking them various questions.
- *Questionnaires and polls*: Sometimes in place of persons contact mailed questionnaire is also used for the purpose of getting opinions. Similarly public opinion polls are conducted to know peoples opinion on various issue.

In order to measure the degree of intensity of the attitude various kinds of scales have been devised.

These scales may be divided into the following categories:

- Point scales
- Ranking scales
- Rating of intensity scales etc

Other scales for the measurement of attitudes are social distance, scale of Bogardus Thurston Scale, Likert scale and socio-metric scale by Moreno. However standard scales with universal application are yet to be devised.

Likert Scale

The Likert technique presents a set of attitude statements. Subjects are asked to express agreement or disagreement of a five-point scale. Each degree of agreement is given a numerical value from one to five. Thus a total numerical value can be calculated from all the responses.

Analysis and Interpretation of Data

The purpose of assembling data is to present some theoretical analysis or interpretation of it. But the processes of observation and analysis are rarely independent of one another.

The problems become redefined as the research proceeds and this means changing accounts of observations made. In the social survey the pilot stage is very important since the sociologist derives preliminary information from it which he then uses to test existing hypotheses in a crude way. He may then have to modify both the hypothesis and in consequence the techniques for example he may change the schedule that he is using.

Unstructured interview techniques and observations are particularly suitable where the questions must be changed when an analysis begins to throw up new problems which demand new information in order to answer them.

Analysis of data involves seeking through observations with object of determination in what circumstances they do not or to check that if sociologist can support one interpretation rather then another. At this stage it is necessary to point out two difficulties in the use of sociological information for analytical or interpretative purposes. The first of these is called the reliability of data. This refers to the extent to which investigation are repeatable that is if the same procedures of data collection the same object categories and the same rules for establishing the veracity are used on the same subject by different observers or by the same observers on different occasions, no relevant changes have taken place on the main attempt results comparable with earlier studies can be obtained.

If different answer emerged from the enquiries which should yield the same response then the date may not be used to represent and establish underlying regularity. The measures that sociologist can take to overcome unreliability in response will depend upon what procedures are used to collect the information and what type of analysis is to be made.

The second difficulty is that of the validity of data. Validity refers to the extent to which sociologist interpretation of underlying characteristics he wishes to reflect is in fact the faithful representation of the characteristics. The sociologists working with a positivistic framework may wish to represent some abstract notion such as Alienation by a set of relatively easily identified indicators.

He may attempt to combine these into a single indicator of characteristics he wants to represent. Having done this however how can he be sure that his indicator reflects the characteristics of alienation effectively. The usual way to ascertain the suitability of indicators is to test them empirically on samples of subjects which are known from other evidence to be alienated or not alienated. Given however that the sociologist is reasonable satisfied with both the reliability and validity of data how does the analysis or interpretation proceed?

This depends upon the framework within which the sociologist is working. Within a positivistic framework the sociologist will be interested in some hypothesis which he has derived from theory by examining the connection in his data between some specified dependent variable which he suspects have some causal influence.

This implies that the initial stages of analysis which may be going on while the data are being assembled must be concerned with identifying the variables and in deciding what criteria may be reasonably used to represent these variables. Only after the positivist sociologist has satisfactorily defined and operationalised the variables he wants to test the casual proposition he is postulating can be proceed to test this.

Chapter 7

Report Writing

WRITING RESEARCH

Writing is easy. All you do is stare at a blank sheet of paper until drops of blood form on your forehead. --- Gene Fowler

A major goal of this course is the development of effective technical writing skills. To help you become an accomplished writer, you will prepare several research papers based upon the studies completed in lab. Our research papers are not typical"lab reports." In a teaching lab a lab report might be nothing more than answers to a set of questions. Such an assignment hardly represents the kind of writing you might be doing in your eventual career.

Written and oral communications skills are probably the most universal qualities sought by graduate and professional schools as well as by employers. You alone are responsible for developing such skills to a high level.

RESOURCES FOR LEARNING TECHNICAL WRITING

Before you begin your first writing assignment, Consult all of the following resources, in order to gain the most benefit from the experience.

- General form of a typical research substance.
- Specific guidelines (if any) for the assignment
- McMillan, VE."Writing Papers in the Biological Sciences, Third Ed." New York: Bedford/St. Martin's, 2001. ISBN 0-312-25857-7 (REQUIRED for Bios 211,

311, recommended for other science courses that include writing)

As you polish up your writing skills please make use of the following resources:

- Instructor feedback on previous assignments
- Common errors in student research papers
- Selected writing rules (somewhat less serious than the other resources)

For Biosciences majors the general guidelines apply to future course work, as can be seen by examining the guidelines for the advanced experimental sciences research paper. Instructions for authors from the Journal of Biological Chemistry editorial board may be helpful as well. Their statement of editorial policies and practices may give you an idea of how material makes its way into the scientific literature.

GENERAL FORM OF A RESEARCH PAPER

An objective of organizing a research paper is to allow people to read your work selectively. When we research a topic,we may be interested in just the methods, a specific result, the interpretation, or perhaps we just want to see a summary of the paper to determine if it is relevant to my study. To this end submitted in the order listed. There are variations of course. Some journals call for a combined results and discussion, for example, or include materials and methods after the body of the paper. The well known journal Science does away with separate parts altogether, except for the abstract.

Your papers are to adhere to the form and style required for the Journal of Biological Chemistry, requirements that are shared by many journals in the life sciences.

General Style

Specific editorial requirements for submission of a manuscript will always supercede instructions in these general guidelines.

To make a paper readable:

- Print or type using a 12 point standard font, such as Times, Geneva, Bookman, Helvetica, etc.

- Text should be double spaced on 8 1/2" x 11" paper with 1 inch margins, single sided
- Number pages consecutively
- Start each new parts on a new page
- Adhere to recommended page limits

Mistakes to avoid:

- Placing a heading at the bottom of a page with the following text on the next page (insert a page break!)
- Dividing a table or figure - confine each figure/table to a single page
- Submitting a paper with pages out of order

In all parts of your paper:

- Use normal prose including substances ("a","the," etc.)
- Stay focused on the research topic of the paper
- Use paragraphs to separate each important point (except for the abstract)
- Indent the first line of each paragraph
- Present your points in logical order
- Use present tense to report well accepted facts - for example,'the grass is green'
- Use past tense to describe specific results - for example,'When weed killer was applied, the grass was brown'
- Avoid informal wording, don't address the reader directly, and don't use jargon, slang terms, or superlatives
- Avoid use of superfluous pictures - include only those figures necessary to presenting results

Title Page

Select an informative title as emphasized in the examples in your writing portfolio example package. Include the name(s) and address(es) of all authors, and date submitted."Biology lab #1" would not be an informative title, for example.

General intent

An abstract is a concise single paragraph summary of completed work or work in progress. In a minute or less a reader can learn the rationale behind the study, general approach to the problem, pertinent results, and important ceases or new questions.

Writing an abstract

Write your summary after the rest of the paper is completed. After all, how can you summarize something that is not yet written? Economy of words is important throughout any paper, but especially in an abstract. However, use complete sentences and do not sacrifice readability for brevity. You can keep it concise by wording sentences so that they serve more than one purpose. For example,"In order to learn the role of protein synthesis in early development of the sea urchin, newly fertilized embryos were pulse-labeled with tritiated leucine, to provide a time course of changes in synthetic rate, as measured by total counts per minute (cpm)." This sentence provides the overall question, methods, and type of analysis, all in one sentence. The writer can now go directly to summarizing the results. Summarize the study, including the following elements in any abstract.

Try to keep the first two items to no more than one sentence each:

- *Purpose of the study*: Hypothesis, overall question, objective
- Model organism or system and brief description of the experiment
- *Results, including specific data*: If the results are quantitative in nature, report quantitative data; results of any statistical analysis shoud be reported
- Important ceases or questions that follow from the experiment(s)

Style:

- Single paragraph, and concise
- As a summary of work done, it is always written in past tense
- An abstract should stand on its own, and not refer to any other part of the paper such as a figure or table

- Focus on summarizing results - limit background information to a sentence or two, if absolutely necessary
- What you report in an abstract must be consistent with what you reported in the paper
- Corrrect spelling, clarity of sentences and phrases, and proper reporting of quantities are just as important in an abstract as they are anywhere else

Introduction

Your introductions should not exceed two pages (double spaced, typed).

General Intent

The purpose of an introduction is to aquaint the reader with the rationale behind the work, with the intention of defending it. It places your work in a theoretical context, and enables the reader to understand and appreciate your objectives.

Writing an Introduction

The abstract is the only text in a research paper to be written without using paragraphs in order to separate major points. Approaches vary widely, however for our studies the following approach can produce an effective introduction.

- *Describe the importance (significance) of the study*: Why was this worth doing in the first place? Provide a broad context.
- *Defend the model*: Why did you use this particular organism or system? What are its advantages? You might comment on its suitability from a theoretical point of view as well as indicate practical reasons for using it.
- *Provide a rationale*: State your specific hypothesis(es) or objective(s), and describe the reasoning that led you to select them.
- Very briefy describe the experimental design and how it accomplished the stated objectives.

Style:

- Use past tense except when referring to established facts. After all, the paper will be submitted after all of the work is completed.
- Organize your ideas, making one major point with each paragraph.
- Present background information only as needed in order support a position. The reader does not want to read everything you know about a subject.
- State the hypothesis/objective precisely - do not oversimplify.
- As always, pay attention to spelling, clarity and appropriateness of sentences and phrases.

Materials and Methods

There is no specific page limit, but a key concept is to keep this part as concise as you possibly can. People will want to read this material selectively. The reader may only be interested in one formula or part of a procedure. Materials and methods may be reported under separate subheadings within this part or can be incorporated together.

General Intent

This should be the easiest part to write, but many students misunderstand the purpose. The objective is to document all specialized materials and general procedures, so that another individual may use some or all of the methods in another study or judge the scientific merit of your work. It is not to be a step by step description of everything you did, nor is a methods part a set of instructions. In particular, it is not supposed to tell a story.

WRITING A MATERIALS AND METHODS PART

Materials:

- Describe materials separately only if the study is so complicated that it saves space this way.
- Include specialized chemicals, biological materials,

and any equipment or supplies that are not commonly found in laboratories.

- Do not include commonly found supplies such as test tubes, pipet tips, beakers, etc., or standard lab equipment such as centrifuges, spectrophotometres, pipettors, etc.
- If use of a specific type of equipment, a specific enzyme, or a culture from a particular supplier is critical to the success of the experiment, then it and the source should be singled out, otherwise no.
- Materials may be reported in a separate paragraph or else they may be identified along with your procedures.
- In biosciences we frequently work with solutions - refer to them by name and describe completely, including concentrations of all reagents, and pH of aqueous solutions, solvent if non-aqueous.

Methods:

- Report the methodology
- Describe the mehodology completely, including such specifics as temperatures, incubation times, etc.
- To be concise, present methods under headings devoted to specific procedures or groups of procedures
- *Generalize*: Report how procedures were done, not how they were specifically performed on a particular day. For example, report"samples were diluted to a final concentration of 2 mg/ml protein;" don't report that"135 microliters of sample one was diluted with 330 microliters of buffer to make the protein concentration 2 mg/ml." Always think about what would be relevant to an investigator at another institution, working on his/her own project.
- If well documented procedures were used, report the procedure by name, perhaps with reference, and that's all. For example, the Bradford assay is well known. You need not report the procedure in full - just that you used a Bradford assay to estimate

protein concentration, and identify what you used as a standard. The same is true for the SDS-PAGE method, and many other well known procedures in biology and biochemistry.

Style:

- It is awkward or impossible to use active voice when documenting methods without using first person, which would focus the reader's attention on the investigator rather than the work. Therefore when writing up the methods most authors use third person passive voice.
- Use normal prose in this and in every other part of the paper - avoid informal lists, and use complete sentences.

What to avoid:

- Materials and methods are not a set of instructions.
- Omit all explanatory information and background - save it for the discussion.
- Omit information that is irrelevant to a third party, such as what colour ice bucket you used, or which individual logged in the data.

Results:

- The page length of this part is set by the amount and types of data to be reported. Continue to be concise, using figures and tables, if appropriate, to present results most effectively.

General Intent

The purpose of a results part is to present and emphasize your findings. Make this part a completely objective report of the results, and save all interpretation for the discussion.

Writing a Results Part

Important: You must clearly distinguish material that would normally be included in a research from any raw data material that would not be published. In fact, such material should not be submitted at all unless requested by the instructor.

Content:

- Summarize your findings in text and emphasize them, if appropriate, with figures and tables.
- In text, describe each of your results, pointing the reader to observations that are most relevant.
- Provide a context, such as by describing the question that was addressed by making a particular observation.
- Describe results of control experiments and include observations that are not presented in a formal figure or table, if appropriate.
- Analyse your data, then prepare the analysed (converted) data in the form of a figure (graph), table, or in text form.

What to avoid:

- Do not discuss or interpret your results, report background information, or attempt to explain anything.
- Never include raw data or intermediate calculations in a research paper.
- Do not present the same data more than once.
- Text should complement any figures or tables, not repeat the same information.
- Please do not confuse figures with tables - there is a difference.

Style:

- As always, use past tense when you refer to your results, and put everything in a logical order.
- Place figures and tables, properly numbered, in order at the end of the report (clearly distinguish them from any other material such as raw data, standard curves, etc.)
- If you prefer, you may place your figures and tables appropriately within the text of your results part.

Figures and tables:

- Either place figures and tables within the text of the result, or include them in the back of the report (following Literature Cited) - do one or the other

- If you place figures and tables at the end of the report, make sure they are clearly distinguished from any attached materials, such as raw data
- Regardless of placement, each figure must be numbered consecutively and complete with caption
- Regardless of placement, each table must be titled, numbered consecutively and complete with heading
- Each figure and table must be sufficiently complete that it could stand on its own, separate from text

Discussion

Journal guidelines vary. Space is so valuable in the Journal of Biological Chemistry, that authors are asked to restrict discussions to four pages or less, double spaced, typed. That works out to one printed page. While you are learning to write effectively, the limit will be extended to five typed pages. If you practice economy of words, that should be plenty of space within which to say all that you need to say.

General Intent

The objective here is to provide an interpretation of your results and support for all of your ceases, using evidence from your experiment and generally accepted knowledge, if appropriate. The significance of findings should be clearly described.

Writing a Discussion

Interpret your data in the discussion in appropriate depth. This means that when you explain a phenomenon you must describe mechanisms that may account for the observation. If your results differ from your expectations, explain why that may have happened. If your results agree, then describe the theory that the evidence supported. It is never appropriate to simply state that the data agreed with expectations, and let it drop at that.

- Decide if each hypothesis is supported, rejected, or if you cannot make a decision with confidence. Do not simply dismiss a study or part of a study as"inconclusive."

- Research papers are not accepted if the work is incomplete. Draw what ceases you can based upon the results that you have, and treat the study as a finished work
- You may suggest future directions, such as how the experiment might be modified to accomplish another objective.
- Explain all of your observations as much as possible, focusing on mechanisms.
- Decide if the experimental design adequately addressed the hypothesis, and whether or not it was properly controlled.
- Try to offer alternative explanations if reasonable alternatives exist.
- One experiment will not answer an overall question, so keeping the big picture in mind, where do you go next? The best studies open up new avenues of research. What questions remain?
- Recommendations for specific papers will provide additional suggestions.

Style:

- When you refer to information, distinguish data generated by your own studies from published information or from information obtained from other students (verb tense is an important tool for accomplishing that purpose).
- Refer to work done by specific individuals (including yourself) in past tense.
- Refer to generally accepted facts and principles in present tense. For example,"Doofus, in a 1989 survey, found that anemia in basset hounds was correlated with advanced age. Anemia is a condition in which there is insufficient hemoglobin in the blood."

The biggest mistake that students make in discussions is to present a superficial interpretation that more or less re-states the results.

It is necessary to suggest why results came out as they did, focusing on the mechanisms behind the observations.

Literature Cited

You will not be required to properly document sources of all of your information. One reason is that your major source of information is this website, and websites are inappropriate as primary sources. Second, it is problematic to provide a hundred students with equal access to potential reference materials. List all literature cited in your paper, in alphabetical order, by first author. In a proper research paper, only primary literature is used. Be cautious about using web sites as references - anyone can put just about anything on a web site, and you have no sure way of knowing if it is truth or fiction. If you are citing an on line journal. Some of your papers may not require references, and if that is the case simply state that"no references were consulted."

Writing Research Reports

After you have done your Market Research work, you have to write a report. However, the best research can get put aside without being read. Following are a few tips for writing a good Market Research Report that you can be proud of.

The first thing you have to do is to get your reader's attention with a powerful headline and a good opening summary. If you fail to get your prospects' attention, you will fail to communicate and deliver the benefits of your research.

Always remember that if your report is not read and action taken, your company will receive no benefits from all the research that you have done, and that's a pretty darn shame. But if you do the report right, you are probably about 70 per cent of the way to a promotion. So read on and pay attention.

The trick is writing a research report that will grab the reader's attention without allowing his or her mind to wander even for a second. Or worse: Making a copy mistake that turns her or him off entirely -- and gets your research report instantly tossed into the nearest virtual or literal trash can.

In a very real sense, your body copy is a minefield that must be navigated with the greatest of care: Every word, every sentence and paragraph of body copy represents the chance to either intensify your prospect's focus... or to completely lose him. But take care, in long research reports -- the headline and opening summary represent only about 4 per cent of the total volume of the report copy required. There's a lot of pages where you can loose your reader's attention. Lose him, even for a split second, and you've probably lost him -- and your promotion -- for good!

There are three unforgivable sins that you must be aware of and avoid when writing your report.

Avoid the following three unforgivable sins when crafting your research report:

- Do not confuse your reader...
- Do not bore your reader, and
- Do not set off his BS detector...

By following the seven simple rules, you can avoid all three dangers and produce a top quality Market Research Report.

Rule Number 1: Keep Your Report Logically Organized

Humans are NOT logical animals. But when reading or learning, they generally require that the material be presented in a clear, logical way. That generally means starting at point"A"... progressing to point"B"... moving on to point"C"... and so on, until you have reached your ultimate cease.

To do that, you must build your case logically and methodically -- much like a mason builds a brick wall. You must lay a solid foundation of research and then build upon each completed analysis argument with the next... brick by brick... in a logical order, proving your research points.

Ask yourself,"What must my reader know first... second... third... and so on, in order to conclude that this research offers the opportunity of a lifetime?"

Rule Number 2: Keep the Report Moving

When a reader's eyes first fall upon your report, a little stopwatch starts ticking in his head. If at any point, he feels you're not moving along quickly enough, you will lose him.

Creating a dynamic flow of information in your research report is absolutely essential for maximum readability. There are three ways to do it...

- Creating and following a"chain of logic" outline helps a lot in this regard -- by ensuring that you make each point once, then move on. If prospects feel like you're going back over stuff you already covered, any sense of momentum you may have established is instantly destroyed.
- Check the momentum of each draft by reading it aloud. Mark the places where you -- as a reader -- begin to become distracted or bored. Once again, highlight any parts that begin to lose you. Each of these parts will kill readership and response if they're still there in the final draft. Edit them or delete them.
- Making each part of copy shorter than the one before is a great way to create momentum. For example -- let's say you have to make ten analysis points in order to complete the report. You could spend 1 1/2 pages making your first analysis... 1 page making your second... 3/4 of a page making your third... 1/2 page making your fourth... and then wrap up the final six points in a series of bullets covering a single page.

Rule Number 3: Keep Your Report Simple

Never ask your prospect to work in order to figure out what you're saying. Two-dollar words, esoteric references and complex sentences are killers in research reports. Subtlety, nuance and complexity are for poets -- NOT market reports!

Try to limit yourself to one complete, clearly presented thought per sentence. When you connect two thoughts in a sentence, make sure they connect directly and clearly with each other. Also be sure to avoid inserting undeveloped or underdeveloped thoughts in sentences or paragraphs. They're like little boobytraps in the report. They stop readers cold.

Rule Number 4: Keep the Report Fat-Free

Readers should feel as though they're getting good value in

return for the number of words they're made to read. Your challenge is to never use three words when two will do the job.

Here are four ways to say more with less:

- Use more precise word choices: When you fail to use the word that most precisely and accurately communicates a thought, you wind up using five, six or even ten words instead. When searching for the most precise word, checking synomyms in a thesaurus often gives you the answer.
- Eliminate unnecessary words: Here again, reading copy aloud really helps. Much of the time, for example, the word"that" is totally unnecessary. When in doubt, leave it out!
- Avoid unhelpful repitition: Repetition of key sales points -- a USP or major benefit, for example -- is a beautiful thing. Repeating minor thoughts only slows the copy and bores the reader.
- Figures of speech can help you say more, faster: If a pictures is worth a thousand words, metaphors, similes, and other figures of speech are as well.

Rule Number 5: Keep Your Report Believable

Your reader is already skeptical. Making grandiose claims that you can't (or don't) prove beyond the shadow of a doubt will only confirm what he or she already suspects: That you're full of beans. And this will get your promotion trashed in a heartbeat.

Rule Number 6: Keep Your Report Potent

One of the fastest ways to lose your prospect's attention is to fail to focus on his favourite subject: HIM or HER! The word"You" has been called the most powerful word in the English language -- and for good reason. Finding ways to personalize the report -- applying each passage as if had been written for the reader -- is a key to keeping his attention.

Rule Number 7: Avoid Unintended Impressions

Here's where insisting that friends read your report can

pay huge dividends. By the time you're ready to stick a fork in your new promotion, you can almost recite it word for word -- frontwards and backwards. That means you're too close to the report to catch things that may be misread... even things that may raise objections or implant an erroneous impression in your reader's mind.

HOW TO WRITE A SCHOLARLY RESEARCH REPORT

Researchers communicate their results and help accumulate knowledge through conference papers, reports, on-line journals and print journals. While there are many rewards for having research disseminated in a scholarly outlet, the preparation of a good research report is not a trivial task.

The common parts of a research report along with frequently made mistakes. While the emphasis here is on reports prepared for scholarly, peer-reviewed publication, these points are applicable to other forms of research reports. Dissertations and theses, for example, provide more detail than scholarly publications yet they adhere to the same basic scientific writing principles. Since all scientific research involves observation, description and analysis as well as to experimental, research. More detail can be found in the Publication Manual of the American Psychological Association, proposed revisions to the manual.

First Steps In Writing A Research Report

You should constantly think about writing your report at every stage of your research activities. The Publication Manual provides detailed information about the entire process of publication -- from organizing, writing, keying and submitting your manuscript, to seeing the accepted manuscript through production and publication. Of special interest in the fourth edition are the updated parts on reporting statistics, writing without bias, preparing manuscripts with a word processor for electronic production and publishing research in accordance with ethical principles of scientific publishing. You should have a copy.

Plan your report to focus on a single important finding or highly related group of findings. In the process of analyzing your data, you probably uncovered many relationships and gained numerous insights into the problem. Your journal submission, however, should contain only one key point. The point should be so fundamental that you should be able express it in one sentence or, at most, in a paragraph. If you have several key points, consider writing multiple manuscripts.

When writing your manuscript, keep in mind that the purpose is to inform the readers of what you investigated, why and how you conducted your investigation, the results and your ceases. As the investigator and writer, your job is simply to report, not to convince and usually not to advocate. You must provide enough detail so readers can reach their own ceases about the quality of your research and the veracity of your ceases.

Parts of Your Report

Thus, the title should not contain jargon or vernacular. Rather, the title should be short (generally 15 words or less) and clearly indicate what the study is about. If in doubt, try to specify the cause and effect relationship in your key point. Avoid trite and wasteful phrases such as"A study of..." or"An investigation to determine..."

Abstract: The abstract serves two major purposes: it helps a person decide whether to read the paper, and it provides the reader with a framework for understanding the paper if they decide to read it. Thus, your abstract should describe the most important aspects of the study within the word-limit provided by the journal. As appropriate for your research, try to include a statement of the problem, the people you studied, the dependent and independent variables, the instruments, the design, major findings, and ceases. If pressed for space, concentrate on the problem and, especially, your findings.

Introduction: You will usually start your report with a paragraph or two presenting the investigated problem, the importance of the study, and an overview of your research strategy. You do not need to label this part. Its position within the paper makes that obvious.

The introductory paragraphs are usually followed by a review of the literature. Show how your research builds on prior knowledge by presenting and evaluating what is already known about your research problem. Assume that the readers possess a broad knowledge of the field. Discuss the findings of works that are pertinent to your specific issue. You usually will not need to elaborate on methods.

The goal of the introduction and literature review is to demonstrate"the logical continuity between previous and present work". This does not mean you need to provide an exhaustive historical review. Analyse the relationships among the related studies instead of presenting a series of seemingly unrelated abstracts or annotations. The introduction should motivate the study. The reader should understand why the problem was researched and why the study represents a contribution to existing knowledge. Unless the study is an evaluation of a programmme, it is generally inappropriate to attempt to motivate the study based on its social importance.

Method: The method part includes separate descriptions of the sample, the materials, and the procedures. These are subtitled and may be augmented by further parts, if needed.

Describe your sample with sufficient detail so that it is clear what population(s) the sample represents. A discussion of how the sample was formed is needed for replicability and understanding your study." Convenience samples are not unusual in scientific inquiry; their use should not discourage you from seeking a publication outlet for your report.

A description of your instruments, including all surveys, tests, questionnaires, interview forms, and other tools used to provide data, should appear in the materials subsection. Evidence of reliability and validity should be presented. Since reliability is a property of scores from a specific use of a specific instrument for a specific population, you should provide reliability estimates based on your data.

The design of the study, whether it is a case study, a survey, a controlled experiment, a meta-analysis, or some other type of research, is conveyed through the procedures subsection. It is here that the activities of the researcher are described, such as what was said to the participants, how groups were formed, what control mechanisms were employed, etc. The description is sufficient if enough detail is present for the reader to replicate the essential elements of the study. It is important for the procedures to conform to ethical criteria for researchers.

Results: Present a summary of what you found in the results part. Here you should describe the techniques that you used, each analysis and the results of each analysis.

Start with a description of any complications, such as protocol violations and missing data that may have occurred. Examine your data for anomalies, such as outliers, points of high influence, miscoded data, and illogical responses. Use your common sense to evaluate the quality of your data and make adjustments if need be. Describe the process that you used in order to assure your readers that your editing was appropriate and purified rather than skewed your results.

With today's availability of statistical packages, it is fairly easy to use very sophisticated techniques to analyse your data. Understand the techniques you are using and the statistics that you are reporting. Try to use the simplest, appropriate technique for which you can meet the underlying assumptions.

If you are going to use inferential statistics, you should determine the power a priori based on your anticipated distribution, design, and definition of practical significance. This information must stem from your related literature and not the data that you collected. If you fail to reach statistical significance, then this analysis can be used to show that the finding does not stem from low power.

Where appropriate, compute and report effect sizes or, at a minimum, be sure you provide enough information so effect sizes can be computed. Effect sizes provide a common metric for evaluating results across studies and aid in the design of future studies. They will be needed by anyone who attempts a quantitative synthesis of your study along with the others in your area of research.

For most research reports, the results should provide the summary about what you found rather than an exhaustive listing of every possible analysis and every data point. Use carefully planned tables and graphs. While tables and graphs should be self-explanatory, do not include a table or graph unless it is discussed in the report. Limit them to those that help the reader understand your data as they relate to the investigated problem.

Discussion: At this point, you are the expert on your data set and an authority on the problem you addressed. In this part, discuss and interpret your data for the reader, tell the reader of the implications of your findings and make recommendations. Do not be afraid to state your opinions.

Many authors chose to begin the discussion part by highlighting key results. Return to the specific problem you investigated and tell the reader what you now think and why. Relate your findings to those of previous studies, by explaining relationships and supporting or disagreeing with what others have found. Describe your logic and draw your ceases. Be careful, however, not to over generalize your results. Your ceases should be warranted by your study and your data.

Be sure to recognize the limitations of your study. Try to anticipate the questions a reader will have and suggest what problems should be researched next in order to extend your findings into new areas.

References: There should be a one-to-one match between the references cited in the report and the references listed in the reference part.

PUBLISHING YOUR REPORT

If you intend to publish in a journal, these journals will be the most likely candidates. Review the target audience and publication guidelines for these journals to decide which is best suited to your research. Regardless of scholarly quality, a key question in any editor's mind will be whether your manuscript is suited to the journal's purpose and audience. When considering where to submit, note the style of the in the journal.

Remember that the review process is conducted by human staff, and so is a fallible process. Peters and Ceci made this point abundantly clear.

Because of high rejection rates and the usual long length of time journals need to make a selection decision, it is tempting to submit a manuscript simultaneously to more than one journal. This, however, is clearly unethical. Most journals appropriately specify that manuscripts under consideration cannot be submitted elsewhere. The editors and reviewers will be taking a considerable amount of time examining your manuscript, usually as volunteers.

You should expect your manuscript to be rejected when it is submitted for the first time. If a manuscript is rejected, you should evaluate the comments and then decide whether to revise, resubmit, or submit it elsewhere. In order to facilitate both your revision and its subsequent evaluation, a resubmission should be accompanied by a description of the issues raised in the review process and your manuscript modifications and other substantive reactions to them.

While very little has been written about ethical standards for authors in the education field, the Uniform Requirements for Manuscripts Submitted to Biomedical Journals, which have been adopted by more than 500 scientific and biomedical journals, address criteria for authorship, acknowledgments, redundant publication, competing manuscripts, and conflict of interest. A concise summary of the Uniform Requirements can be found in Syrett and Rudner.

A key concept in the Uniform Requirements is that individuals identified as authors should have made significant contributions to the conception and design, or analysis and interpretation of data, or both; to drafting of the manuscript or revising it critically for intellectual content; and on final approval of the version of the manuscript to be considered for publication. Being an advisor or head of a research group, does not, in itself, warrant authorship credit.

Chapter 8

Application of a Case Study Methodology

The goals and objectives were presented and explained in detail. The methodology to accomplish those goals and objectives will be examined. The reader will become familiar with the specific techniques that are used in the current study.

That methodology will follow the recommendation of Yin and has four stages:

- Design the case study,
- Conduct the case study,
- Analyse the case study evidence, and
- Develop the ceases, recommendations and implications.

That includes some of the background information that is intended to inform the reader. Following that part, each step of the methodology will be explored in detail. Finally a summary will connect all the information in a concise manner.

INTRODUCTION

Case study is an ideal methodology when a holistic, in-depth investigation is needed. Case studies have been used in varied investigations, particularly in sociological studies, but increasingly, in instruction. Yin, Stake, and others who have wide experience in this methodology have developed robust procedures. When these procedures are followed, the researcher will be following methods as well developed and tested as any in the scientific field. Whether the study is experimental or quasi-experimental, the data collection and analysis methods are known to hide some details. Case studies, on the other hand, are designed to bring out the details from the viewpoint of the participants by using multiple sources of data.

Yin has identified some specific types of case studies: Exploratory, Explanatory, and Descriptive. Stake included three others: Intrinsic - when the researcher has an interest in the case; Instrumental - when the case is used to understand more than what is obvious to the observer; Collective - when a group of cases is studied. Exploratory cases are sometimes considered as a prelude to social research. Explanatory case studies may be used for doing causal investigations. Descriptive cases require a descriptive theory to be developed before starting the project. Pyecha used this methodology in a special education study, using a pattern-matching procedure. In all of the types of case studies, there can be single-case or multiple-case applications.

Case study research is not sampling research; that is a fact asserted by all the major researchers in the field, including Yin, Stake, Feagin and others. However, selecting cases must be done so as to maximize what can be learned in the period of time available for the study.

The unit of analysis is a critical factor in the case study. It is typically a system of action rather than an individual or group of individuals. Case studies tend to be selective, focusing on one or two issues that are fundamental to understanding the system being examined.

Case studies are multi-perspectival analyses. This means that the researcher considers not just the voice and perspective of the actors, but also of the relevant groups of actors and the interaction between them. This one aspect is a salient point in the characteristic that case studies possess. They give a voice to the powerless and voiceless. When sociological investigations present many studies of the homeless and powerless, they do so from the viewpoint of the"elite".

Case study is known as a triangulated research strategy. Snow and Anderson asserted that triangulation can occur with data, investigators, theories, and even methodologies. Stake stated that the protocols that are used to ensure accuracy and alternative explanations are called triangulation. The need for triangulation arises from the ethical need to confirm the validity of the processes. In case studies, this could be done by using multiple sources of data. The problem in case studies is to establish meaning rather than location.

Denzin identified four types of triangulation: Data source triangulation, when the researcher looks for the data to remain the same in different contexts; Investigator triangulation, when several investigators examine the same phenomenon; Theory triangulation, when investigators with different view points interpret the same results; and Methodological triangulation, when one approach is followed by another, to increase confidence in the interpretation.

The issue of generalization has appeared in the literature with regularity. It is a frequent criticism of case study research that the results are not widely applicable in real life. Yin in particular refuted that criticism by presenting a well constructed explanation of the difference between analytic generalization and statistical generalization:"In analytic generalization, previously developed theory is used as a template against which to compare the empirical results of the case study". The inappropriate manner of generalizing assumes that some sample of cases has been drawn from a larger universe of cases. Thus the incorrect terminology such as"small sample" arises, as though a single-case study were a single respondent.

Stake argued for another approach centred on a more intuitive, empirically-grounded generalization. He termed it"naturalistic" generalization. His argument was based on the harmonious relationship between the reader's experiences and the case study itself. He expected that the data generated by case studies would often resonate experientially with a broad cross part of readers, thereby facilitating a greater understanding of the phenomenon.

Yin presented at least four applications for a case study model:

- To explain complex causal links in real-life interventions

- To describe the real-life context in which the intervention has occurred
- To describe the intervention itself
- To explore those situations in which the intervention being evaluated has no clear set of outcomes.

Information technologies involve all four of the categories, but this study will only report on the last two. Since the Levy case study of the University of Arizona, there has been very little literature relating to the pace of acquisition of information technology at institutions of higher education. For this reason, Levy conducted a case study after consulting with experts in the field and with senior case researchers. Their recommendation was to conduct an in-depth study of the institution using the case methodology. This study replicates and extends that study and thereby adds to the body of knowledge on the nature of information technology acquisition at universities.

Levy used a single-case design for the study at the University of Arizona. Single cases may be used to confirm or challenge a theory, or to represent a unique or extreme case. Single-case studies are also ideal for revelatory cases where an observer may have access to a phenomenon that was previously inaccessible. These studies can be holistic or embedded, the latter occurring when the same case study involves more than one unit of analysis. Multiple-case studies follow a replication logic. This is not to be confused with sampling logic, where a selection is made out of a population, for inclusion in the study. This type of sample selection is improper in a case study. Each individual case study consists of a"whole" study, in which facts are gathered from various sources and ceases drawn on those facts.

As in all research, consideration must be given to construct validity, internal validity, external validity, and reliability. Levy established construct validity using the single-case exploratory design, and internal validity using the single-case explanatory design. Yin suggested using multiple sources of evidence as the way to ensure construct validity. The current study used multiple sources of evidence; survey instruments, interviews, and documents. The specification of the unit of analysis also provides the internal validity as the theories are developed and data collection and analysis test those theories. External validity is more difficult to attain in a single-case study. Yin provided the assertion that external validity could be achieved from theoretical relationships, and from these generalizations could be made. It is the development of a formal case study protocol that provides the reliability that is required of all research.

The design of this case study closely follows that of the Levy study. The methodology selected by Levy was based on the seminal work by Yin and confirmed by Feagin, Orum, and Sjoberg. That single-case study methodology was used in the current study. Danziger has established the"context of use" as a mitigating factor in the study of computing in organizations. The"pattern matching" of acquisition and use established in other environments may be shown to be applicable in higher education. Yin Listed six sources of evidence for data collection in the case study protocol: documentation, archival records, interviews, direct observation, participant observation, and physical artifacts. Not all need be used in every case study. In this study, the last three types of sources are not relevant, since they are related to direct sociological investigation, and are not used.

For this case study, the researcher replicated Levy's study, but also adds to the field by examining aspects of client/server computing, the Internet. It is based on a modification of the methodology devised by Yin. Each stage of the methodology will consist of a discussion of procedures recommended in the literature, followed by a discussion of the application of those procedures in the proposed study:

- *Design the case study protocol*:
  - Determine the required skills
  - Develop and review the protocol
- *Conduct the case study*:
  - Prepare for data collection
  - Distribute questionnaire
  - Conduct interviews

- *Analyse case study evidence:*
  - Analytic strategy
- Develop ceases, recommendations, and implications based on the evidence

In the order in which they are executed in the current study. Each part begins with the procedures recommended in the literature, followed by the application of the recommended procedure in the current study.

DESIGN THE CASE STUDY PROTOCOL

The first stage in the case study methodology recommended by Yin is the development of the case study protocol. This stage is composed of two subheadings: Determine the Required Skills and Develop and Review the Protocol. These are presented in the following discussion.

DETERMINE THE REQUIRED SKILLS

Recommended Procedures

Yin suggested that the researcher must possess or acquire the following skills: the ability to ask good questions and to interpret the responses, be a good listener, be adaptive and flexible so as to react to various situations, have a firm grasp of issues being studied, and be unbiased by preconceived notions. The investigator must be able to function as a"senior" investigator.

Application of Recommended Procedures

This researcher has had thirty years of experience in both academic and administrative computing and was adequately prepared for the investigation. This researcher's training in systems analysis is adequate preparation for the project.

A draft of the protocol will be developed by the researcher. This follows extensive relevant readings on the topic which would help in developing the draft questions. Yin recommended that this be conducted in a seminar format if there are multiple investigators. The purpose of the seminar or review, in the case of a single investigator, is to discover problems in the plans or any phase of the study design. If there is a team of investigators, the seminar format would perhaps highlight team-member incompatibilities and perhaps potentially productive partnerships amongst the members. If there are unreasonable or unattainable deadlines in the plan, this will most likely be discovered by the team.

Some of the early criticism of the case study as a research methodology was that it was unscientific in nature, and because replication was not possible. The literature contains major refutations by Yin, Stake, Feagin, and others whose work resulted in a suggested outline for what a case study protocol could include. Yin reminded the researcher that there is more to a protocol than the instrument. He asserted that the development of the rules and procedures contained in the protocol enhance the reliability of case study research. While it is desirable to have a protocol for all studies, Yin stated that it is essential in a multiple-case study.

The protocol should include the following parts:

- *An overview of the case study project*: This will include project objectives, case study issues, and presentations about the topic under study
- *Field procedures*: Reminders about procedures, credentials for access to data sources, location of those sources
- *Case study questions*: The questions that the investigator must keep in mind during data collection
- *A guide for the case study report*: The outline and format for the report.

The discipline imposed on the investigator by the protocol is important to the overall progress and reliability of the study. It helps keep the investigator's focus on the main tasks and goals, while the process of development brings out problems that would only be faced during the actual investigation. The overview of the project is a useful way to communicate with the investigator, while the field procedures are indispensable during data collection. The case study questions are those under study, not those contained in the survey instrument. Each question should also have a list of probable sources.

The guide for the case study report is often omitted from case study plans, since investigators view the reporting phase as being far in the future. Yin proposed that the report be planned at the start.

Case studies do not have a widely accepted reporting format - hence the experience of the investigator is a key factor. Some researchers have used a journal format which was suitable for their work, but not necessarily for other studies. Indeed the case study at. Fairfield University is not served by such a format, nor was the Levy study before it. The reason for the absence of a fixed reporting format is that each case study is unique. The data collection, research questions and indeed the unit of analysis cannot be placed into a fixed mold as in experimental research.

Application of Recommended Procedures

Yin presented three conditions for the design of case studies: a) the type of research question posed, b) the extent of control an investigator has over actual behavioural events, and c) the degree of focus on contemporary events. In the Levy study and this study, there are several"what" questions. This type of research question justifies an exploratory study.

Examples of such questions include:

- What patterns of acquisition emerge from the current computing environment and the perceived needs for computing?
- What patterns are revealed from historical inventory records?
- Was there any change in the perceived needs related to the Internet?
- What characteristics of the categories of computing use contribute to the patterns of acquisition?
- What managerial issues arise from the rapid acquisition of information technology and how important have those technologies become to the organization?
- Since replacement and enhancement of information technologies are projected to increase, what economic

impact will that have on the planning and budgeting of the university?

- Was there any particular budgetary and/or systematic preparation for the implementation of client/server computing?
- What was the level of managerial commitment to information technology?
- What was the level of faculty commitment to information technology?
- What was the degree of decentralization/ decentralization of information technologies?
- What resources were or will be needed for conversion to a client/server environment?
- What additional resources will be needed now and in the future for university community access to the WWW?

The existence of several"how" questions in the questionnaires make the study explanatory as well, which is not uncommon.

Examples of such questions include:

- How do the respondents view the availability of computing resources in comparison to peer institutions?
- How are information technology resources allocated?
- How are information technology resources financed?
- How will the institution balance the need for technological changes with the need to continue the accomplishment of routine tasks?
- How does Fairfield University plan to meet current demand for service while preparing for strategic long term goals?
- How does the university evaluate the cost-benefit of its computing environment?

The researcher had no control over the behavioural events, which is a characteristic of case studies. The third condition, that was present in the Levy study and is evident in the current study, is that the events being examined are contemporary, although historic information was used.

An empirical investigation of a contemporary phenomenon within its real-life context is one situation in which case study methodology is applicable. Yin cautioned that case study designs are not variants of other research designs.

Yin proposed five components of case studies:

- A study's questions,
- Its propositions, if any,
- Its unit(s) of analysis,
- The logic linking the data to the propositions, and
- The criteria for interpreting the findings.

The research questions framed as"who","what","where", "how", and"why" determine the relevant strategy to be used. In the Levy study and the current study, the nature of the questions lead to an explanatory-exploratory case study. The Levy study and this proposed study, both being exploratory, need not, and do not have a proposition. The unit of analysis in a case study could be"an individual, a community, an organization, a nation-state, an empire, or a civilization". The Levy study used the case study organization as the unit of analysis. The linking of the data to the propositions and the criteria for interpretation of the findings are not well developed in case studies. However they are represented in the data analysis and report. Levy established the single-case explanatory- exploratory methodology as the most suitable choice for the investigation of information technology. The explanatory strategy came from the need to determine the extent to which the patterns of acquisition and use that were established in other environments were applicable to higher education environment also. The exploratory strategy was used to examine the economic aspects of information technologies. As a replication of the Levy study, this study also followed that methodology.

DATA COLLECTION, DISTRIBUTION OF THE QUESTIONNAIRE, AND CONDUCTING INTERVIEWS

RECOMMENDED PROCEDURES

The second stage of the methodology recommended by

Yin and which were used in the current study, is the Conduct of the case study. There are three tasks in this stage that must be carried out for a successful project: Preparation for Data Collection, Distribution of the Questionnaire, and Conducting Interviews.

These stages are presented together in the following part, since they are interrelated. Once the protocol has been developed and tested, it puts the project into the second phase - the actual execution of the plan. In this phase the primary activity is that of data collection.

The protocol described the types of evidence that are available in the case organization. In case studies, data collection should be treated as a design issue that will enhance the construct and internal validity of the study, as well as the external validity and reliability.

Most of the field methods described in the literature treat data collection in isolation from the other aspects of the research process but that would not be productive in case study research.

Yin identified six primary sources of evidence for case study research. The use of each of these might require different skills from the researcher.

Not all sources are essential in every case study, but the importance of multiple sources of data to the reliability of the study is well established.

The six sources identified by Yin are:

- Documentation,
- Archival records,
- Interviews,
- Direct observation,
- Participant observation, and
- Physical artifacts.

No single source has a complete advantage over the others; rather, they might be complementary and could be used in tandem.

Thus a case study should use as many sources as are relevant to the study.

Table indicates the strengths and weaknesses of each type:

Table. Types of Evidence

Source of Evidence	Strengths	Weaknesses
Documentation	Stable - repeated review unobtrusive - exist prior to case study exact - names etc. broad coverage - extended time span	Retrievability - difficult biased selectivity reporting bias - reflects author bias access - may be blocked
Archival Records	Same as above precise and quantitative	Same as above privacy might inhibit access
Interviews	Targeted - focuses on case study topic insightful - provides perceived causal inferences	Bias due to poor questions response bias incomplete recollection reflexivity - interviewee expresses what interviewer wants to hear
Direct Observation	Reality - covers events in real time contextual - covers event context	Time-consuming selectivity - might miss facts reflexivity - observer's presence might cause change cost - observers need time
Participant Observation	Same as above insightful into interpersonal behavior	Same as above bias due to investigator's actions
Physical Artifacts	Insightful into cultural features insightful into technical operations	Selectivity availability

Documents could be letters, memoranda, agendas, study reports, or any items that could add to the data base. The validity of the documents should be carefully reviewed so as to avoid incorrect data being included in the data base.

One of the most important uses of documents is to corroborate evidence gathered from other sources.

The potential for over-reliance on document as evidence in case studies has been criticized. There could be a danger of this occurrence if the investigator is inexperienced and mistakes some types of documents for unmitigated truth.

Archival records could be useful in some studies since they include service records, maps, charts, lists of names, survey data, and even personal records such as diaries. The investigator must be meticulous in determining the origin of the records and their accuracy.

Interviews are one of the most important sources of case study information. The interview could take one of several forms: open-ended, focused, or structured. In an open-ended interview, the researcher could ask for the informant's opinion on events or facts. This could serve to corroborate previously gathered data.

In a focused interview, the respondent is interviewed for only a short time, and the questions asked could have come from the case study protocol. The structured interview is particularly useful in studies of neighborhoods where a formal survey is required. The use of tape recorders during the interviews is left to the discretion of the parties involved. Direct observation in a case study occurs when the investigator makes a site visit to gather data. The observations could be formal or casual activities, but the reliability of the observation is the main concern. Using multiple observers is one way to guard against this problem.

Participant observation is a unique mode of observation in which the researcher may actually participate in the events being studied. This technique could be used in studies of neighborhoods or organizations, and frequently in anthropological studies. The main concern is the potential bias of the researcher as an active participant. While the information may not be available in any other way, the drawbacks should be carefully considered by the researcher.

Physical artifacts could be any physical evidence that might be gathered during a site visit. That might include tools, art works, notebooks, computer output, and other such physical evidence.

Yin suggested three principles of data collection for case studies:

- Use multiple sources of data
- Create a case study database
- Maintain a chain of evidence

The rationale for using multiple sources of data is the triangulation of evidence. Triangulation increases the reliability of the data and the process of gathering it. In the context of data collection, triangulation serves to corroborate the data gathered from other sources. The cost of using multiple sources and the investigator's ability to carry out the task, should be taken into account prior to deciding on the use of this technique.

The data that are collected during this phase need to be organized and documented just as it is in experimental studies. The two types of databases that might be required are the data and the report of the investigator. The design of the databases should be such that other researchers would be able to use the material based on the descriptions contained in the documentation. All types of relevant documents should be added to the database, as well as tabular materials, narratives, and other notes.

In recommending that a chain of evidence be maintained, Yin was providing an avenue for the researcher to increase the reliability of the study. The procedure is to have an external observer follow the derivation of evidence from initial research questions to ultimate case study ceases.

Application of Recommended Procedures

This study used the methodology established by Levy in his investigation of the impacts of information technology at the University of Arizona. The methodology recommended by Yin and others was adapted for use at Fairfield University.

The questionnaire developed by Levy was modified for use at Fairfield University. The modifications were approved by Levy. The modified instruments reflect both the current case organization and the technology environment under study. The modified instruments were tested on a group of individuals from the administration and from the faculty at Fairfield University, the case organization. The results from the test group indicated that changes to the instruments would be beneficial, and these changes were made. The remodified instruments were reviewed by Levy. King and Kraemer provided the logical categories for context of use in computing environments and were adapted by Levy in the 1988 study: technological development, structural arrangements, socio-technical interface, political/economic environment, and benefits/problems. Specific questionnaire items cover these areas. These categories were also employed in the analysis.

The primary data gathering was accomplished using the"Administrator Assessment of Computing" and the"Faculty Assessment of Computing" questionnaires developed for the Levy study, appropriately modified to reflect recent developments and concerns specific to Fairfield University. The purpose of the modifications to the instruments was to gather data on the client/server aspects of the computing environment, as well as the use of the Internet. Permission to use the questionnaires from Levy's study was obtained.

Some of the items in the instruments that relate to each of the categories are:

- *Technological Development:*
  - There is considerable support for the acquisition of PC networks within my department/unit
  - More local area networks
  - Access to the Internet
  - Access to networked CD's from classroom
  - Ability to create class material for use on the WWW
  - Video Conference capability
  - Microcomputer classrooms for instruction only
  - More classrooms connected to networks
  - More instructional software
  - Support for Multimedia course development
  - Ability to transfer large files with sound, images, etc.
- *Structural Arrangements:*
  - University policy has provided effective guidelines for computing use in the university
  - The university's central administration has been equitable in allocating available resources for computing

- Satisfied with our level of computing decisions

- *Socio-Technical Interface*:
  - Hands-on workshops designed specifically for faculty and research uses of information technology tools would be useful for me
  - Current support programmmes
  - Sufficient data communications capabilities
  - Access to Internet, WWW, E-mail, from the Office
  - Access to Internet, WWW, E-mail, from the Classroom
  - Access to Internet, WWW, E-mail, from the Home
  - Use the services of an Instructional Computing group to help faculty use computing for instruction
  - Use the services of a Research Computing group to help faculty use computing for instruction
- *Political/Economic Environment*:
  - All students should have access to computing, regardless of the course in which they are enrolled
  - Faculty positions
  - Support positions
  - Plant and Equipment maintenance
  - Current instructional programmmes
  - There is sufficient support for instructional computing in my department
- *Benefits/Problems*:
  - The scope of the work we are able to undertake is directly increased by the use if computing
  - Attracting undergraduate students
  - Attracting faculty
  - Able to adequately discuss needs with mainframe support staff
  - Satisfied with system response time
  - Satisfied with institutional data sets available for analysis

The questionnaires were distributed through the office of the Academic Vice President to all full-time faculty and academic administrators, and specific others recommended by the deans and the AVP. This data gathering activity was co-sponsored by the Education Technology committee. The questionnaire for faculty was also distributed to the permanent faculty of the School of Engineering, although they are not full-time faculty. They are heavy users of technology and their views were considered valuable. Including part-time faculty other than the School of Engineering, carried the risk of including several hundred instructors who teach in the School of Continuing Education and whose access to computing resources is limited. They are adjunct lecturers who could be classified as part-time instructors. Their number is too large to warrant the potential distortion in the results. The completed questionnaires were returned to the office of the Academic Vice President.

A reminder notice was sent to all faculty and administrators one week after the original contact, so as to encourage participation. This action increased the response rate. The Educational Technology Committee made phone calls to colleagues to encourage participation.

Levy used open-ended interviews as recommended by Yin to expand the depth of data gathering, and to increase the number of sources of information. In this study the researcher used the same interview questions and protocol that were used in the Levy study.

As in the Levy study, the survey was enhanced by interviews of key individuals so as to acquire information that might not have become available through the questionnaire. The interviews were conducted according to the interviewee's schedule and availability, as suggested by Feagin, Orum, and Sjoberg.

The list of those to be interviewed included the Academic Vice President, the Vice President of Administration, the Director of Telecommunications, the Deans of Arts and Sciences, Business, and Engineering, and the Chair of the academic Educational Technology committee. The interview protocol used by Levy was free form and followed the recommendations of Yin. It was ideal for the case organization under study. The researcher is well qualified to conduct this form of inquiry.

The source of the quantitative data was various university records in the public domain. The historic financial information, Financial Statements, 1989-1995 was available through the appropriate university officers. Permission was obtained from the Fairfield University Controller, for use of the documents. The Long Range Planning Committee Report and the Computer User Group Report were the primary sources of information on future projections. Both the documents were available in the university Library. The academic Educational Technology Committee minutes would have been very informative for some of the historic and anecdotal issues, but were unavailable for non-committee use.

ANALYSE CASE STUDY EVIDENCE

The following discussion will present the Analytic Strategy that should be followed in the course of evaluating data gathered in the previous stage of the study. There are various viewpoints relating to this phase of the study, and one of them is that statistical robustness is not an absolute necessity in all case studies.

"Data analysis consists of examining, categorizing, tabulating, or otherwise recombining the evidence to address the initial propositions of a study". The analysis of case study is one of the least developed aspects of the case study methodology. The researcher needs to rely on experience and the literature to present the evidence in various ways, using various interpretations. This becomes necessary because statistical analysis is not necessarily used in all case studies. This case study employs a series of statistical tests to help in the presentation of the data to the reader. However not all case studies lend themselves to statistical analysis, and in fact the attempt to make the study conducive to such analysis could inhibit the development of other aspects of the study. Miles and Huberman have suggested alternative analytic techniques of analysis in such situations, such as using arrays to display the data, creating displays, tabulating the frequency of events, ordering the information, and other methods. This must be done in a way that will not bias the results.

Yin suggested that every investigation should have a general analytic strategy, so as to guide the decision regarding what will be analysed and for what reason. He presented some possible analytic techniques: pattern-matching, explanation-building, and time-series analysis. In general, the analysis will rely on the theoretical propositions that led to the case study. If theoretical propositions are not present, then the researcher could consider developing a descriptive framework around which the case study is organized.

Trochim considered pattern-matching as one of the most desirable strategies for analysis. This technique compares an empirically based pattern with a predicted one. If the patterns match, the internal reliability of the study is enhanced. The actual comparison between the predicted and actual pattern might not have any quantitative criteria. The discretion of the researcher is therefore required for interpretations.

Explanation-building is considered a form of pattern-matching, in which the analysis of the case study is carried out by building an explanation of the case. This implies that it is most useful in explanatory case studies, but it is possible to use it for exploratory cases as well as part of a hypothesis-generating process. Explanation-building is an iterative process that begins with a theoretical statement, refines it, revises the proposition, and repeating this process from the beginning. This is known to be a technique that is fraught with problems for the investigator. One of those problems is a loss of focus, although keeping this in mind protects the investigator from those problems.

Time-series analysis is a well-known technique in experimental and quasi-experimental analysis. It is possible that a single dependent or independent variable could make this simpler than pattern-matching, but sometimes there are multiple changes in a variable, making starting and ending points unclear.

There are some things that the researcher must be careful to review to ensure that the analysis will be of high quality, including: showing that all relevant evidence was used, that all rival explanations were used, that the analysis addressed the most significant aspect of the case study, and that the researchers knowledge and experience are used to maximum advantage in the study.

APPLICATION OF RECOMMENDED PROCEDURE

The data analysis for the current case study follows the logical categories used in the Levy study, and was adapted from the categories developed by King and Kraemer.

The categories are:

- Technological development
- Structural arrangements
- Socio-technical interface
- Political economic environment, and
- Benefits/problems.

Those categories were supported by the selection of indicators that were"functionally equivalent" items for each concept. Functional equivalence means that the same variable may be measured by a variety of different indicators, all of which have some bearing on the concept.

This researcher modified the Levy questionnaires to reflect current technology developments and items of interest to Fairfield University.

All references to the University of Arizona were replaced by references to Fairfield University. Several items were added to gather data concerning the Internet. A factor analysis was executed to determine if the current case population produced the same groupings as in the Levy study. Loehlin recommended an exploratory factor analysis for the type of data that was gathered in this study.

Some of the items added to the original instrument include:

- Current use/could use/would enhance future use
  - Internet resources (Gopher, FTP etc.)
  - World Wide Web resources (Netscape, etc.)
  - Networked PC access from classroom

- The following contribute to the effectiveness of my work
  - Access to the Internet, WWW, Email from the office, classroom, and home
- These developments could be important in five years
  - Access to the Internet and WWW
  - Access to networked CD's from classroom
  - Ability to create class material for use on WWW
- High priority should be placed on the following
  - More powerful network servers
  - Microcomputer/Multimedia classrooms for instruction only
  - More classrooms connected to the network
  - Support for WWW/Multimedia course development
  - More instructional software
  - Ability to transfer large files with sound, images etc.
  - Ability to scan and store documents on WWW for instruction
- Table adding up to one hundred per cent
  - Use of the Internet for: Instruction, Research, Professional Interest, Email, and Personal Interest/Surfing.

Aczel recommended cross tabulations to explore a hypothesis such as that relating to differences between faculty and administration within the King and Kraemer categories. The hypothesis was that there is no significant difference between the responses of the two groups of respondents with regard to the factors relating to the rate of technology acquisition.

Cross tabulations were used to explore the differences in responses of the faculty by school. Cross tabulations and the chi- square were computed to determine if the differences that appeared among the sub groups of the university community such as faculty and administrators, were significant. A contingency coefficient for each cross tabulation indicated the strength of the relationship.

The Likert-type variables were analysed using frequency distributions. The ordinal items in the questionnaires were analysed using the mean and median.

For those items in the questionnaires that are common to the Levy study and the current case organization (Fairfield University), a paired comparison of the sample populations was run. The statistical tests were the Cross tabulation and Chi square, so that inferences may be drawn about the comparison of the two very different institutions. Those inferences could lead to grounded theory regarding the aspects of information technology at universities of different sizes. The Chi-square was used to assess whether the differences that emerged were significant. All analyses were carried out using SPSSx version 7.1 on an IBM Pentium 75 megahertz PC compatible running Windows 95. These resources were available to the researcher at Fairfield University. The data capture was carried out on a DEC Vax 6430 using Accent R, creating a database and screen driven programmmes. The researcher created the programmmes to validate the data as it was entered so as to minimize data entry errors.

There are hundreds of private colleges that are about the same size as Fairfield University. By applying the case study to this type of institution, the analytic generalizations could be informative to other similar institutions. The literature has pointed to increasing costs and declining revenues. Those are issues that many higher education institutions face.

DEVELOP CEASES, RECOMMENDATIONS, AND IMPLICATIONS BASED ON THE EVIDENCE

Recommended Procedure

The reporting aspect of a case study is perhaps most important from the user perspective. It is the contact point between the user and the researcher. A well designed research project that is not well explained to the reader, will cause the research report to fall into disuse. The researcher must refrain from technical jargon and resort to clear explanations. Those explanations are necessary to help the user understand the implications of the findings.

Application of Recommended Procedure

These results are presented not exclusively as statistical results, but with accompanying explanations of the meaning of those test results. In that way both the technical requirements and the informational needs are met.

Summary

The case study methodology has been subjected to scrutiny and criticism at various times since the 1930's. As a research tool, it has not been a choice that is listed in the major research texts in the social sciences. However, case study is a reliable methodology when executed with due care. The literature, while not extensive, contains specific guidelines for researchers to follow in carrying out case studies. Yin and Stake have designed protocols for conducting the case study, which enhance the reliability and validity of the investigation.

The current study followed the design used by Levy in his case study of the impacts of information technology at the University of Arizona. The survey instruments used by Levy were modified for use at Fairfield University. The modifications included replacing"Fairfield University" for references to the"University of Arizona", deleting environmental references not appropriate for Fairfield University, and adding items to the instruments for the purpose of gathering data on the client/server computing, the Internet, and the World Wide Web.

Once the instruments were modified and the testing completed, the surveys were distributed to the full-time faculty and educational administrators. One week after the initial distribution, a reminder was sent to the groups so as to encourage participation.

The analysis followed conventional analytic techniques using statistical as well as anecdotal analysis. Differences between the responses of the administrators and faculty were explored using cross tabulations. These differences were examined within the categories described by King and Kraemer (1985) and adapted for use by Levy (1988) in a case study of the University of Arizona. For the Likert-type variables frequency distributions were used to analyse the data. For those items where the original Levy (1988) instruments and the current instruments were identical, a cross tabulation and chi-square were executed to examine the significance of the differences, if any, between the groups. All these tests were run at Fairfield University using SPSSX version 7.1 on an IBM Pentium 75 megahertz PC compatible running Windows 95.

The methodology that was used to conduct the current study. In a future edition of this journal, the results will be presented in accord with the goals and objectives of the study so as to confirm that what was proposed was in fact executed. Once again follow the goals and objectives outlined in the introductory and confirm that what was proposed was in fact accomplished.

FIVE MISUNDERSTANDINGS ABOUT CASE STUDY RESEARCH

When we first became interested in in-depth case-study research,we was trying to understand how power and rationality shape each other and form the urban environments in which we live. It was clear to me that in order to understand a complex issue like this, in-depth case-study research was necessary.

It was equally clear, however, that my teachers and colleagues kept dissuading me from employing this particular research methodology.'You cannot generalize from a single case', some would say,'and social science is about generalizing.' Others would argue that the case study may be well suited for pilot studies but not for full-fledged research planss. Others again would comment that the case study is subjective, giving too much scope for the researcher's own interpretations. Thus the validity of case studies would be wanting, they argued. At first, we did not know how to respond to such claims, which clearly formed the conventional wisdom about case-study research. we decided therefore to find out where the claims come from and whether they are correct.

THE CONVENTIONAL WISDOMABOUT CASE-STUDY RESEARCH

Looking up'case study' in the Dictionary of Sociology as a beginning. The detailed examination of a single xample of a class of phenomena, a case study cannot provide reliable information about the broader class, but it may be useful in the preliminary stages of an investigation since it provides hypotheses, which may be tested systematically with a larger number of cases. This description is indicative of the conventional wisdom of case-study research, which, if not directly wrong, is so oversimplified as to be grossly misleading. It is correct that the case study is a'detailed examination of a single example', it is not true that a case study'cannot provide reliable information about the broader class'.

It is also correct that a case study can be used'in the preliminary stages of an investigation' to generate hypotheses, but it is misleading to see the case study as a pilot method to be used only in preparing the real study's larger surveys, systematic hypotheses testing, and theory-building. The conventional view, a case and a case study cannot be of value in and of themselves; they need to be linked to hypotheses, following the well-known hypothetico-deductive model of explanation.

Mattei Dogan and Dominique Pelassy put it like this:'one can validly explain a particular case only on the basis of general hypotheses. All the rest is uncontrollable, and so of no use'. Similarly, the early Donald Campbell did not mince words when he relegated single-case studies to the methodological trash heap: [S]uch studies have such a total absence of control as to be of almost no scientific value. ... Any appearance of absolute knowledge, or intrinsic knowledge about singular isolated objects, is found to be illusory upon analysis. ... It seems well-nigh unethical at the present time to allow.

FIVE MISUNDERSTANDINGS ABOUTCASE-STUDY RESEARCH

If you read such criticism of a certain methodology enough times, or if you hear your thesis advisers repeal it, you begin to believe it may be true. This is what happened to me, and it made me uncertain about case-study methodology. As we continued our research, however,we found out that Campbell had later made a 180-degree turn in his views of the case study and had become one of the strongest proponents of this method.we eventually found, with the help of Campbell's later works and other works like them, that the problems with the conventional wisdom about case-study research can be summarized in five misunderstandings or oversimplifications about the nature of such research: Misunderstanding no.

- General, theoretical (context-independent) knowledge is more valuable than concrete, practical (contextdependent) knowledge. Misunderstanding no.
- One cannot generalize on the basis of an individual case; therefore the case study cannot contribute to scientific development. Misunderstanding no.
- The case study is most useful for generating hypotheses, that is, in the first stage of a total research process, whil other methods are more suitable for hypotheses testing and theory-building. Misunderstanding no.
- The case study contains a bias towards verification, that is, a tendency to confirm the researcher's preconceived notions. Misunderstanding no.
- It is often difficult to summarize and develop general propositions and theories on the basis of specific case studies.

These five misunderstandings indicate that it is theory, reliability and validity that are at issue; other words, the very status of the case study as a scientific method. In what follows, we shall focus on these five misunderstandings and correct them one by one. First, however,we shall outline the role of cases in human learning.

THE ROLE OF CASES IN HUMAN LEARNING

In order to understand why the conventional view of case-study research is problematic, we need to grasp the role of cases and theory in human learning. Here two points can be made. First, the case study produces the type of context-dependent knowledge that research on learning shows to be necessary to allow people to develop from rule-based beginners to virtuoso experts. Second, in the study of human affairs, there appears to exist only context-dependent knowledge, which thus presently rules out the possibility of epistemic theoretical construction.

The full argument behind these two points can be found in Flyvbjerg. For reasons of space, we can only give an outline of the argument here. At the outset, however, we can assert that if the two points are correct, it will have radical consequences for the conventional view of the case study in research and teaching. This view would then be problematic. Phenomenological studies of human learning indicate that for adults there exists a qualitative leap in their learning process from the rulegoverned use of analytical rationality in beginners to the fluid performance of tacit skills in what Pierre Bourdieu calls virtuosos and Hubert and Stuart Dreyfus (1986) true human experts. Here we may note that most people are experts in a number of everyday social, technical and intellectual skills like giving a gift, riding a bicycle or interpreting images on a television screen, while only few reach the level of true expertise for more specialized skills like playing chess, composing a symphony or flying a fighter jet.

Common to all experts, however, is that they operate on the basis of intimate knowledge of several thousand concrete cases in their areas of expertise. Context-dependent knowledge and experience are at the very heart of expert activity. Such knowledge and expertise also lie at the centre of the case study as a research and teaching method; or, to put it more generally still, as a method of learning. Phenomenological studies of the learning process therefore emphasize the importance of this and similar methods: it is only because of experience with cases that one can at all move from being a beginner to being an expert. If people were exclusively trained in context-independent knowledge and rules, that is, the kind of knowledge that forms the basis of textbooks and computers, they would remain at the beginner's level in the learning process. This is the limitation of analytical rationality: it is inadequate for the best results in the exercise of a profession, as student, researcher or practitioner. In a teaching situation, well-chosen case studies can help the student achieve competence, while context-independent facts and rules will bring the student just to the beginner's level. Only a few institutions of higher learning have taken the consequence of this. Harvard University is one of them.

Here both teaching and research in the professional schools are modelled to a wide extent on the understanding that case knowledge is central to human learning. At one stage in my research, we was invited to Harvard to learn about case methodology'in action'. During my stay, it became clear to me that if we was going to aspire to become an expert in my field of expertise, and if we wanted to be an effective help to my students in their learning processes, we would need to master case methodologyin research and teaching. My stay atHarvard also became a major step forward in shedding my uncertainties about the conventional wisdom about cases and case studies. At Harvard we found the literature and people who effectively argued,'Forget the conventional wisdom, go ahead and do a case study'.

There is much to gain, for instance, by transforming the lecture format still dominant in most universities to one of case learning. It is not that rule-based knowledge should be discounted: it is important in every area and especially to novices. But to make rule-based knowledge the highest goal of learning is regressive. There is a need for both approaches. The highest levels in the learning process, that is, virtuosity and true expertise, are reached only via a person's own experiences as practitioner of the relevant skills. Therefore, beyond using the case method and other experiential methods for teaching, the best that teachers can do for students in professional programmes is to help them achieve real practical experience; for example, via placement arrangements, internships, summer jobs, and the like. For researchers, the closeness of the case study to real-life situations and its multiple wealth of details are important in two respects. First, it is important for the development of a nuanced view of reality, including the view that human behaviour cannot be meaningfully understood as simply the rule-governed acts found at the lowest levels of the learning process, and in much theory. Second, cases are important forresearchers' own learning processes in developing the skills needed to do good research.

If researchers wish to develop their own skills to a high level, then concrete, context-dependent experience is just as central for them as to professionals learning any other specific skills. Concrete experiences can be achieved via continued proximity to the studied reality and via feedback from those under study. Great distance to the object of study and lack of feedback easily lead to a stultified learning process, which in research can lead to ritual academic blind alleys, where the effect and usefulness of research becomes unclear and untested. As a research method, the case study can be an effective remedy against this tendency. The second main point in connection with the learning process is that there does not and probably cannot exist predictive theory in social science.

Social science has not succeeded in producing general, context-independent theory and has thus in the final instance nothing else to offer than concrete, context-dependent knowledge. And the case study is especially well suited to produce this knowledge. In his later work, Donald Campbell arrives at a similar cease, explaining how his work has undergone'an extreme oscillation away from my earlier dogmatic disparagement of case studies'. In a logic that in many ways resembles that of the phenomenology of human learning, Campbell now explains: After all, man is, in his ordinary way, a very competent knower, and qualitative common-sense knowing is not replaced by quantitative knowing. ... This is not to say that such common-sense naturalistic observation is objective, dependable, or unbiased. But it is all that we have.

It is the only route to knowledge - noisy, fallible, and biased though it be. Campbell is not the only example of a researcher who has altered his views about the value of the case study. Hans Eysenck, who originally did not regard the case study as anything other than a method of producing anecdotes, later realised that'sometimes we simply have to keep our eyes open and look carefully at individual cases - not in the hope of proving anything, but rather in the hope of learning something!' Proof is hard to come by in social science because of the absence of'hard' theory, whereas learning is certainly possible. More recently, similar views have been expressed by Charles Ragin, Howard Becker and their colleagues in explorations of what the case study is and can be in social inquiry.

As for predictive theory, universals and scientism, the study of human affairs is thus at an eternal beginning. In essence, we have only specific cases and context-dependent knowledge. The first of the five misunderstandings about the case study - that general theoretical knowledge is more valuable than concrete, practical (context-dependent) knowledge - can therefore be revised as follows:

CASES AS'BLACK SWANS'

The view that one cannot generalize on the basis of a single case is usually considered to be devastating to the case study as a scientific method. This second misunderstanding about the case study is typical among proponents of the natural science ideal within the social sciences. Yet even researchers who are not normally associated with this ideal may be found to have this viewpoint.

Anthony Giddens, for example, Research which is geared primarily to hermeneutic problems may be of generalized importance in so far as it serves to elucidate the nature of agents' knowledgeability, and thereby their reasons for action, across a wide range of action-contexts. Pieces of ethnographic research like ... say, the traditional small-scale community research of fieldwork anthropology - are not in themselves generalizing studies. But they can easily become so if carried out in some numbers, so that judgements of their typicality can justifiably be made.

It is correct that one can generalize in the ways Giddens describes, and that often this is bothappropriate and valuable. But it would be incorrect to assert that this is the only way to work, just as it is incorrect to conclude that one cannot generalize from a single case. It depends upon the case one is speaking of, and how it is chosen. This applies to the natural sciences as well as to the study of human affairs. For example, Galileo's rejection of Aristotle's law of gravity was not based upon observations'across a wide range', and the observations were not'carried out in some numbers'.

The rejection consisted primarily of a conceptual experiment and later of a practical one. These experiments, with the benefit of hindsight, are self-evident. Nevertheless, Aristotle's view of gravity dominated scientific inquiry for nearly two thousand years before it was falsified. In his experimental thinking, Galileo reasoned as follows: if two objects with the same weight are released from the same height at the same time, they will hit the ground simultaneously, having fallen at the same speed. If the two objects are then stuck together into one, this object will have double the weight and will according to the Aristotelian view therefore fall faster than the two individual objects. This cease operated in a counter-intuitive way for Galileo.

The only way to avoid the contradiction was to eliminate weight as a determinant factor for acceleration in free fall. And that was what Galileo did. Historians of science continue to discuss whether Galileo actually conducted the famous experiment from the leaning tower of Pisa, or whether it is simply a myth. In any event, Galileo's experimentalism did not involve a large random sample of trials of objects falling from a wide range of randomly selected heights under varying wind conditions, and so on, as would be demanded by the thinking of the early Campbell and Giddens. Rather, it was a matter of a single experiment, that is, a case study, if any experiment was conducted at all. Galileo's view continued to be subjected to doubt, however, and the Aristotelian view was not finally rejected until half a century later, with the invention of the air pump. The air pump made it possible to conduct the ultimate experiment, known by every pupil, whereby a coin or apiece of lead inside a vacuum tube falls with the same speed as a feather. After this experiment, Aristotle's view could be maintained no longer. What is especially worth noting in our discussion, however, is that the matter was settled by an individual case due to the clever choice of the extremes of metal and feather. One might call it a critical case: for if Galileo's thesis held for these materials, it could be expected to be valid for all or a large range of materials. Random and large samples were at no time part of the picture.

Most creative scientists simply do not work this way with this type of problem. Carefully chosen experiments, cases and experience were also critical to the development of the physics of Newton, Einstein and Bohr, just as the case study occupied a central place in the works of Darwin, Marx and Freud. In social science, too, the strategic choice of case may greatly add to the generalizability of a case study. In their classic study of the'affluent worker', John Goldthorpe et al. deliberately looked for a case that was as favourable as possible to the thesis that the working class, having reached middle-class status, was dissolving into a society without class identity and related conflict.

If the thesis could be proved false in the favourable case, then it would most likely be false for intermediate cases. Luton, a prosperous industrial centre with companies known for high wagesand social stability - fertile ground for middleclass identity - was selected as a case, and through intensive fieldwork the researchers discovered that even here an autonomous workingclass culture prevailed, lending general credence to the thesis of the persistence of class identity. As suggested, discuss more systematically this type of strategic sampling. As regards the relationship between case studies, large samples and discoveries,W.I.B. Beveridge observed immediately prior to the breakthrough of the quantitative revolution in the social sciences:'[M]ore discoveries have arisen from intense observation than from statistics applied to large groups.' This does not mean that the case study is always appropriate or relevant as a research method, or that large random samples are without value. The choice of method should clearly depend on the problem under study and its circumstances.

Finally, it should be mentioned that formal generalization, be it on the basis of large samples or single cases, is considerably overrated as the main source of scientific progress. Economist Mark Blaug —a self-declared adherent to the hypothetico-deductive model of science - hasdemonstrated that while economists typically pay lip service to the hypothetico-deductive model and to generalization, they rarely practise what they preach in actual research. More generally, Thomas Kuhn has shown that the most important precondition for science is that researchers possess a wide range of practical skills for carrying out scientific work. Generalization is just one of these.

In Germanic languages, the term'science' means literally'to gain knowledge'. And formal generalization is only one of many ways by which people gain and accumulateknowledge. That knowledge cannot be formally generalized does not mean that it cannot enter into the collective process of knowledge accumulation in a given field or in a society. A purely descriptive, phenomenological case study without any attempt to generalize can certainly be of value in this process and has often helped cut a path towards scientific innovation. This is not to criticize attempts at formal generalization, forsuch attempts are essential and effective means of scientific development.

It is only to emphasize the limitations, which follows when formal generalization becomes the only legitimate method of scientific inquiry. The balanced view of the role of the case study in attempting to generalize by testing hypothese has been formulated by Eckstein: Comparative and case studies are alternative means to the end of testing theories, choices between which must be largely governed by arbitrary or practical, rather than logical, considerations. ... It is impossible to take seriously the position that case study is suspect because problem-prone and comparative study deserving of benefit of doubt because problem-free.

Eckstein here uses the term'theory' in its'hard' sense, that is, comprising explanation and prediction. This makes Eckstein's dismissal of the view that case studies cannot be used for testing theories or for generalization stronger than my own view, which is here restricted to the testing of'theory' in the'soft' sense, that is, testing propositions or hypotheses. Eckstein shows that if predictive theories existed in social science, then the case study could be used to test these theories just as well as other methods. More recently, John Walton has similarly observed that'case studies are likely to produce the best theory'.

Eckstein observes, however, the striking lack of genuine theories within his own field, political science, but apparently fails to see why this is so: Aiming at the disciplined application of theories to cases forces one to state theories more rigorously than might otherwise be done - provided that the application is truly'disciplined,' i.e., designed to show that valid theory compels a particular case interpretation and rules out others. As already stated, this, unfortunately, is rare (if it occurs at all) in political study. One reason is the lack of compelling theories. The case study is ideal for generalizing using the type of test that Karl Popper called'falsification', which in social science forms part of critical reflexivity. Falsification is one of the mostrigorous tests to which a scientific proposition can be subjected: if just one observation does not fit with the proposition, it is considered not valid generally and must therefore be either revised or rejected.

Popper himself used the now famous example of'All swans are white', and proposed that just one observation of a single black swan would falsify this proposition and in this way have general significance and stimulate further investigations and theory-building. The case study is well suited for identifying'black swans' because of its in-depth approach: what appears to be'white' often turns out on closer examination to be'black'. Finding black swans was an experience with which we became thoroughly familiar when we did our first in-depth case study, of urban politics and planning in the city of Aalborg, Denmark.

For instance, at university we had been trained in the neoclassical model of'economic man', competition and free markets. As we dug into what happened behind closed doors in Aalborg, we found that economic man does not live here. The local business community were power-mongers who were busy negotiating illicit deals with politicians and administrators on how to block competition and the free market and create special privileges for themselves. The neoclassical model was effectively falsified by what we saw in Aalborg. Similarly, the model of representative democracy, which on the surface of things appears to apply, and by law is supposed to apply in Aalborg and Denmark, was strangely absent in the deep detail of the case.

Here we found a highly undemocratic, semi-institutionalized way of making decisions, where leaders of the business community and of the city government had formed a secret council, which in actual fact replaced the democratically elected city council as the place where important decisions on urban politics and planning were made. My colleagues in third-world nations, who appear to hold fewer illusions about markets and democracy than academics in the first world, get a good laugh when we tell our Aalborg stories. They see that, after all, we in the North are not so different; we are thirdworld in some ways too. For the present, however, we can correct the second misunderstanding - that one cannot generalize on the basis of a single case and that the case study cannot contribute to scientific development - so that it now reads: One can often generalize on the basis of a single case, and the case study may be central to scientific development via generalization as supplement or alternative to other methods. But formal generalization is overvalued as a source of scientific development, whereas'the force of example' is underestimated.

STRATEGIES FOR CASE SELECTION

The third misunderstanding about the case study is that the case method is claimed to be most useful for generating hypotheses in the first steps of a total research process, while hypothesistesting and theory-building is best carried out by other methods later in the process. This misunderstanding derives from the previous misunderstanding that one cannot generalize on the basis of individual cases. We can now correct the third misunderstanding as follows: The case study is useful for both generating and testing of hypotheses but is not limited to these research activities alone.

Eckstein - contravening the conventional wisdom in this area - goes so far as to argue that case studies are better for testing hypotheses than for producing them. Case studies, Eckstein asserts,'are valuable at all stages of the theory-building process, but most valuable at that stage of theory-building where least value is generally attached to them: the stage at which candidate theories are tested'. Testing of hypotheses relates directly to the question of'generalizability', and this in turn relates to the question of case selection. Here generalizability of case studies can be increased by the strategic selection of cases.

When the objective is to achieve the greatest possible amount of information on a given problem or phenomenon, a representative case or a random sample may not be the most appropriate strategy. This is because the typical or average case is often not the richest in information. Atypical or extreme cases often reveal more information because they activate more actors and more basic mechanisms in the situation studied. In addition, from both an understanding-oriented and an action-oriented perspective, it is often more important to clarify the deeper causes behind a given problem and its consequences than to describe the symptoms of the problem and how frequently they occur. Random samples emphasizing representativeness will seldom be able to produce this kind of insight; it is more appropriate to select some few cases chosen for their validity.

The extreme case can be well suited for getting a point across in an especially dramatic way, which often occurs for well-known case studies such as Freud's'Wolf-Man' and Foucault's'Panopticon'. In contrast, a critical case can be defined as having strategic importance in relation to the general problem. For example, an occupational medicine clinic wanted to investigate whether people working with organic solvents suffered brain damage. Instead of choosing a representative sample among all those enterprises in the clinic's area that used organic solvents, the clinic strategically located a single workplace where all safety regulations on cleanliness, air quality and the like had been fulfilled. This model enterprise became a critical case: if brain damage related to organic solvents could be found at this particular facility, then it was likely that the same problem would exist at other enterprises that were less careful with safety regulations for organic solvents.

Via this type of strategic choice, one can save both time and money in researching a given problem. Another example of critical case selection is the strategic selection of lead andfeather for the test of whether different objects fall with equal velocity. The selection of materials provided the possibility to formulate a generalization characteristic of critical cases, a generalization of the sort,'If it is valid for this case, it isvalid for all (or many) cases'. In its negative form, the generalization would be,'If it is notvalid for this case, then it is not valid for any (or only few) cases'. How does one identify critical cases? This question is more difficult to answer than the question of what constitutes a critical case. Locating a critical case requires experience, and no universal methodological principles exist by which one can with certainty identify a critical case. The only general advice that can be given is that when looking for critical cases, it is a good idea to look for either'most likely' or'least likely' cases, that is, cases that are likely to either clearly confirm or irrefutably falsify propositions and hypotheses.

I was mistaken, however, but to my chagrin we did not realise this until we was halfway through the research process. Initially, we conceived of Aalborg as a'most likely' critical case in the following manner: if rationality and urban planning were weak in the face of power in Aalborg, then, most likely, they would be weak anywhere, at least in Denmark, because in Aalborg the rational paradigm of planning stood stronger than anywhere else. Eventually we realised that this logic was flawed, because my research of local relations of power showed that one of the most influential'faces of power' in Aalborg, the Chamber of Industry and Commerce, was substantially stronger than their equivalents elsewhere.

This had not been clear at the outset because much less research existed on local power relations than research on local planning. Therefore, instead of a critical case, unwittingly we ended up with an extreme case in the sense that both rationality and power were unusually strong in Aalborg, and my case study became a study of what happens when strong rationality meets strong power in the arena of urban politics and planning.

But this selection of Aalborg as an extreme case happened to our, we did not deliberately choose it. It was a frustrating experience when it happened, especially during those several months from when we realised we did not have a critical case until it became clear that allwas not lost because we had something else.

As a Type of selection purpose:

- Random selection To avoid systematic biases in the sample.The sample's size is decisive for generalization.
  - Random sample To achieve a representative sample that allows forgeneralization for the entire population.
  - Stratified sample To generalize for specially selected sub-groups within the population.
- Information-oriented selection To maximize the utility of information from small samples and single cases. Cases are selected on the basis of expectations about their information content.
  - Extreme/deviant cases To obtain information on unusual cases, which can be especially problematic or especially good in a more closely defined sense.
  - Maximum variation cases To obtain information about the significance of various circumstances

for case process and outcome, e.g. three to four cases that are very different on one dimension: size, form of organization, location, budget, etc.

- Critical cases To achieve information that permits logical deductions of the type,'if this is (not) valid for this case, then it applies to all (no) cases'.
- Paradigmatic cases To develop a metaphor or establish a school for the domain that the case concerns.

case researcher charting new terrain one must be prepared for such incidents, we believe.A model example of a'least likely' case is Robert Michels's (1962) classical study of oligarchy in organizations. By choosing a horizontally structured grass-roots organization with strong democratic ideals - that is, a type of organization with an especially low probability of being oligarchical - Michels could test the universality of the oligarchy thesis, that is,'If this organization is oligarchic, so are most others'. A corresponding model example of a'most likely' case is W.F. Whyte's (1943) study of a Boston slum neighbourhood but in fact showed quite the opposite. Cases of the'most likely' type are especially well suited to falsification of propositions, while least likely' cases are most appropriate to tests of verification. It should be remarked that a most likely case for one proposition is the least likely for its negation.

For example, Whyte's slum neighbourhood could be seen as a least likely case for a hypothesis concerning the universality of social organization. Hence, the identification of a case as most or least likely is linked to thedesign of the study, as well as to the specific properties of the actual case. A final strategy for the selection of cases is choice of the paradigmatic case. Thomas Kuhn has shown that the basic skills, or background practices, of natural scientists are organized in terms of'exemplars', the role of which can be studied by historians of science. Similarly, scholars like Clifford Geertz and Michel Foucault have often organized their research around specific cultural paradigms: a paradigm for Geertz lay for instance in the'deep play' of the

Balinesecockfight, while for Foucault, European prisons and the'Panopticon' are examples.

Both instances are examples of paradigmatic cases, that is, cases that highlight more general characteristics of the societies in question. Kuhn has shown that scientific paradigms cannot be expressed as rules or theories. There exists no predictive theory for how predictive theory comes about. A scientific activity is acknowledged or rejected as good science by how close it is to one or more exemplars, that is, practicalprototypes of good scientific work. A paradigmatic case of how scientists do science is precisely such a prototype. It operates as a reference point and may function as a focus for the founding of schools of thought. As with the critical case, we may ask,'How does one identify a paradigmatic case?'

How does one determine whether a given case has metaphorical and prototypical value? These questions are even more difficult to answer thanfor the critical case, precisely because the paradigmatic case transcends any sort of rule-based criteria. No standard exists for the paradigmatic case because it sets the standard. Hubert and Stuart Dreyfus see paradigmatic cases and case studies as central to human learning. In an interview with Hubert Dreyfus (author's files),we therefore asked what constitutes a paradigmatic case and how it can be identified.

Dreyfus replied: Heidegger says, you recognize a paradigm case because it shines, but I'm afraid that is not much help. You just have to be intuitive. We all can tell what is a better or worse case - of a Cézanne painting, for instance. But we can't think there could be any rules for deciding what makes Cézannne a paradigmatic modern painter. ... [I]tis a big problem in a democratic society where people are supposed to justify what their intuitions are. In fact, nobody really can justify what their intuition is. So you have to make up reasons, but it won't be the real reasons.

One may agree with Dreyfus that intuition is central to identifying paradigmatic cases, but one may disagree that it is a problem to have to justify one's intuitions. Ethnomethodological studies of scientific practice have demonstrated that all variety of such practice relies on takenfor- granted procedures that feel largely intuitive. However, those intuitive decisions are accountable, in the sense of being sensible to other practitioners or often explicable if not immediately sensible. That would frequently seem to be the case with the selection of paradigmatic cases. We may select such cases on the basis of takenfor- granted, intuitive procedures but are often called upon to account for that selection. That account must be sensible to other members of the scholarly communities of which we are part.

This may even be argued to be a general characteristic of scholarship, scientific or otherwise, and not unique to the selection of paradigmatic social scientific case studies. For instance, it is usually insufficient to justify an application for research funds by stating that one's intuition says that a particular research should be carried out. A research council ideally operates as society's test of whether the researcher can account, in collectively acceptable ways, for his or her intuitive choice, even though intuition may be the real, or most important, reason why the researcher wants to execute the project. It is not possible consistently, or even frequently, to determine in advance whether or not a given case - Geertz's cockfights in Bali, for instance - is paradigmatic. Besides the strategic choice of case, the execution of the case studywill certainly play a role, as will the reactions to the study by the research community, the group studied and, possibly, a broader public.

The value of the case study will depend on the validity claims that researchers can place on their study, and the status these claims obtain in dialogue with other validity claims in the discourse to which the study is a contribution. Like other good craftsmen, all that researchers can do is use their experience and intuition to assess whether they believe a given case is interesting in a paradigmatic context,and whether they can provide collectivelyacceptable reasons for the choice of case. Finally, concerning considerations of strategy in the choice of cases, it should be mentioned that the various strategies of selection are not necessarily mutually exclusive.

For example, a casecan be simultaneously extreme, critical and paradigmatic. The interpretation of such a case canprovide a unique wealth of information, because one obtains various perspectives and ceaseson the case according to whether it is viewed and interpreted as one or another type of case.

DO CASE STUDIES CONTAINA SUBJECTIVE BIAS?

The fourth of the five misunderstandings about case-study research is that the method maintains a bias towards verification, understood as a tendency to confirm the researcher's preconceived notions, so that the study therefore becomes of doubtful scientific value. Diamond, for example, holds this view. He observes that thecase study suffers from what he calls a'cripplingdrawback', because it does not apply'scientificmethods', by which Diamond understandsmethods useful for'curbing one's tendencies to stamp one's pre-existing interpretations on data as they accumulate'. Francis Bacon saw this bias towards verification not simply as a phenomenon related to the case study in particular, but as a fundamental human characteristic. Bacon expressed it like this: The human understanding from its peculiar nature, easily supposes a greater degree of order and equality in things than it really finds. When any proposition has been laid down, the human understanding forces everything else to add fresh support and confirmation.

It is the peculiar and perpetual error of the human understanding to be more moved and excited by affirmatives than negatives. Bacon certainly touches upon a fundamental problem here, a problem that all researchers must deal with in some way. Charles Darwin, in his autobiography, describes the method he developed in order to avoid the bias towards verification: we had ... during many years followed a golden rule, namely, that whenever a published fact, a new observation or thought came across me, which was opposed to my general results, to make a memorandum of it without fail and at once; for we had found by experience that such facts and thoughts were far more apt to escape from the memory than favourable ones. Owing to this habit, very few objections were raised against my views, which we had not at least noticed and attempted to answer.

The bias towards verification is general, but the alleged deficiency of the case study and other qualitative methods is that they ostensibly allow more room for the researcher's subjective and arbitrary judgement than other methods: they are often seen as less rigorous than are quantitative, hypothetico-deductive methods. Even if such criticism is useful, because it sensitizes us to an important issue, experienced case researchers cannot help but see the critique as demonstrating a lack of knowledge of what is involved in casestudy research. Donald Campbell and others have shown that the critique is fallacious, because the case study has its own rigour, different to be sure, but no less strict than the rigour of quantitative methods.

The advantage of the case study is that it can'close in' on real-life situations and test views directly in relation to phenomena as they unfold in practice. Campbell, Ragin, Geertz, Wieviorka, Flyvbjerg and others, researcherswho have conducted intensive, in-depth casestudies typically report that their preconceived views, assumptions, concepts and hypotheseswere wrong and that the case material has compelled them to revise their hypotheses on essential points. Ragin calls this a'special feature of small-N research', and goes on to explain that criticizing single-case studies for being inferiorto multiple-case studies is misguided, since even single-case studies'are multiple in most research efforts because ideas and evidence may be linked in many different ways'.Geertz says about the fieldwork involved in most in-depth case studies that'TheField' itself is a'powerful disciplinary force:assertive, demanding, even coercive'. Like anysuch force, it can be underestimated, but it cannot be evaded.

'It is too insistent for that', says Geertz. That he is speaking of a general phenomenon can be seen by simply examining case studies, as Eckstein, Campbell and Wieviorka have done. Campbell discusses the causes of this phenomenon in the following passage: In a case study done by an alert social scientist who has thorough local acquaintance, the theory he uses to explain the focal difference also generates prediction or expectations on dozens of other aspects of the culture, and he does not retain the theory unless most of these are also confirmed. ... Experiences of social scientists confirm this. Even in a single qualitative case study, the conscientious social scientist often finds no explanation that seems satisfactory.

Such an outcome would be impossible if the caricature of the single case study ... were correct - there would instead be a surfeit of subjectively compelling explanations. It is falsification and not verification that characterizes the case study. Moreover, the question of subjectivism and bias towards verification applies to all methods, not just to the case study and other qualitative methods. For example, theelement of arbitrary subjectivism will be significant in the choice of categories and variables for a quantitative or structural investigation, such as a structured questionnaire to be used across a large sample of cases. And the probability is high that

- This subjectivism survives without being thoroughly corrected during the study and
- That it may affect the results, quite simplybecause the quantitative/structural researcher does not get as close to those under study as does the case-study researcher and therefore is less likely to be corrected by the study objects'talking back'.

Ragin: this feature explains why small-N qualitative research is most often at the forefront of theoretical development. When N's are large, there are few opportunities for revising a casing [that is, the delimitation of a case]. At the start of the analysis, cases are decomposed into variables, and almost the entire dialogue of ideas and evidence occurs through variables. One implication of this discussion is that to the extent that large-N research can be sensitized to the diversity and potential heterogeneity of the cases included in an analysis, large-N research may play a more important part in the advancement of social science theory.

If one thus assumes that the goal of the researcher's work is to understand andlearn about the phenomena being studied, then research is simply a form of learning. If one assumes that research, like other learning processes, can be described by the phenomenologyfor human learning, it then becomes clear that the most advanced form of understanding is achieved when researchers place themselves within the context being studied. Only in thisway can researchers understand the viewpoints and the behaviour that characterizes social actors. Relevant to this point, Giddens states that valid descriptions of social activities presume that researchers possess those skills necessary to participate in the activities described:'Accepted that it is right to say that the condition of generating descriptions of social activity is being able in principle to participate in it.

It involves"mutual knowledge", shared by observer and participants whose action constitutes and reconstitutes the social world'. From this point of view, the proximity to reality that the case study entails, and the learningprocess that it generates for the researcher, willoften constitute a prerequisite for advanced understanding. In this context, one begins to understand Beveridge's cease that there are more discoveries stemming from the type of intense observation made possible by the case study than from statistics applied to large groups.

With the point of departure in the learning process, we understand why the researcher who conducts a case study often ends up by casting off preconceived notions and theories. Such activity is quite simply a central element in learning and in the achievement of new insight. More simple forms of understanding must yield to more complex ones as one moves from beginner to expert.

On this basis, the fourth misunderstanding - that the case study supposedly contains a bias towards verification, understood as a tendency to confirm the researcher's preconceived ideas - is revised as follows: The case study contains no greater bias towards verification of the researcher's preconceived notions than other methods of inquiry. On the contrary, experience indicates that the case study contains a greater bias towards falsification of preconceived notions than towards verification.

THE IRREDUCIBLE QUALITY OF GOOD CASE NARRATIVES

Case studies often contain a substantial element of narrative. Good narratives typically approach the complexities and contradictions of real life. Such narratives may be difficult or impossible to summarize into neat scientific formulae, general propositions, and theories. This tends to be seen by critics of the case study as a drawback. To the case-study researcher, however, a particularly'thick' and hard-to-summarize narrative is not a problem. Rather, it is often a sign that the study has uncovered a particularly rich problematic. The question, therefore, is whether the summarizing and generalization, which the critics see as an ideal, is always desirable.

Nietzsche is clear in his answer to this question,' he says about doing science,'one should not wish to divest existence of its rich ambiguity' (emphasis in original). In doing the Aalborg study, we tried to capture the rich ambiguity of politics and planning in a modern democracy. We did this by focusing in depth on the particular events that made up the case and on the minutiae that made up the events. Working with minutiae is time-consuming, and we must concede that during the several years when we was toiling in the archives, doing interviews,making observations, talking with my informants, writing, and getting feedback, a nagging question kept resurfacing in my mind. This is a question bound to haunt many carrying out indepth, dense case studies:'Who will want to learn about a case like this, and in this kind of detail?' We wanted the Aalborg case study to be particularly dense because we wished to test the thesis that the most interesting phenomena in politics and planning, and those of most general import, would be found in the most minute and most concrete of details.

Or to put the matter differently, we wanted to see whether the dualisms general-specific and abstract-concrete would metamorphose and vanish if we went into sufficiently deep detail. Richard Rorty has perceptively observed that the way to re-enchant the world is to stick to the concrete. Nietzsche similarly advocates a focus on'little things'. Both Rorty and Nietzsche seem right to me. We saw the Aalborg case as being made up of the type of concrete, little things they talk about. Indeed, we saw the case itself as such a thing, what Nietzsche calls a discreet and apparently insignificant truth, which, when closely examined, would reveal itself to be pregnant with paradigms, metaphors and general significance. That was my thesis, but theses can be wrong and case studies may fail. We was genuinely relieved when, eventually, the strategy of focusing on minutiae proved to be worth the effort. Lisa Peattie explicitly warns against summarizing dense case studies:'It is simply that the very value of the case study, thecontextual and interpenetrating nature of forces, is lost when one tries to sum up in large andmutually exclusive concepts.'

The dense case study is more useful for the practitioner and more interesting for social theory than either factual'findings' or the highlevel generalizations of theory. The opposite of summing up and'closing' a case study is to keep it open. Here we have foundthe following two strategies to work particularly well in ensuring such openness. First, when writingup a case study, we demur from the role of omniscient narrator and summarizer. Instead, we tell the story in its diversity, allowing the story to unfold from the many-sided, complex and sometimes conflicting stories that the actors in the case have told me. Second, we avoid linking the case with the theories of any one academic specialization.Instead we relate the case to broader philosophical positions that cut across specializations.In this way we try to leave scope for readers of different backgrounds to make different interpretations and draw diverse ceases regarding the question of what the case is a case of. The goal is not to make the case study be all things to all people.

The goal is to allow the study to be different things to different people. we try to achieve this by describing the case with so many facets - like life itself - that different readers may be attracted, or repelled, by different things in the case. Readers are not pointed down any one theoretical path or given the impression that truth might lie at the end of such a path.

Readers will have to discover their own path and truth inside the case. Thus, in addition to the interpretations of case actors and case narrators, readers are invited to decide the meaning of the case and to interrogate actors' and narrators' interpretations in order to answer that categorical question of any case study:'What is this case a case of ?' Case stories written like this can neither be briefly recounted nor summarized in a few main results. The case story is itself the result. It is a'virtual reality', so to speak.

For the reader willing to enter this reality and explore it inside and out, the payback is meant to be a sensitivity to the issues at hand that cannot be obtained from theory. Students can safely be let loose in this kind of reality, which provides a useful training ground with insights into real-life practices that academic teaching often does not provide. If we return briefly to the phenomenology for human learning, we may understand why summarizing case studies is not always useful and may sometimes be counterproductive.

Knowledge at the beginner's level consists precisely in the reduced formulas that characterize theories, while true expertise is based on intimate experience with thousands of individual cases and on the ability to discriminate between situations, with all their nuances of difference, without distilling them into formulas or standard cases. The problem is analogous to the inability of heuristic, computer-based expert systems to approach the level of virtuoso human experts, even when the systems are compared with the experts who have conceived the rules upon which these systems operate. This is because the experts do not use rules but operate on the basis of detailed case experience.

This is real expertise. The rules for expert systems are formulated only because thesystems require it; rules are characteristic of expert systems, but not of real human experts. In the same way, one might say that the rule form ulation that takes place when researchers summarize their work into theories is characteristic of the culture of research, of researchers, and of theoretical activity, but such rules are not necessarily part of the studied reality constituted by

Bourdieu's'virtuoso socialactors'. Something essential may be lost by this summarizing - namely the possibility to understandvirtuoso social acting, which, as Bourdieu has shown, cannot be distilled into theoretical formulas - and it is precisely their fear of losing this'something', that makes case researcherscautious about summarizing their studies.

Case researchers thus tend to be sceptical about erasingphenomenological detail in favour of conceptual closure. Ludwig Wittgenstein shared this scepticism. Gasking and Jackson, Wittgenstein used the following metaphor when he described his use of the case-study approach in philosophy: In teaching you philosophy I'm like a guide showing you how to find your way round London. We have to take you through the city from north to south, from east to west, from Euston to the Embankment and from Piccadilly to the Marble Arch.

After we have taken you many journeys through the city, in all sorts of directions, we shall have passed through any given street a number of times - each time traversing the street as part of a different journey. At the end of this you will know London; you will be able to find your way about like a born Londoner. Of course, a good guide will take you through the more important streets more often than he takes you down side streets; a bad guide will do the opposite. In philosophy I'm a rather bad guide.

This approach implies exploring phenomena first-hand instead of reading maps of them. Actual practices are studied before their rules, and one is not satisfied by learning only about those parts of practices that are open to publicscrutiny; what Erving Goffman calls the'backstage' of social phenomena must be investigated, too, like the side streets that Wittgenstein talks about. With respect to intervention in social and political affairs, Abbott has rightly observed that a social science expressed in terms of typical case narratives would provide'far better access for policy intervention than the present social science of variables'.

MacIntyre similarly says,'*I can only answer the question"What am I to do?" if I can answer the prior question"Of what story or stories do I find myself a part?"*' Several observers have noted that narrative is an ancient method and perhaps our most fundamental form for making sense of experience It must again be emphasized that, despite the difficulty or undesirability of summarizing case studies, the case-study method in general can certainly contribute to the cumulative development of knowledge. Today, when students and colleagues present me with the conventional wisdom about case-study research - for instance, that one cannot generalize on the basis of a single case or that case studies are arbitrary and subjective. By and large, the conventional wisdom is wrong or misleading. For the reasons, the case study is a necessary and sufficient method for certain important research tasks in the social sciences, and it is a method that holds up well when compared to other methods in the gamut of social science research methodology. Let me reiterate, however, that this cease, and the revision of the five misunderstandings should not be interpreted as a rejection of research that focuses on large random samples or entire populations; for example, questionnaire surveys with related quantitative analysis.

This type of research is also essential for the development of social science; for example, in understanding the degree to which certain phenomena are present in a given group or how they vary across cases. The advantage of large samples is breadth, while their problem is one of depth. For the case study, the situation is the reverse. Both approaches are necessary for a sound development of social science. Here as elsewhere, the sharp separation often seen in th literature between qualitative and quantitative methods is a spurious one. The separation is an unfortunate artefact of power relations and time constraints in graduate training; it is not a logical consequence of what graduates and scholars need to know to do their studies and do them well.

In my interpretation, good social science is opposed to an either/or and stands for a both/and on the question of qualitative versus quantitative methods. Good social science is problem-driven and not methodology-driven, in the sense that it employs those methods that for a given problematic best help answer the research questions at hand. More often than not, a combination of qualitative and quantitative methods will do the task best. Fortunately, there seems currently to be a general relaxation in the old and unproductive separation of qualitative and quantitative methods. This being said, it should nevertheless be added that the balance between case studies and large samples is currently biased in favour of the latter in social science, so biased that it puts case studies at a disadvantage within most disciplines.

In this connection, it is worth repeating the insight of Thomas Kuhn that a discipline without a large number of thoroughly executed case studies is a discipline without systematic production of exemplars, and that a discipline without exemplars is an ineffective one. In social science, more good casestudies could help remedy this situation. NOTE 1 The quotation is from the original first edition of the dictionary. In the third edition, a second paragraph has been added about the case study. Theentry is still highly unbalanced, however, and still promotesthe mistaken view that the case study is hardly a methodology in its own right, but is best seen as subordinateto investigations of larger samples.

Chapter 9

Demographics in Market Research

AN OVERVIEW

Consumers no longer fit into yesterday's molds. Here's how to get a grip on the new demographics -- and get inside your customers' heads. Demographics are the physical characteristics of a population such as age, sex, marital status, family size, education, geographic location, occupation, income, and educational level. For decades, companies large and small have depended on these demographic categories to shape their marketing campaigns and make sense of their potential customers.

It is time to rethink this strategy. Demographics -- the quantifiable social and economic characteristics of a population -- are not as powerful as they used to be. Demographics are increasingly becoming less important.

Demographics are not as significant as they used to be because the world society has evolved and new subgroups are emerging within the traditional demographic groups. For example, mixed-races, multiethnic individuals and so forth. Today in the United States, 1 in 16 Americans under 18 is of mixed racial heritage. Several celebrities fall into these subgroups, for example golf champ Tiger Woods, Halle Berry, Derek Jeter, and many others.

Shifts are also taking place between married vs. single households, a major component of traditional demographics. In the 1950s, 80 per cent of U.S. Households were married households. Today, the figure is only slightly more than 50 per cent. The typical American family is no longer typical.

Yankelovich studied 170 variables ranging from spirituality to brands, and it found a much greater diversity of attitudes among single people compared to married couples. Today just knowing that someone is single these days does not tell you much about what he or she really thinks and believes.

Adding to the difficulty of categorizing consumers is their refusal to be stereotyped on the basis of race, age, education and income level. Americans living in a more accepting, multicultural society no longer fit neatly into one demographic profile that lets companies determine their lifestyles and the best way to market to them. The demographic categories that were traditionally understood are now breaking down. The boundries between categories are blurring.

In Europe the demographics are also changing. Asia is also undergoing demographic changes. So the consumers and the markets situation worldwide have to be studied, analysed and quantified to reflect the present population and today's trends.

The End of Mass Market

Goodbye Mass Market, Welcome Nanomarket. Today's increasing diversity has transformed the mass market into what some researchers call the"nanomarket". Marketplaces are fragmenting into tiny pieces due to an explosive growth in consumer segments, preferences, tastes and lifestyles that's beyond the measuring ability of traditional demographics. This implies the need to look at the marketplaces in a new way.

Demographics alone no longer work in a mass market that's more or less dead. Today's marketplaces are individualized, customised, and personalized. The implication is that the producers and sellers --companies, manufacturers, marketers and retailers-- need to adapt to the new realities of the Internet Era.

Many companies, however, continue to operate on old beliefs based on demographic data, and it's leading to a disconnect between companies and consumers. Many advertisements, for example, continue to portray women as married, stay-at-home moms in a world where an increasing number of women stay single into their 40s, become single moms by choice and take on primary-breadwinner roles within their families.'

Amid such shifts, simply saying your campaign targets women 18 to 49 has become meaningless. Demographics today don't tell you the whole story, marketers know that old demographic targeting isn't working for them. It gives them nothing.

Big companies are going deeper into consumers' heads to understand what drives them to buy--and this, in turn, is driving market research methods such as ethnography. Ethnographers are cultural anthropologists who observe how consumers use products and services in their natural environments. They write reports using the words and phrasing of the people they study, and the information helps companies figure out the behaviours and reasoning behind people's purchasing decisions.

Instead of boxing their customers into one profile, large companies are segmenting customers into ever-narrower lifestyle profiles and categories to understand their core values. They're targeting the 20 per cent of customers who generate 80 per cent of their business, based on the Pareto Principle.

Electronics retailer Best Buy, for example, now focuses its business on five customer profiles instead of trying to broadly tailor its marketing to fit every customer profile. Most entrepreneurs, however, still try to be everything to everyone by targeting a wide demographic. Focusing on a specific, high-value profitable target audience, and then doing everything you can to engage them, requires a change of mentality for the mass-market marketers.

Demographics aren't becoming obsolete, they are just taking on a new role as marketers get smarter in how to apply them. Entreprenuers have understode that there are other ways of looking at your customers. Consumer attitudes will replace demographics as the basis for marketing execution, and companies will have to incorporate attitudes into their databases the same way they have used demographics in the past. Today you have to speak with lifestyle relevance to your customers to get their attention. Understanding lifestyles is crucial to understanding your customers.

Two things are necessary for understanding customers, one is intuition and the other is data mining. Market research is used to gather customer household income, age and other lifestyle information that helps make marketing and product-design decisions. The Internet is a great tool for learning about your customers. It's much more up-to-date than an old demographics list.

Demographics is in Evolution into the Age of Genergraphics

The Age of Genergraphics

Understanding the influence one generation has on another will be the key to successful marketing in the future, contends Phil Goodman, president of market research and planning company Generation Transitional Marketing in San Diego. He's the creator of"Genergraphics," a method of marketing to customers of different generations by taking into account their generational mind-sets.

The Internet, Goodman says, is tailor-made for Genergraphics. Companies will retool their websites using buzzwords geared to each of the major generations: seniors, boomers, Gen X and echo boomers. Customers visiting a company's website will click intuitively on the link meant for their generation, and then they'll see products and services described with generational buzzwords and images that fit their mind-sets.

Goodman claims Genergraphics will triple the chance of making a sale."People buy different products and services according to their generations," he says."You're not just wasting space or time on whatever advertising and marketing you're doing. You're gearing it toward that mind-set."

Goodman thinks boomer grandparents will be one of the most powerful groups 10 years from now. Some boomers are working on their third or fourth marriages and are bringing kids into the mix--from previous relationships and kids they have together--making blended families of forty- and fiftysomethings an emerging trend. Donald Trump is a famous recent example of a boomer blending two or more families.

But of all the major demographic categories, the most overlooked could be the Generation X consumer in his or her 30s and early 40s."Up to this point, it's been the stepchild generation behind the powerful baby-boom generation, but Gen Xers are entering their peak earning years and peak buying years for many product categories," Chung says."Marketers are only now trying to understand them." Basic demographics still play a role in drilling down consumers, but companies need to go beyond demographics to spot emerging customer categories in a rapidly changing marketplace."We're in the middle of a huge transformation in the shape of marketing," Smith says."You've got to have better information about consumers." Call it the shape of things to come...

The Demographic Revolution

The following demographic groups should be on the radar of every smart marketer in 2005 and beyond.

- *Cablinasians*: Tiger Woods coined this term to refer to his mixed racial heritage, and he's not alone: 1 in 16 Americans under 18 today is of mixed racial heritage. Marketers who tap into the multiethnic experience could win big.
- *Unmarried, professional women in their 30s and 40s*: These highly educated women aren't weighed down by family responsibilities and have disposable income that high-end marketers are chasing, says James Chung, founder of Reach Advisors, a Belmont, Massachusetts, strategy and research firm.
- *Empty nesters*: These are the boomers whose kids have moved out, creating a new stream of disposable income for these parents--and new marketing prospects for entrepreneurs.
- *Twixters*: These are twentysomethings who've been so fussed over by their boomer parents that they can't deal with adulthood. University of Michigan, Ann

Arbor, economics and public policy Bob Schoeni, cited in Time, the percentage of 26-year-olds living with mom and dad rose from 11 per cent to 20 per cent between 1970 and 2004. If they hold jobs, these young people have disposable income that's probably not spent on rent or mortgages. They also have parents willing to spend on them, too.

- *Gen X*: The 44 million Gen Xers born between 1965 and 1975 are entering their peak earning years. They're raising families, they're tech savvy and they love to shop.
- Boomer grandparents: Grandparents are becoming day-care providers to their grandkids, and in some cases even more: As of 2003, 900,000 grandparents had been responsible for most of the basic needs of their grand-children for at least five years, according to the Census. The number of boomer grandparents will only rise and increase in power as boomers age.
- *Progressive Prioritizers*: Thirty-one per cent of women 25 to 29 held a bachelor's degree or higher in 2003, compared to 26 per cent of their male peers. What's emerging is a generation of young, educated women who are prepared to leave their jobs to stay home with kids and then return to the work force when they're ready. Savvy marketers will find ways to catch women as they go between both mind-sets.
- *Blended families*: Younger boomers are remarrying. Some are even working on their third or fourth marriages and have kids in the mix, says Phil Goodman, president of Generation Transitional Marketing in San Diego.
- *Single mothers by choice*: More women are having children without partners. In 2002, 12 per cent of births were to unmarried women ages 30 to 44.

The Demographics Evolution in Market Research

Demographics is an important element in modern market research. It is always changing in response to changes in population and lifestyle changes.

Following is a Brief History of Demographics:

- *1940s*: The mass market reigns. TV and radio are dominated by sponsored shows such as"Bob Hope's Texaco Star Theater" with ads for big brands aimed at wide audiences.
- *1946*: The"baby boom" begins. 77 million boomers will be the first generation to grow up with TV. The field of modern demographics develops around this explosion of births and migration patterns following World War II.
- *1950s*: Marketers use demographics and socioeconomics to segment the market into smaller groups of consumers who might buy their brands.
- *1960s*:"Psychographics," which describes how attitudes and interests can be used to produce more effective advertisements, is on the rise.
- *1965*: Forty-four million"baby busters," later known as Gen Xers, start to be born. This generation isn't considered big enough for marketers to bother with.
- *1971*: Claritas is founded. Its products will allow companies to segment consumers into smaller and smaller groups based on psychographics and Census Bureau data. In 1978, Claritas developed ways of classifying whole neighborhoods with catchy names. New database"geo-demographic" systems let marketers apply psychographics to small, geographic areas. The information helps large retailers figure out where to build stores.
- *1978*: Baby boomers start having kids. This 71-million strong"echo boom" generation will drive the Britney Spears-dominated youth market of the early 21st century.
- *1980s*: Marketers realise transactional data can drive marketing decisions. Bar code scanners are used in stores, and retailers begin to collect consumers' behavioural data.
- *1995*: Websites start helping companies data-mine

transactional data that's used to track customers' buying habits and drive marketing decisions.

- *1998*: Web analysis tools like HitBox Professional start tracking web users using cookies, a precursor to today's annoying pop-up ads and spyware. Words like synergy are used endlessly to describe more sophisticated cross-promotions.
- *2000*: Fledgling attempts at"neuromarketing," using brain scans to study consumer mind-sets. Ethnography, applying principals of anthropology to study consumers, is also emerging as a marketing tool.
- *2002*: More thirtysomething Gen Xers are starting families. This yet-unnamed generation won't know a world without the web or wireless technology.
- *2005*: Marketers are studying individual demographics and attitudes to create one-to-one marketing campaigns that can be sent to individual cell phones and PDAs. Genergraphics begins to be accepted.
- *2015*: One-to-one marketing is the name of the game. Marketers gather the demographics and behavioural patterns of individual consumers to create individualized marketing messages. Even TV product placements can be geared to each household.

The Complete Guide to Internet Statistics and Demographics

We have been on the Internet for a few years now and, if we remember correctly, one of the first questions we had from the very beginning about the web was"How Many People are Using the Internet?"

We started to search for a reply to this very simple question and we started to get many different answers. The numbers were incomplete and the ones available were generally from many years back. Research reports with full information by specialized firms were available but for purchase at a high price...

Out of personal curiosity, more than for any other reason, we decided to start writing down all the countries we could find with the number of Internet users. Slowly at first, the list started to grow. Soon the help of an Excel dBase became necessary. More countries were added and updated figures started to come in.

The percentage of the population using the Internet in each country was investigated in order to complete the information. This number is called the Internet Penetration Rate and is expressed as a percentage. Once again, the need for accurate updated population statistics in my data base. These are very dynamic numbers and change constantly.

The following data reports regarding Internet Usage, Penetration and Population are available for free online viewing:

- Internet Usage and Population by World Regions
- The Top 10 Languages Used in the Internet
- The Top 20 Countries in Internet Usage
- The 30 Most Penetrated Countries by the Internet
- Internet Usage and Population in Africa
- Internet Usage and Population in America
- Internet Usage and Population in Latin America
- Internet Usage and Population in Asia
- Internet Usage and Population in Europe
- Internet Usage and Population in the European Union
- Internet Usage and Population in the Middle East
- Internet Usage and Population in Oceania
- Growth of the Internet from 1995 to 2006

Online Survey in Market Research

Type the phrase"paid surveys" in Google, and you will see a countless list of paid survey web sites. Some claim $150/hr payment, others say it's the perfect work at home job, while others say online paid surveys are just a scam. With all of these conflicting links, it's hard to know what to believe. Are online paid surveys an Internet Jackpot, an online scam, or somewhere in between? Are you missing a great opportunity or should you stay away? The first thing that you must understand is that market research is a real business. Market Research firms have been paying customers to take surveys and participate in focus groups long before the internet was a household commodity. It's just that with the increasing number of people online, the internet has become an effective and efficient way for marketing companies to collect data and test their advertisements. Also the internet gives these market research firms access to a wide demographic of users, which allows them to get a better idea of how their products will perform with people of different age, sex, nationality, etc.

Unfortunately, many questionable sites have popped up on the internet which has ruined the image on online paid surveys. These sites usually make outrageous claims about how much money you can make by working from home. They usually charge a"membership fee" to gain access to a list of web sites that conduct online paid surveys. They claim that their lists are special, and offer the highest paying surveys. But the truth is that the survey sites they list can be found for free on the internet.

Legitimate market research firms do not charge panel members any fees or try to sell you any products. With a little research you can find all of the quality market research firms yourself. Also, there are several good sites on the internet that offer free reviews and listings. You should never have to pay for information or access to online paid surveys.

Assuming that you manage to avoid the scams, and stick with legitimate market research firms, the question remains is it really worth the time? The answer lies in your expectations. If you are looking for the perfect work at home dream job, this is not it. If you would be happy with an extra couple hundred dollars a month then read on.

The typical pay for any given survey varies, but most offer between $2 to as high as $50 or more per survey. The problem is that these firms are usually looking for a certain demographic, and you may not always qualify for all the paid surveys that are sent your way. These survey invitations are usually sent to you via an email, with details about the incentive offered, and a link to the survey. Usually you are asked to fill out a short screener survey, and if you qualify then you can continue on and earn the full amount promised. If you do not qualify, you are dismissed, with some sites offering a small incentive or a sweepstakes entry for your time. The screener survey usually takes less than 5 minutes, and the full survey can take anywhere from 15 to 30 minutes.

If you sign up with several quality market research firms, and can qualify for several surveys, you should be able to make anywhere from $50 to several hundred dollars a month for the household petty cash piggy bank. It's not exactly a fortune, but it can help offset some of your monthly bills, and it only takes a couple hours a week.

Teen Surveys - A Safe, Rewarding Online Activity for Teens

In a world of Dateline predators and inappropriate content on MySpace, we sometimes lose sight of the fact that there are good internet sites for teens. There are many sites dedicated to higher learning and fun teen activities for the millions of teenagers that access the internet each day. An often overlooked online activity that can be both fun and rewarding for teenagers is online teen surveys. Each year corporations spend billions of dollars on advertising. They hire market research companies to test there advertisements and do research on the best ways to market to certain demographics. One of these key demographics is teenagers 13 to 17 years of age. Several of these companies offer cash and prizes in exchange for teen opinions on new products, movies, and teen trends in general. Online teen surveys are a great way for teens to express their ideas, influence the new products and services that enter the teen market, and earn cash and prizes.

Sounds good, but how does it all work? The market research companies usually host an online panel that they invite you to join. After you join, they then gather information about you, specifically age, hobbies, interest, etc. so that they can match you up with the surveys that are best suited for you. After you become a member, you will begin to receive survey invitations via email. Upon completion of the survey you will receive any incentives that were promised in the email. While volunteering this type of information online does not seem like a good idea, especially for teens, it is actually a safe, confidential environment for teens to express their opinions. This is of course if you stick to the legitimate market research companies, and not the thousands of scam sites on the internet.

Taking online surveys is a completely free process, and if a site requests money then that is usually the first sign that it is a scam and should be avoided. True market research firms are prohibited from charging fees. Also, if a site asks questions too personal in nature and seems suspicious (no company street address, contact information, etc) it should be avoided. Some quality paid survey sites that offer teen membership are WhaddYaKnow (A division of GreenField Online), E-Poll, NFO MY Survey, Your2Cents, and American Consumer Opinion to name a few. Teen Surveys can be a good after school activity, and serve as a mini-part-time-online-job for teens that will allow them to earn a little cash, gift certificates, and prizes. Parents, it is important for you to monitor your teen's online activities. There are several web sites with good information on the International Markets. The following links are sources of basic market data that are useful for starting your market research without spending a bundle.

World Markets 101

BBC News Country Profiles

Excellent profiles for all the world regions and most countries that provide an instant guide to history, politics, madia, and economic background of countries and territories. The site also features profiles on key institutions.

International Trade Centre

The ITC is the executing agency of the United Nations Development Programme, directly responsible for implementing UNDP-financed projects in developing countries and economies in transition related to trade promotion. The site has a useful infobase and links to market information sources.

Internet World Stats

An International website featuring worldwide Internet Usage, Population Data, and Market Statistics, for over 233 countries and world regions. This is a useful resource for global market research, containing Internet statistics, broadband penetration, country population data and global trade information.

Organisation For Economic Co-operation and Development

For more than 40 years, OECD has been one of the world's largest and most reliable sources of comparable statistics and economic and social data. As well as collecting data, OECD monitors trends, analyses and forecasts economic developments and researches social changes or evolving patterns in trade, environment, agriculture, technology, taxation and more.

Portals of the World

Portals to the World contains selective links providing authoritative, in-depth information about the nations and other areas of the world. They are arranged by country or area with the links for each sorted into a wide range of broad categories. The links were selected by Area Specialists and other Library staff using Library of Congress selection criteria.

PMA - Produce Marketing Association

The PMA is a global trade association serving the entire produce and floral supply chains by enhancing the marketing of produce, floral, and related products and services worldwide. In addition to advocating for the industry in Washington, PMA is a source for late-breaking news, information on industry trends, consumer and industry research, education and networking opportunities, and industry standards and technologies.

SICE

SICE, for short, from its Spanish acronym - Sistema de Información al Comercio Exterior (The"Foreign Trade Information System") is part of the Organization of American States (OAS). Their goal is to provide complete information and documents on trade in the Western Hemisphere. The website is in the four official languages of the OAS - English, Spanish, Portuguese and French - Information about trade in North America, Carribean States and Latin America.

The Economist - Country Briefings

The Economist is the premier online source for the analysis of world business and current affairs, providing authoritative insight and opinion on international news, world politics, business, finance, science and technology, as well as overviews of cultural trends and regular industry, business and country special reports.

Trade Port

TradePort is a well designed tool offering one place to go for comprehensive trade information, trade leads, and other types of useful information. The main menu offers a large selection of market research information.

World Factbook

Profiles for all main world countries and basic information background about the geography, people, government, the economy, communications, transports, military power, and transnational issues.

United States Trade Administration

This U.S. Department of Commerce web site features top Imports and Exports by country and product. Other information is available.

QUALITY OF WORK LIFE IN CALL CENTRE

ABSTRACT

Quality of work life is one of the most important topics of

every organization. It is related mainly with the productivity of the employees working in the organization. It is related with the better working conditions of the employees which will further result in better performance. Thus increasing the productivity of the organization which will further help to enhance the profits of the organization (call centres).I am studying quality of work life because it will enhance my efficiency in context to the productivity of the organization (call centres).

In such a context, we thought it is worthwhile doing this project on the working conditions provided in the different call centres.

The main motive of this research is to study the different working conditions provided to the employees in call centres, to study the job satisfaction level of employees in call centres, to check the satisfaction level regarding facilities provided in the call centres and to know the extent of awareness among the employees regarding the facilities they are getting in the call centres.

The descriptive research design is chosen with the use of exploratory approach keeping the time constraint in perspective. For the purpose of study both primary and secondary data was needed. Primary data was collected by the survey done in call centres through Questionnaire and Interview. Secondary data was gathered, through magazines, Internet etc. Random Sampling Method was used with sample size 100.

The study shows that call centres have shifts and lengthy working hours,majority of employees are not getting accommodation facility but then else majority of employees are satisfied with their job and about 52% of employees are aware with all the facilities they are getting. From all the analysis and findings of the study it can be concluded that the employees being internal customers should be provided accommodation, transportation and hygienic food. The employees should get continuous learning environment through training and development. The working hours should be flexible so that employees may not feel stressed out.

INTRODUCTION TO RESEARCH PROBLEM

Why we choose"quality of work life" as a topic for my research project?

India is a developing country. This means that majority of the population belong to the working class. They have to struggle to make both ends meet. In their daily life struggle, they loose sight of the individual development, productivity, self-actualization etc.

There are certain special characteristics with regard to the Indian employee, such as coming from villages to city in search of work, being away from loved ones, having to accept work at poor working conditions, low wages, etc. Quality of work life is one of the most important topics of every organization. Employers who provide employees with the structural and individual support to help them balance work and personal life will benefit both of them. It is related mainly with the productivity of the employees working in the organization. It is related with the better working conditions of the employees which will further result in better performance. Thus increasing the productivity of the organization which will further help to enhance the profits of the organization, quality of work life plays an ample role.

I am studying quality of work life because it will enhance my efficiency in context to the productivity of the organization. We have taken call centres because there is the rising growth of the call centres in India. Call center industry has been a good scope for India and it is having its contribution in Indian economy also. It is providing employment to large number of youths in the country. Not only call center industry but also whole B.P.O industry is a great source of foreign revenue and employment opportunities for India. Call center industry has been a boom in Indian economy. It also evolved the life style and social standards of people working there as call center employees. Call center jobs are lucrative. They pay you in five figures even if you are a fresher. All you need is good command over written and spoken English and excellent communication skills.

Besides the monetary gains, call center management insure every employee for his medical reimbursements. PF and other coverage of expenses such as free meals and transportation. Working in call centres can be hectic and against to the normal body clock. The work processes of call centres are on 24/7 basis. So, you have to adjust according to it. Working in nights can affect your family or personal life adversely.

Also, dealing with different customers of different temperaments can be very stressful and challenging. To tackle this situation well, call centres should arrange motivational campaigns regularly to help their employees deal with stress easily. They should try to provide work and play atmosphere to boost the positive attitude of workers.

In such a context, we thought it is worthwhile doing this project on the working conditions provided in the different call centres.

JUSTIFICATION OF THE STUDY

We have taken up to do this study, first of all, considering the importance of Quality of work life both in the life of the employees -for they constitute the largest population of the country -and important for the employers as well, since their concern to have the employee morale kept high and productivity kept high with healthy working conditions. Besides the morale of the employees are kept high their loyalty gained, if only the management is concerned about the relationship between the working conditions prevailing in the environment and the employees. It is in this context that we decided to study the aspect of working conditions in the call centres by taking rounds of the call centres and interacting with different class of employees working there.

Objectives of the Study

- To study the different working conditions provided to the employees in call centres.
- To study the satisfaction level of employees in call centres.

- To check the satisfaction level regarding facilities provided in the call centres.
- To know the extent of awareness among the employees regarding facility.
- To know how they cope up with lengthy working hours.
- To know whether they are satisfied with their job or not.
- To check if they are satisfied with the Quality of Work Life they are getting.
- To study how they maintain balance between their personal and professional lives.

Introduction to the Subject

. The principal objectives of HRM may be listed thus- In simple words, HRM means employing people, developing their capacities, utilizing, maintaining and compensating their services in tune with the job and organizational requirement.

The goal of human resource management is to help an organization to meet strategic goals by attracting, and maintaining employees and also to manage them effectively.

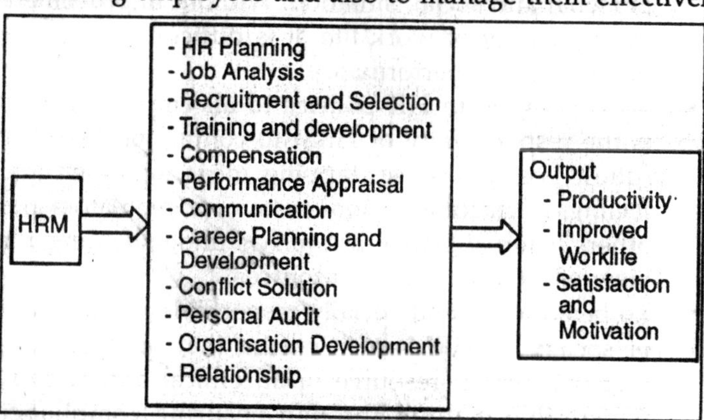

Objectives of Human Resource Management

- To help the organization reaches its goals-HR department, like other departments in an organization, exists to achieve the goals of the organization first and if it does not meet this purpose HR department will wither or die.

- To employ the skills and abilities of the work force efficiently- The primary purpose of HRM is to make peoples strengths productive and to benefit customers, stock holders and employees.
- To provide the organization with well- trained and well- motivated employees-HRM requires that the employees should be motivated to exert maximum efforts, so that their performance could be evaluated properly with results and thus they can be remunerated on the basis of their contributions to the organizations.
- To increase to the fullest the employees job satisfaction and self actualization - It tries to prompt and programmes have to be designed aimed at improving the quality of stimulate every employee to realise its potential. To this end suitable work life (QWL).
- To develop and maintain a quality of work life-It makes employment in the organization a desirable, personal and social, situation. Without improvement in the quality of work life, it is difficult to improve organizational performance.
- To communicate HR policies to all employees ----it is the responsibility of HRM to communicate in the fullest possible sense, tapping ideas, opinions and feelings of customers, non- customers, regulators and others external public as well as understanding the view of internal human resources.
- To be ethically and socially responsible to the needs of society --- HRM must ensure that organizations manage human resource in an ethical and socially responsible manner through ensuring compliance with legal and ethical standards.

Quality of Work Life

The degree of personal satisfaction experienced at work.

Quality of working life is dependent on the extent to which an employee feels valued, rewarded, motivated, consulted, and empowered. It is also influenced by factors such as job security, opportunities for career development, work patterns, and work-life balance. Taylor (1979),more pragmatically identified the essential components of Quality of working life as; basic extrinsic job factors of wages, hours and working conditions, and the intrinsic job notions of the nature of the work itself. He suggested that a number of other aspects could be added, including; individual power, employee participation in the management, fairness and equity, social support, use of one's present skills, self development, a meaningful future at work, social relevance of the work or product, effect on extra work activities.

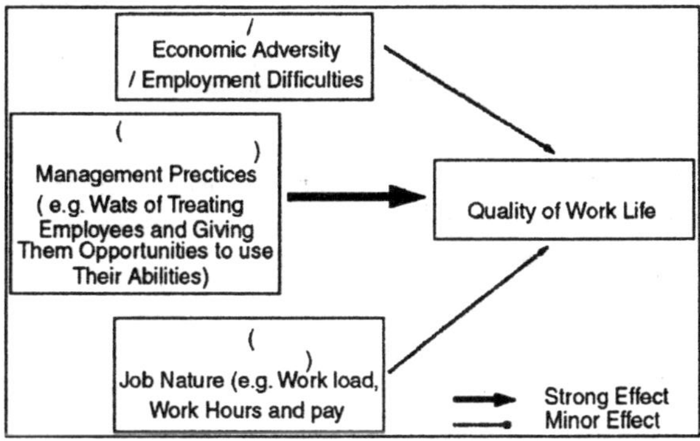

Taylor suggested that relevant Quality of working life concepts may vary according to organization and employee group. Qwl refers to the favourableness or unfavourableness of a job environment for people. It refers to the quality of relationships between employees and the total environment. Harrison, Qwl is the degree of work in an organization contributes to material and psychological well being of its members.

Qwl as"a process of joint decision making,collaboration and building mutual respect between management and employees."It is concerned with increasing labour management cooperatives to solve the problems of improving organizational performance ad employee satisfaction.

How to Measure Quality if work life?

The following parametres are used to judge the quality of work life are as follows:

- *Job involvement*: It represents the degree of an individual's identification with or ego involvement in the job. The more central the job is to the individual's life, the greater is his involvement in it. people with high involvement are more motivated and are highly productive.

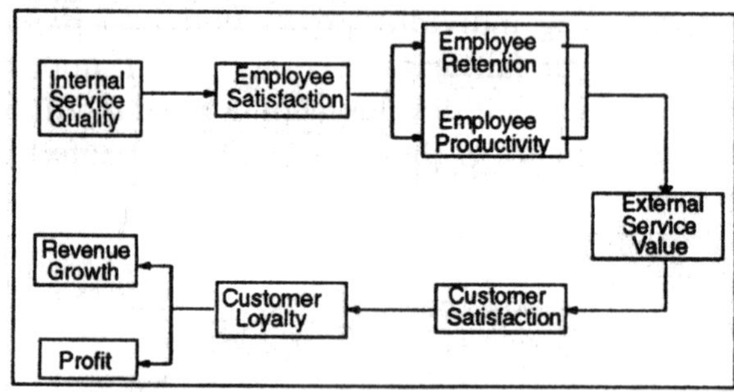

- *Job satisfaction*: It implies the workers satisfaction with the environment on his job environment consisting of nature of work, quality of supervision, pay, coworkers, opportunities for promotion, etc. job satisfaction is related with job involvement and people involved in their jobs are satisfied with their jobs and vice-versa.
- *Sense of competence*: It refers to the feeling of confidence that an individual has in his own competence. Sense of competence and job involvement reinforce each other. When he feels more competent, he becomes more involved in his job and thus becomes better motivated.
- *Job performance*: When an individual's job involvement, job satisfaction and sense of competence increases, there is a rise in job performance.
- *Productivity*: When the level of job performance increases the output per unit of input goes up. Thus match between job characteristics and productivity

traits of employees generally result in higher productivity.

Dimensions of Quality of Work Life

Qwl is a multidimensional concept implying a concern for the members of the organization.

It is ultimately defined by the workers himself. The main aspects of Qwl are as follows:

- *Adequate and fair compensation*: There should be just and equitable balance between effort and reward. The compensation should help the employee in maintaining a socially desirable standard of living and should be comparable to the pay for similar work elsewhere.
- *Safe and healthy working conditions*: Qwl cannot be high unless the work environment is free from all hazards detrimental to the health and safety of employees. Reasonable hours of work, cleanliness, pollution free atmosphere, risk free work, etc. are the main elements of a good physical environment for work.
- *Opportunity to use and develop human capacities*: The job should contain sufficient variety of tasks to provide challenge and to ensure the utilization of talents. Today the work has become repetitive and mechanical so that the worker has little control on it. Quality of work life can be improved if the job allows sufficient autonomy and control, provides timely feedback on performance and uses a wide range of skills.
- *Opportunity for career growth*: The work should provide career opportunities for development of new abilities and expansion of existing skills on a continuous basis.
- *Social integration in workforce*: The worker should make to feel a sense of identity with the organization and develop a feeling of self- esteem. Openness, trust, sense of community feeling, scope for upward mobility, equitable treatment are essential for this purpose.

- *Constitutionalisation in the work organization*: Qwl provides constitutional protection to the employees. Management action can be challenged. Constitutional protection is provided to the employees on such matters as free speech, equity and due process.
- *Work and personal life*: There should be proper balance between work life and personal life of employees. The demand of work such as late hours, frequent travel, quick transfers are both psychologically and socially very costly and detrimental to quality of wok life.
- *Social relevance of works*: Work should not be a source of material and psychological satisfaction but a means of social welfare like pollution, consumer protection, national integration, employment etc can improve the quality of work life.

THE HUMAN RESOURCE DEPARTMENT'S ROLE

The role of human resource department in QWL efforts varies widely. In some organisations, top management appoints an executive to ensure that QWL and productivity efforts occur throughout the organisation. In most cases, these executives have a small staff and must rely on the human resource department for help with employee training, communications, attitude survey feedback, and similar assistance. In other organisations, the department is responsible for initiating and directing the firm's QWL and productivity efforts.Perhaps the most crucial role of the department is winning the support of key managers. Management support - particularly top management support appears to be an almost universal prerequisite for successful QWL programmmes. By substantiating employee satisfaction and bottom-line benefits, which range from lower absenteeism and turnover to higher productivity and fewer accidents, the department can help convince doubting managers. The department also has both a direct and indirect influence on employee motivation and satisfaction.

The department makes direct contact with employees and supervisors through orientation, training and development, career planning, and counselling activities. At the same time, these activities may help a supervisor do a better job of motivating employees. The policies and practices of the department also influence motivation and satisfaction indirectly. Rigorous enforced safety and health programmmes, for example, can give employees and supervisors a greater sense of safety from accidents and industrial health hazards. Likewise, compensation policies may motivate and satisfy employees through incentive plans, or they may harm motivation and satisfaction through insufficient raises or outright salary freezes. The motivation and satisfaction of employees act as feedback on the organisation's QWL and on the department's day-to-day activities.

QUALITY OF WORK LIFE AS HR STARTEGY - AN ANALYSIS

In the modern scenario, QWL as a strategy of Human Resource Management is being recognized as the ultimate key for development among all the work systems, not merely as a concession. This is integral to any organization towards its wholesome growth. This is attempted on par with strategies of Customer Relation Management.

Strategy and Tactics

Over the years, since industrial revolution, much experimentation has gone into exploiting potential of human capital in work areas either explicitly or implicitly. Thanks to the revolution in advanced technology, the imperative need to look into QWL in a new perspective is felt and deliberated upon. Major companies are tirelessly implementing this paradigm in Human Resources Development (some call it People's Excellence). Globalization has lowered national boundaries, creating a knowledge-based economy that spins and spans the world. Major economies are converging technologically and economically, and are highly connected at present moment. The new global workplace demands certain prerequisites such as higher order of thinking skills like abstraction system thinking and experimental inquiry, problem-solving and team work. The needs are greater in the new systems, which are participative ventures involving workers managed by so-called fictional proprietors.

QWL THROUGH EMPLOYEE INVOLVEMENT

One of the most common methods used to create QWL is employee involvement. Employee involvement(EI) consists of a variety of systematic methods that empower employees to participate in the decisions that affect them and their relationship with the organisation. Through (EI), employees feel a sense of responsibility, even"ownership" of decisions in which they participate. To be successful, however, EI must be more than just a systematic approach; it must become part of the organisation's culture by being part of management's philosophy. Some companies have had this philosophy ingrained in their corporate structure for decades; Hewlett-Packard, IBM, General Motors, Ford, etc.

Pygmalion Effect

The implications for managers and human resource specialists are to create an organisational culture that truly treats people as though they are experts at their jobs and empowers them to use that expertise. When management does this, a Pygmalion effect may result, which occurs when people live up to the high expectations that others have of them. If management further assumes that people want to contribute and seek ways to tap that contribution, better decisions, improved productivity and a higher QWL are likely.

QWL and EI Interventions

A wide variety of companies have undertaken interventions to create employee involvement or improved QWL. Examples include Motorola's participative management approach, Boeing's tiger teams, etc. Boeing's'Tiger Teams' Boeing uses a single-focus task force approach called'tiger teams'.Generally these teams are assembled to solve some production-delaying problem that the supervisor and employees cannot overcome. Various approaches to team building share a common underlying philosophy. Groups of people usually are better at solving problems than an individual. And even though the"purpose" of these approaches may be to find a solution, a by-product is improved quality of work life.

Quality Circles

Quality circles are small groups of employees who meet regularly with their common leader to identify and solve work-related probems. They are a highly specific form of team building, which are common in Japan and gained popularity in North America in the late 1970s and early 1980s. by the 1980s most medium- and large-sized Japanese firms had quality control circles for hourly employees. This effort began as a quality improvement programmme but has since become a routine procedure for many Japanese managers and a cornerstome of QWL efforts in many Japanese firms.

Several characteristics make this approach unique. First, membership in the circle is voluntary for both the leader (usually the supervisor) and the members (usually hourly workers). Secondly, the creation of quality circles is usually preceded by in-house training. For supervisors these sessions typically last for two or three days. Most of the time is devoted to discussions of small-group dynamics, leadership skills, and indoctrination in the QWL and quality circle philosophies. About a day is spent on the different approaches to problem-solving techniques. The workers also receive an explanation of the supervisor's role as the group's discussion leader and information on the quality circle concept. Thirdly, as is pointed out in the training, the group is permitted to select the problems it wants to tackle. Management may suggest problems of concern, but the group is empowered to decide which ones to select. Ideally, the selection process is not by democratic vote but is arrived at by consensus, whereby everyone agrees on the problem to be tackled. (If management has been pressing problems that need to be solved, these problems can be handled in the same way that they were resolved before the introduction of quality circles). When employees are allowed to select the problems they want to work on, they are likely to be more motivated to find solutions. And they are also more likely to be motivated to stay on as members of the circle and solve additional problems in the future.

Socio-technical Systems

Another intervention to improve QWL is the use of socio-technical systems. Socio-technical systems are interventions in the work situation that restructure the work, the work groups, and the relationship between workers and the technologies they use to do their jobs. More than just enlarging or enriching a job, these approaches may result in more radical changes in the work environment.

Autonomous Work Groups

A common approach to employee involvement is the use of autonomous work groups. These are teams of workers, without a formal company-appointed leader, who decide among themselves most decisions traditionally handled by supervisors. The key feature of these groups is a high degree of self-determination by employees in the management of their day-to-day work. Typically this includes collective control over the pace of work, distribution of tasks, organisation of breaks, and collective participation in the recruitment and training of new members. Direct supervision is often necessary.QWL is more likely to improve as workers demand jobs with more behavioural elements. These demands will probably emerge from an increasingly diverse and educated work force that expects more challenges and more autonomy in its jobs - such as worker participation in decisions traditionally reserved for management.

The following table shows the effect of various management activities on QWL:

S.No.	Management activity	Effect on the quality of work life
1	Job analysis	Finding out what human requirements are necessary so that people with the necessary skills and aptitudes can be placed into jobs where they can perform best and be satisfied.
2	Selection	Placing the right person on the right job should provide the person with the more satisfying, rewarding experience.
3	Job evaluation	Having adequate, equitable wages is a major consideration of most people in defining the quality of their work life.
4	Job enrichment	By tapping higher order needs the employees are encouraged to grow and use all his/her abilities.
5	Safety and health	A safe, healthy work environment is an obvious element contributing to the QWL.
6	Grievance procedure	Helps protect employee rights and dignity and therefore contributes to the QWL.
7	Equal employment opportunities	Protects rights of minority workers and thereby contributes to their QWL.
8	The reward system	Adequate rewards, wages that are equitable externally and internally and individuality of incentive systems and benefits, for instance.

Barriers to QWL

Though the positive effect of QWL is already established, all parties of the organization still resist to any planss or procedure to improve QWL. The management may feel the QWL at the present level is satisfactory and more steps need be taken to improve it. Employee on the other hand resist to changes with a pre conceived notion that any plans that the management takes up to would be to increase production without extra cost. Another barrier to the improvement of QWL is lack of financial resources. Strategies for improving QWL are self managed work teams, job redesign and enrichment, effective leadership and supervisory behaviour, career development, alternative work schedules, job security, administrative or organizational justice and participating management. By implementing such changes management can create a sense of involvement, commitment and togetherness among the employees which paves way for better QWL.

BALANCING THE WORK AND LIFE OF EMPLOYEES

Researches indicate that balanced work-life can lead to greater employee productivity. With the progressive shift of the economy towards a knowledge economy, the meaning and Importance of tile quality of work life is also assuming a new significance.

Sigmund Freud, family is an essential ingredient for the love that exists in the life of the employees. Many researchers indicate that maintaining a good balance in work and life has become a priority for the corporates in the developed nations. At the dawn of industrialisation, the needs and priorities of employees were at the lower end of Maslow's need hierarchy pyramid. The priority was given more to physical and material security.

However, with rapid cultural and economic developments, the priorities outside job became very different. Employees started looking for higher and meaningful quality of life as a result of the outcomes of their work. With the increasing shift of the economy towards knowledge economy, the meaning and importance of the quality of work life is also assuming a new significance.

Today, the connotation of the term'work' has also become different. It has more to do with the intellectual exercise than physical labour. As a result, the corporates need to streamline and restructure their work schedules in order to bring about a balance in work life of their employees. Understanding and managing the levels and complexities of diverse motivational needs is another area, which requires careful attention from the corporates to bring about work-life balance. Various researchers have pointed out the factors that have created the need for maintaining work life balance.

Shifts in Societal Patterns

Today's nuclear families with both the partners working, have created new dynamics that has become emotionally demanding to the employees. Financial and social obligations have assumed a different level of significance today. The needs of organisations today have also changed. Money is getting accumulated in tiny pockets, among those parts of people who possess the'most wanted' knowledge. And these so-called'knowledge workers' are the ones who are in acute need to balancing their work and life.

Technological Breakthroughs

Tremendous progress in the fields of information technology and communication system has changed our worldview. At the same time, it demands more from today's employees. Strict deadlines, tighter schedules and ever-escalating corporate targets are the natural outcome of it.

New Horizon of Expectations

Due to the reasons there has been a total shift in the level of expectations for today's employees. In fact, Thomas and Bennis explain how attitudes towards work and life balance varies from generation to generation. Baby boomers are no longer ready to give their lives to the company they work for. Whereas the Generation X's and Y's are more committed to meet the demands of both work and family life. In turn, they seek a newly defined and restructured way of getting jobs assigned to them.

Researchers have pointed out that a balance between work and life is maintained when there is no conflict between work and family demands. Though this seems to be idealistic situation, what the corporates need to remember is that the conflicts should not reach unacceptable levels where it would tend to affect the productivity of the employee.

In 1998 America study conducted by Aon Consulting Worldwide Inc., an HR consulting firm based in Chicago, the employees of today put their commitment to organizations they work for only if the management recognizes the importance of their personal and family life. Striking a balance between work and life is as difficult for the corporates as it is for the employees.

However, the onus of maintaining this is more on the corporates because, as pointed out by the famous Hawthorne Experiment, the world of individuals primarily centres on their place of work.

So a careful perusal of the working patterns and scheduling of jobs will be one of the first steps in designing work schedule that can balance life and work. The HR managers, along with the functional heads and line mangers, should try to bring in flexibility to the working patterns within the organizations. A trade off between organizational needs and personal needs of the employees has to be worked out. Following are some of the ways in which it can be done. Though this is in no way an exhaustive list, yet it does provide a starting point for corporates to develop flexible work schedules that can balance work and life.

CREATING INSTITUTIONAL SUPPORT MECHANISMS

The first and the foremost requirement is to create conditions that will provide organizational support towards maintaining the flexibility of work and life of the employees. These entail the propagation of the culture of work flexibility,

HR policies and other organizational regulations that allow the employees to maintain a good mix of personal lives with their career.

There is a need to clearly chalk out the connection between maintaining this flexibility and the corporate objectives. For instance, managers at Eli Lilly begin their job in the company with a clear understanding of what the company expects.

They undergo a weeklong programmme, called Supervisor School that blends the business case for work life initiatives. Thus, the management ensures that the flexibility in work is linked with the objectives of the organisation. But this is not enough.

What is needed is to ensure and communicate the support of the senior management. The top management of the company must clearly communicate its eagerness and willingness to restructure the work schedules in such a manner that it can balance the work and life of the employees. This will require clear articulation from the company that it values the personal lives of its employees.

The employees must understand that their organisation also keeps in mind the value of their life and personal relationship. Such articulation can be done through the company's vision and mission statements.

Providing Managerial Support

Organisations must make sure that there are proper organisational systems of work design that allows employees to have flexible time. This may even require a new look towards HR manual, which the organisation may have.It is also necessary to evaluate such systems of flexibility from time to time.

Otherwise, stagnancy will creep into the work schedules, which might create new dimensions of the problem in the work life patterns. To keep pace with the changing patterns of work and life of employees, the organisations can arrange special training programmmes that will inform the employees about the new working trends. This can be done through sharing successful models of work schedules and real life case studies.

Practising what you Preach

The organisations need to execute their flexible work schedules. Flexible work patterns must become a part of organisational initiatives. This will require the creation of a networked environment that can provide a'back up' system to support work relationship.

Essentially this will require employees to become cross functional, so that a temporary emergency or a shortfall in one department can be met by other departments. Thus, the role of HR department needs to be revisited and made more expansive and supportive towards organisational and individual needs.

Sustain It

Once the organisation follows and internalises the practice of flexible work schedules for its employees, it is very necessary that it sustains it over a long period of time. Such sustainability can e brought about by clear demarcations of accountability and means to measure it. In other words, the focus and purpose of creating balanced work life should be maintained at any cost. This will also call for review and evaluation of the current work environment and make modifications in the schedules accordingly. Several researchers have shown that a balanced work-life creates greater employee productivity.

What important is the long-term and not the short-term, which seems to become the focus of many organisations. So, though it may apparently seem that employees are having more leisure, the effect of a balanced work-life will show up positively in the bottom line of the company.

Benefits of Improving Work-life Balance

- Aiding employee recruitment and retention
- Reducing absenteeism
- Improving the quality of people's working lives
- Matching people who wouldn't otherwise work with jobs
- Benefiting families and communities

Top Ten Tips for Improving the Quality of Work Life

The following ten tips apply as much to the CEO as they do to the front line worker:

- *Have a personal vision of who you want to be and what you want to do*: Keep in mind that if you do not have one for yourself, you will likely become part of someone else's vision!
- *Test out your own personal vision with that of your organization's*: In how many ways do they support each other? Ask questions to better understand your organization's mission, vision and values.
- *Learn, and keep on learning*: Go to training sessions and in-services, enroll in college courses, read books. Know why, not just how.
- *Buddy-up*: Find ways to share the load with other team members. Sharing the load makes work easier to manage and less stressful.
- *Share your successes*: This allows you to learn from the successes of others, as well as giving you a boost when you need
- *Get it off your chest*: Talk things over with your buddy, friend, supervisor when things trouble you, don't keep it bottled up inside.
- *Find joy in being of service to others*: Think about how the person you are serving is better off as a result of your work, and rejoice in that knowledge.
- *Take time for breaks*: Pay particular attention to the need to refresh body, mind and spirit.
- *Try out new ideas*: To innovate is to grow. By using your creativity and innovation life becomes exciting and fulfilling.
- *Have fun at work*: Laughter is the best medicine, but use only appropriate humour. Damaging someone else's self-esteem for the fun of it is no laughing matter.

What is"Call Center"?

The beginning of an industry: Carrying out transactions over the telephone has a long history, beginning with operator services and later, reservations lines, particularly for airlines. But in the last 15 to 20 ears, he introduction of information technologies and telecommunications advances have expanded the types of work it is possible to undertake, while reducing costs. Concurrently, ideas of'service' and service relationships continue to be redefined as technology becomes increasingly ubiquitous, rendering the public more receptive to mediated service interactions.

Call center is a centralised office used for the purpose of receiving and transmitting a large volume of requests by telephone. A call centre is operated by a company to administer incoming product support or information inquiries from consumers. Outgoing calls for telemarketing, clientele, product services, and debt collection are also made. In addition to a call centre, collective handling of letters, faxes, live chat, and e-mails at one location is known as a contact centre. A call centre is often operated through an extensive open workspace for call centre agents, with work stations that include a computer for each agent,

A telephone set/headset connected to a telecom switch, and one or more supervisor stations. It can be independently operated or networked with additional centres, often linked to a corporate computer network, including mainframes, microcomputers and LANs. Increasingly, the voice and data pathways into the centre are linked through a set of new technologies called Computer Telephony Integration (CTI).

DEFINATION OF CALL CENTRE

Most major businesses use call centres to interact with their customers. Examples include utility companies, mail order catalogue retailers, and customer support for computer hardware and software. Some businesses even service internal functions through call centres. Examples of this include help desks, retail financial support, and sales support.As a first step, it is useful to establish a definition of a call center. This is not a completely straightforward task, as there are considerable variations between types of call centres, which are spread across several sectors of the economy, and which perform different functions for different organizations, both within and across sectors.

The broadest definition in the call center literature is that provided by Norling, who states"a call center is any communications platform from which firms deliver services to customers via remote, real-time contact".

Callaghan and Thompson apply a similarly inclusive definition, stating that call centres may be"broadly defined as workplaces that integrate telephone and computer technologies". While these definitions usefully highlight the centrality of communication technology integration in the call center field, it leaves the boundaries of the industry somewhat ambiguous. Taylor and Bain narrow the definition by specifying the types of technologies used:"we define a call center as a dedicated operation in which computer-utilising employees receive inbound-or make outbound-telephone calls, with those calls processed and controlled either by an Automatic Call Distribution (ACD) or predictive dialing system. The call center is thus characterized by the integration of telephone and VDU technologies."

Other authors narrow their definitions by focusing on the types of services which these integrated technologies are designed to provide. For example, in an early definition, Richardson states"telephone call centres are specialist technology-intensive offices that are established by organizations in order to deliver services to customers over the telephone, replacing or complementing face-to-face interaction with the public".

Houlihan also includes the types of operations typically performed in a call center within her definition. She lists the tasks most effectively performed by call centres:"Call centres are centralized, specialized operations for both inbound and outbound communication handling. Call center operations are especially suited to information delivery, customer services and sales operations".

Buchanan and Koch-Schulte go one step further and include in their description the organizational rationale for establishing call centres. Call centres are a relatively recent phenomenon made possible by the dissemination of telecommunications and information technologies. The technology enables telephone service representatives to deal quickly and remotely with customer needs by connecting the representative to the customer's account information on his/her computer as the call is relayed to the headset. As call centres can be centralized in locations far from the customers of a business, they allow firms to cut costs by reducing the number of local service outlets.

In reviewing these definitions and descriptions, it becomes clear that although there are variations in stress placed on different elements, there is general agreement about which elements are key. Borrowing from this accumulation, we might, therefore, define a call center as a specialized office where agents remotely provide information, deliver services, and/or conduct sales, using some combination of integrated telephone and information technologies, typically with an aim to enhancing customer service while reducing organizational costs.

UNDERSTANDING - THE CALL CENTER"INDUSTRY"

Call center is a place where calls are either made or received in a high volume by 100s of call center agents sitting together in a large group.

The purposes are:

- Sales
- Marketing
- Telemarketing
- Customer service
- Technical support
- Specialized business activity

The set up can be considered as one of the following:

- Huge telemarketing center
- Customer service center

- Help line
- Service bureau
- Outsourcer

Earlier call center was defined as a place where various business transaction were handled through telephone that used to combine centrally located through telephone that used to combine centrally located database with an automatic call distribution [ACD] system.An agent in a call center means a staff/person who is working in a call center.

Belt, Richardson and Webster (2000), agree that call centres are not an'industry' as the term is generally defined, but rather represent certain ways of delivering various services using the telephone and computer technologies across traditional industry boundaries. However, these authors provide three strong reasons defending the practice of referring to call centres as an industry:

First, the call center community often defines itself as an industry, with numerous national.and international call center conferences and workshops taking place each year, industry journals and call center forums organized at local levels.

Second, the labour force requirements of call centres are often the same across sectors. This means that many, though not all, call centres share a common labour pool.

Third, the organizational templates and technologies used tend to be very similar, regardless of the sector. To this one might add the remarkable similarities that international researchers have found between technologies used, work practices and key issues including monitoring, control, training, and labour demographics for workers in countries as diverse as Germany, Japan, Australia, Greece, Canada, the US, the UK and the Netherlands.

HUMAN ISSUES IN CALL-CENTER INDUSTRYSTRESS

For many employed in the call center sector,"the daily experience is of repetitive, intensive and stressful work, based upon Taylorist principles, which frequently results in employee"burnout". Brown, more vividly, characterizes the work as"repetitive brain strain". These descriptions are hardly surprising, in a way, given that call centres are established by organizations to"create an environment in which work can be standardized to create relatively uniform and repetitious activities so as to achieve economies of scale and consistent quality of customer service". This means, in other words, that workplaces are organized in ways that weaken employee autonomy and enhance the potential for management control, and"a loss of control is generally understood to be an important indicator of work-related stress".

There is almost universal consensus that call center work is stressful. Even in studies that report the observation that some staff actually enjoys their work, mention of stress is still the norm, and a significant portion of the call center literature is devoted to detailing the sources of stress in call center work.

Four Key Stressors

Can we get off the phone for a while?'The primary source of stress reported is inherent to the nature of the job: spending all day on the phone dealing with people one after another, day after day, is difficult. Doing it under constant pressure to keep call volumes up, with no time between calls to"recover from an awkward call or from'customer rejection'" is even more difficult. And doing it with"very little authority or autonomy to rectify problems" that arise is perhaps the most difficult of all. Many studies report agents as wanting to'just get off the phones'.

For example, Belt and colleagues note"agents in all three sectors [financial services, IT, and third-party services] spoke of the phenomenon of'burnout', caused by the pressure of working exclusively'on the phones'". In the same study, the authors mention that the issue of'burnout' was also recognized by some managers:"It was pointed out that managers face an inherent conflict between the need to reduce staff boredom and labour turnover, and the pressure to concentrate staff energies on telephone based work".

"The question of how call center employees deal with stress is an important one, particularly in view of evidence that a build-up of stress leads to illness, absenteeism and turnover," writes Houlihan. Many authors agree, and there are a variety of individual coping mechanisms described in the literature. Tricks to circumvent control mechanisms although they are unreliable in this role as they may also increase stress. Others mention social interaction squeezed into brief moments--Callaghan and Thompson describe agents using humourous (or rude) gestures towards the phone, or making faces at colleagues to defuse stress over angry or abusive callers, and making jokes to combat the tedium of the day.

Lankshear and Mason describe a similarly social approach to reducing tension in one of the sites they observed, where staff often laughed and joked with one another in intervals between calls, with management's approval. More formally, some call centres include stress management as a component in training programmmes, and many have, or claim to have, team de-briefings which permit staff to vent frustrations while discussing difficult calls or dissatisfactions with elements of work.

Knights and McCabe take a different approach to stress in the workplace. They note that although much organizational analysis and most of the call center literature tends to conceptualize stress as an individual problem, it is actually located within"a framework that emphasizes the interrelationships between structural relations of power and the subjective interpretations and actions of employees".

This more nuance positioning may provide more insight into call center conditions, as it allows a researcher to consider the response of employees"forced to interpret the often contradictory demands management place upon them" including"contradictions...over service quality versus the quantity of work output"."Clearly," these authors write,"staff face some fundamental contradictions over unity versus conflict, uncertainty versus certainty, quality versus quantity and these are at the heart of the reproduction of stress, resistance and control".

This focus on the"contradictory" nature of demands strikes at the heart of the second inherent sources of stress in (primarily inbound) call center works: the quality/quantity conflict.

Quality/Quantity Conflict

Typically, organizational rhetoric in inbound call centres is concerned with'customer care', or'keeping customers happy' (providing quality service), yet these goals are juxtaposed with an ongoing pressure to keep call times down and call volumes up. Houlihan describes the difficulty concisely:

Call centres are rooted in contradictory tensions and structural paradoxes, and confront a number of trade-offs on that basis. These set a context for attitudes towards the organization and can impose conflicting role requirements on agents. A core example is that of the pressure for quantity versus the aspiration for quality, the guiding logic of which is the conundrum of trying to get closer to the customer while reutilizing, centralizing, reducing costs and prescribing standards.

The dichotomy is not completely straightforward, it is important to note. Part of providing quality service from a management perspective is making sure customers do not wait too long for their calls to be answered, even though the push to keep queue waiting times short is typically categorized as part of the pressure towards quantity. As Bain points out,"efforts to attain what is perceived to be the desired balance between the quantity and the quality of calls presents a perennial challenge".

The practice of ongoing work practice modification and target revision as management swings from one side to another of the quality/quantity debate is a major source of stress for call center agents. As Houlihan notes:"The practice of putting a'drive' on particular targets for improvement (for example, the collection of renewal dates, the up-selling or cross-selling of products, the quality of data input, or the intensity of sales push) and continual reprioritization means that the'goalposts' are constantly shifting". Virtually all of the call center authors who write about work conditions mention the difficulty of dealing with these competing goals. Korczynski and colleagues suggest that this dilemma is particularly difficult for front-line workers because they may be likely"to identify with embodied individual customers, for interactions with specific customers may be an important arena for meaning and satisfaction within the work".

They contrast this customer-as-individual orientation to the managerial goal of balancing customer orientation with efficiency, which they suggest leads management to prefer workers to identify with a generic category,'the customer', since"such a disembodied image of the customer will encourage workers to deal with individual customers efficiently because they will be conscious of the concerns of other customers waiting in a queue".

Intensity

The third central stressor in call center work is its intensity. As Bain argues,"far from being either in terminal decline or on the wane, Taylorism-in conjunction with a range of other control mechanisms-is not only alive, well and deeply embedded in the call center labour process, but its malevolent influence appears to be spreading to previously uncharted territory". There is widespread consensus that"call centres are a new, and particularly effective, manifestation of the increasingly capital intensive'industrialization' of service sector work, and work performed in them is highly intensive and routine".

Buchanan and Koch-Schulte quote one call center worker who describes the constant pressure graphically: Ellen: It's almost like the army. It's very regimented. You punch in with a time clock. You come in and you sit down, and the numbers are all computerized.

As soon as you finish a call, the minute you hang up another call comes up just this constant, all day, repetitious...constant sort of like beating on a drum, but day after day. The pace of work is determined by the combination of technologies that deliver calls to the headset and account details to the screen, and workers often have no control over this process.

Descriptions such as"exhausting,""robotic,""controlled," and agents discussing the nature of their work often use"machine-like".

Houlihan expands on the idea of controlled, machine-like agents by suggesting that this is in fact exactly the way that the organization conceives of them:

Call centres are information handling organizations. As currently characterized, the job of the agent is to be the voice of the organization, interfacing with the client or customer.

The organization rehearses the things it wants said and feeds them through the agent. The agent is largely constructed as a mouthpiece rather than as a brain. Buchanan and Koch-Schulte spoke with a call-center worker who articulated her feelings about the organization's expectations of its agents in very similar terms: Rosa: You are standing waiting to be used by the technology, and it's a physical embodiment of that. You are standing, waiting until that call comes in to use you to make money.

And you are simply another part of that machine. When this feeling of being a cog in a machine which never stops as it grinds on, repeating the same actions over and over again, is combined with"the cumulative emotional demands by the interpersonal nature of the work", stress is inevitable.

Targets

There is a fourth feature of some call center work that may engender stress: performance targets. There are various types of targets, which may vary between inbound and outbound centres.

Inbound centres typically have targets for call duration,'wrap time', and daily call volume. Outbound centres often also have sales or'completion' targets, which are closely monitored and upon which pay may be partially based. In addition, in some sectors, inbound call centres are attempting to introduce the practice of cross selling, where agents attempt to sell additional products to the customers who call in for another purpose. In these centres, sales targets similar to those in outbound centres are often in place.

Taylor and Bain argue that particularly in the financial services industry in the UK, targets are a significant source of stress for workers as more and more importance is placed upon meeting them in an increasingly competitive business environment. Sales targets, in particular, are difficult to accept, or meet, for staff who often consider themselves as service personnel, particularly when they are set centrally and implemented locally:"Cross-selling is seen by employees, not as an opportunity to engage in creative work, but as an additional and acute source of pressure". This is especially the case when sales targets are parachuted in on top of service targets set originally when there was no pressure to produce sales. As a CSR in Taylor and Bain's study emphasizes:"When somebody phones in for a balance you have to try to get a sale or get them interested as well as turning the call round in 155 seconds".

Even in centres that claim not to prioritize targets, researchers have found that staff often feels significant pressure. Targets simply intensify the stress produced by the quantity/quality debate, or, as one agent is quoted as saying,"They say that they're not really interested in numbers. They say that they are more into quality. Well, that's a lie. They're usually more into numbers than anything". It is important not to over generalize however. While most call centres do have some targets, they are a source of stress that is directly under management control. Some call centres are managed in such a way that targets are set to realistically reflect local conditions, are interpreted in light of other, more subjective information, and are not used punitively or to intensify work.

In some they are even used effectively to motivate and encourage staff. For example, Lankshear and Mason describe a series of conversations with managers in their call center site where management consistently conceptualized their performance reports (for example, one commented that it's'human nature' for productivity to drop before and after a holiday), and used their stats as an excuse to praise good performance and coach those who consistently had difficulty meeting targets:"Our best bet is to develop the people we have got" one manager is quoted as saying.

Other Health Issues

The result of intense, stressful work may be an effect on workers' health. There are often high rates of absenteeism and sick leave reported in the literature, although there is relatively little exploration of these issues, particularly when compared to turnover. Most often, authors provide a brief list of known health issues. For example, Richardson, Belt and Marshall write that"Health concerns have been expressed, including tension, sleeplessness, headaches, eye-strain, repetitive strain injury (RSI), voice loss, hearing problems and burn-out", but they do not develop the point. More detailed descriptions of the causes and effects of these ailments can be found in industry and trades union reports.

Also in the UK, regulators have been proactive in their examination of the industry, with the Health and Safety Executive issuing a bulletin on call center regulations, health risks and best practices in December 2001. They looked specifically at health issues including stress, noise levels, musculoskeletal disorders (such as back problems) and voice loss, and also at display screen issues, working environments, requirements for work stations, daily work routines, training, organizational working practices and shifts.

Sleeping Disorders

No prizes for guessing the most severe ailment afflicting people working in Indian call centres. Since this is a unique Indian problem, again, no solution appears in sight. Obviously this affects first timers more severely, as they take time to acclimatize their biological clocks, but even experienced people or managers are not able to completely escape from it. Some call centres are looking at devising innovative mechanisms like flexible shifts with sleeping arrangements in the office premises as possible solutions. Digestive System Related DisordersWorking long and odd hours without any sleep, and eating food supplied by external caterers everyday, has led to

41.9% of the respondents suffering from digestive problems. Especially for the large number of girls working in the industry, the problem is even more severe. Many call centres are now taking additional care to ensure their caterers supply hygienic food; besides stipulating strict conditions to maintain the quality of the food they serve.

Depression

In last year's survey, this was not among the top disorders, but this year it has climbed up the chart, affecting nearly one-fourth of the respondents. Not surprising, since, as the industry matures, the initial glitz and glamour wears away and the real problems come to the fore. Not only are there several health related issues, but, on top of that, the gradual realization that there is limited scope in developing a career owing to fewer growth opportunities is increasing the frustration levels. Coupled with growing mental fatigue and increasingly punishing physical environments, depression is the obvious end result. Some call centres have now devised different stress management programmmes mainly to counter depression.

Severe Stomach Related Problems

Continuing digestive problems lead to severe stomach disorders like gastroenteritis, as endorsed by more than 24% of the respondents. Even doctors in major cities agree-in recent times many of the patients with various stomach ailments are from call centres.

Eyesight Problems

Globally call center industry employees are considered a high-risk group for eye-related problems. While the quality of monitors might impact these disorders, sitting continually without adequate breaks seems to be the truer reason. The number of people affected seems to be on the rise-last year only 19% complained; this year it has gone up to 23%. At some point of time, this problem might also afflict the IT services industry, but for the call center industry, no remedy seems to be in sight.

Ear Problems

More than 16% of the respondents inform that they have hearing problems. Again, no surprises here, since a call center job involves taking calls throughout the shift, sitting with headphones.

SOME OTHER HUMAN ISSUES, IN CALL-CENTRES, WHICH NEED IMMEDIATE ATTENTION

PERSONAL HABITS

The young executives are getting more than five figure salaries per month in an early age. They tend to develop certain bad habits such as alcohol, smoking etc. It is not easy to identify such individuals. It is also very sensitive to talk to them. The professional counselors can conduct group-counseling, workshops, educative film shows in order to create awareness on effects of bad habits. Such actions will enable individuals to realise the importance of good habits.

Discipline and Behavioural Issues

Call centres provide excellent working environment, free food and transportation. There is always a situation where individual or group of youngsters tend to commit mistakes and abuse the freedom. They start behaving like in college campus where they have more freedom. However, the call center executives have more responsibility and accountability, they need to follow discipline and do well in the job. The most common behaviour is misuse of food, behave erratically in vans, and smoke in public places, misuse of telephones and other resources of the company.

The supervisors always concentrate on performance and achieving targets. They do not have time or interest to go deep into these matters and find out the reasons for such behaviour. The professional counselor can play a major role in educating the youngsters on discipline; provide advice to erring executives. The counselors with their wisdom and experience can tackle such issues tactfully and bring change within the individuals.Sleeping while on duty, reading novels and playing games on the computer during working hours brings down productivity and quality suffers.

The HR representatives and professional counselors jointly have a role to bring behavioural change starting from the training days. Continuous education and Counseling will help to mitigate such problems and it is possible to prevent serious problems.

Inter-Personal Relationship and Friendship

Executives develop friendship quickly and sometime the friendship breaks and there will be misunderstanding among the team members and naturally affects the team performance. The supervisors and counselors can play a major role to sort out the interpersonal relationship and develop team spirit. Healthy relationship among the team members has always helped the team to out perform. When the relationship fails the individuals will also break down mentally. They either absent for duties or fall ill or the performance will come down. It is also true that due to misunderstanding and break in friendship they change jobs quickly.

Love Affair and Marriages

Few of the boys and girls fall in love quickly. They maintain the healthy relationship, behave in a matured manner, plan the future course of action and such persons have got married with the consent of their parents. They work together in the same organization for longer duration. There are instances, where lovers fall apart, start disliking, creating troubles to each other and vitiating the atmosphere. They are immature, take instant decisions to break or unite and sometimes go to an extent of damaging others reputation. The professional counselors can play an important role in explaining the importance of marriage, preparation required for marriage, how to enter the institution of marriage, which is acceptable to both parents and society and about the new role and responsibility after getting married. Counseling services can definitely give emotional support to individuals.

Absenteeism

Absenteeism is very high in calls centres. Employees tend to be very irregular to the duty due to various reasons. The professional counseling services to such irregular employees on one to one basis will help to bring down the absenteeism. The counselor can educate and explain the importance of attending duties to earn the salary and also to meet the organizational goals.

Higher Education and Part Time Jobs

It is possible to do higher education while working in BPO units. Few organizations encourage and offer support services to pursue higher education. However, the time management by the executives is crucial to go forward in education as well as to maintain the performance and career growth. Programmes on time management, tips to study, tips to keep fit and such other programmes can be offered.

These steps would help to seek the loyalty of employees to the organizations and helps greatly for the retention of employees.

Organizations do not grant permission to pursue part time jobs while working in BPO units. In order to make quick money and to have options open to change the jobs in future will drive the employees to do part time work. Human body does not permit to stretch beyond one's capacity. The executives need to take sufficient rest in the daytime so that energy levels are maintained.

Remedial Measures for Stress Management

Understanding that the"Stress" is a major concern for all Call-Center Employees, it is a duty of HR-heads of Call-Centres to address it properly. Some of the common signs and symptoms of stress Although we all experience stress in different ways, there are certain signs that are most frequently reported. These signs fall into two major categories; physical/ behavioural signs and emotional signs. If we become aware of our own stress symptoms, as suggested, be more effective in dealing with them sooner rather than later.

Cease

It is desirable to employ professional HR Professionals with knowledge of Human Psychology in BPO units/call centres. The services offered by professionals may not be felt in the initial stages. Companies like Tata, L&T, MICO and few others have employed professionals in their factories. The professionals can do wonders in BPO sectors as well. People are the backbone of BPO industry and it is certain that professional HR or Human Psychologist can make inroad in this emerging organization and facilitate the growth of organization in an immense way.

VARIOUS CALL CENTRES

Tata Indicom

Tata Teleservices Limited (TTSL) is part of the Tata Group of Companies, an Indian Conglomerate. It runs the brand name Tata Indicom in India in various telecom circles of India. The company forms part of the Tata Group's presence in the Telecommunication Industry in India, along with Tata Teleservices (Maharashtra) Limited (TTML) and VSNL.TTSL was incorporated in 1995 and was the first company to offer CDMA Mobile services in India, specifically in the state of Andhra Pradesh. In December 2002, the company acquired the erstwhile Hughes Telecom (India) Ltd. which was renamed Tata Teleservices (Maharashtra) Limited. In September 2007, Tata Indicom launched the Talk World plan, an International Long Distance Plan.

Tata is the direct competitor with Reliance both CDMA operators in India. The company provides unified telecommunication solutions including mobile, fixed wireless, fixed line and broadband. Other competitors are Vodafone, Airtel, Aircel, Idea, MTNL, BSNL providing GSM based mobile telephony.

The company was first in India to provide free intra network calling within city limits. They launched a unique plans providing lifetime rental free connectivity on its mobile and fixed wireless for a one time charge.

On February this year, TTSL announced to provide CDMA mobile services targeted towards the youth, in a JV with Virgin, UK,on a MVNO basis

Vodafone

The story of Vodafone is an interesting one. Within two decades, Vodafone has become the telecommunications leader in Global Systems for Mobile networks (GSM). Since it's inception, Vodafone's goal has been one of providing innovative and cutting edge telecommunication services on the largest wireless network on earth. Step by step, Vodafone has engaged in key strategic activity to become closer and closer to that goal each day. Being only second to China Mobile (Hong Kong) in subscriber volume, with over 133 million subscribers, Vodafone by far is a MNE with true role in the shaping of telecomm sector.

Culture of Globalization

Vodafone Group Plc, a twenty-year-old multinational enterprise, has become a leading player among global firms. It was ranked the second largest multinational in 2004 by the World Investment report. Vodafone Group Plc provides an extensive range of mobile telecommunications services, including voice and data communications, and is the world's largest mobile telecommunications company, with a significant presence in Continental Europe, the United Kingdom, the United States and the Far East through the Company's subsidiary undertakings, associated undertakings and investments. (hoovers.com) Vodafone's goal is to integrate data services and telecommunication into a worldwide network. The story of Vodafone is one of continued success and growth. In 2004 Vodafone had 60,000 employees, a shocking figure, since in 1995 it only comprised of 5000 employees, and only 50 in 1985. Vodafone is traded on both the New York Stock Exchange and London Stock Exchange.

Reliance

The Late Dhirubhai Ambani dreamt of a digital India -

an India where the common man would have access to affordable means of information and communication. Dhirubhai, who single-handedly built India's largest private sector company virtually from scratch, had stated as early as 1999:" Make the tools of information and communication available to people at an affordable cost. They will overcome the handicaps of illiteracy and lack of mobility." It was with this belief in mind that Reliance Communications (formerly Reliance Infocomm) started laying 60,000 route kilometres of a pan-India fibre optic backbone. This backbone was commissioned on 28 December 2002, the auspicious occasion of Dhirubhai's 70th birthday, though sadly after his unexpected demise on 6 July 2002.

Reliance Communications has a reliable, high-capacity, integrated (both wireless and wire line) and convergent (voice, data and video) digital network. It is capable of delivering a range of services spanning the entire infocomm (information and communication) value chain, including infrastructure and services - for enterprises as well as individuals, applications, and consulting. Today, Reliance Communications is revolutionizing the way India communicates and networks, truly bringing about a new way of life. Listed on the National Stock Exchange and the Bombay Stock Exchange, it is India's leading integrated telecommunication company with over 40 million customers. Our business encompasses a complete range of telecom services covering mobile and fixed line telephony. It includes broadband, national and international long distance services and data services along with an exhaustive range of value-added services and applications. Our constant endeavour is to achieve customer delight by enhancing the productivity of the enterprises and individuals we serve. at affordable rates. We endeavour to further extend our efforts beyond the traditional value chain by developing and deploying complete telecom solutions for the entire spectrum of society.

Spice

Spice Mobiles Ltd. is a part of Spice Corp, a $ 2 billion

multi-faceted group, previously known as MCorp Global. With"Innovation" as the company's mantra, Spice began the process of revolutionizing the Communication and Entertainment sector, with its new age technologically advanced state of the art mobile phones. This led to the birth of Spice Mobile. Spice Mobile phones made its entry two years ago in the Indian market targeting the entry-level handset segment.

Debuting with handsets targeted at the entry-level segment, today, the brand is growing rapidly and has a bouquet of offerings targeting entry, mid and premium segments.

Ms. Katrina Kaif, a leading Bollywood actress, is the Brand Ambassador for Spice Mobiles. She perfectly compliments the youth, fun and vibrancy of the brand with her beauty, intelligence and grace. As an ambassador for the brand she will play a key role in building a strong bond with the Indian consumers.

Riding on the success of its venture, Spice Mobiles Ltd. has strengthened its footprint, built a strong value proposition with the customers and established itself as a competitive brand amongst the host of International players. Moving forward, the company aims to achieve further brand acceptability among all target segments through a broader offering of cutting-edge handsets that combine mobile phone functionality with enriched content and smart device capabilities for greater high-speed voice and data capacity.

Bharti Airtel

Telecom giant Bharti Airtel is the flagship company of Bharti Enterprises. The Bharti Group, has a diverse business portfolio and has created global brands in the telecommunication sector. Bharti has recently forayed into retail business as Bharti Retail Pvt. Ltd. under a MoU with Wal-Mart for the cash and carry business. It has successfully launched an international venture with EL Rothschild Group to export fresh agri products exclusively to markets in Europe and USA and has launched Bharti AXA Life Insurance

Company Ltd under a joint venture with AXA, world leader in financial protection and wealth management.

Airtel comes to you from Bharti Airtel Limited, India's largest integrated and the first private telecom services provider with a footprint in all the 23 telecom circles. Bharti Airtel since its inception has been at the forefront of technology and has steered the course of the telecom sector in the country with its world class products and services. The businesses at Bharti Airtel have been structured into three individual strategic business units (SBU's) - Mobile Services, Airtel Telemedia Services and Enterprise Services. The mobile business provides mobile and fixed wireless services using GSM technology across 23 telecom circles while the Airtel Telemedia Services business offers broadband and telephone services in 94 cities. The Enterprise services provide end-to-end telecom solutions to corporate customers and national and international long distance services to carriers. All these services are provided under the Airtel brand.

Genpact

Genpact has a unique heritage. We built our business by meeting the demands of the leaders of the General Electric Company to increase the productivity of their businesses. We began in 1997 as GE Capital International Services (GECIS) - the India-based business process services operations of GE Capital. During the eight years that followed, we took on a wide range of complex and critical processes and became a provider to many of GE's financial-services and manufacturing businesses.

In 2005, we became an independent company, changing our name to Genpact, which conveys our desire to generate value and business impact for our clients. Since then we have grown rapidly, significantly expanding our range of services and diversifying our client base.

.Genpact manages business processes for companies around the world. We combine our process expertise, information technology and analytical capabilities with operational insight derived from experience in diverse industries to provide a wide range of services using our global delivery platform. Genpact provides a wide range of services, including Finance and Accounting, Collections and Customer Service, Insurance, Supply Chain and Procurement, Analytics, Enterprise Application, IT Infrastructure and Management.

Our goal is to help our clients improve the ways in which they do business by continuously improving their business processes through Six Sigma and Lean principles and by the innovative use of technology. As a service provider, we strive to be a seamless extension of our clients' operations. Genpact manages complex processes in multiple geographic regions, delivering its services from a global network of more than 30 operations centres in nine countries. Our global delivery centres are located in India, China, Hungary, Mexico, the Philippines, the Netherlands, Romania, Spain and the United States.

HCL Bpo

Developed the first indigenous micro-computer at the same time as Apple and 3 years before IBM's PC - in 1978. This micro-computer virtually gave birth to the Indian computer industry. HCL's in-depth knowledge of Unix led to the development of a fine grained multi-processor Unix in 1988, three years ahead of Sun and HP. Along with the swiftly growing software technology industry, HCL, which was hitherto known as the pioneer in modern computing made the advent into software development. HCL's R&D was spun off as HCL Technologies in 1997 to mark their advent into the software services arena.

Today, HCL sells more PCs in India than any other brand, runs Northern Ireland's largest BPO operation, and manages the network for Asia's largest stock exchange network apart from designing zero visibility landing systems to land the world's most popular airplane. And this it does across 18 countries and across 360 service locations in India.

IBM

A report published by the Yankee group stated that in

the US,'67% of online transactions were being abandoned due to inadequate customer support'. And with this, an idea was born. The year - July 1999. In no time, the entrepreneurial drive and the realization of opportunity within India became the two most important factors towards the inception of what would be the largest BPO service provider in India - Daksh. A core team of 4 members sprung into immediate action to put together a sturdy business plan which got them their first client and the first round of funding.It was not a company that was created but a whole new enterprise, a potentially new industry that had no history and no business model to follow. All it had was sound leadership, a focused vision and an undying passion.

And today, IBM Daksh...

- Is a Leading Continuous'BPO' player.
- Has a strong platform of corporate governance.
- Has a 20000 strong team that has embraced the IBM Daksh values.
- Is a winner of multiple globally recognized awards in the domain of employee and customer satisfaction.
- Has built a strong platform of quality around Six Sigma and COPC across the enterprise.
- Has 14 service delivery locations.
- Is known to be profitable since inception.

Literature Review

Different scholars have given large volume of literature regarding Quality Of Work Life of employees in call centre. Although, it is not easy to review each and every work done by all scholars, some studies need special mention which are given in the chronological order.

"Pressure of both qualitative and quantitative overload can result in the need to work excessive hours, which is an additional source of stress." Having to work under time pressure in order to meet deadlines is an independent source of stress. Stress is the outcome of lack of quality of work life. So Quality of Work life should be improved in order to get rid of stress.

- *Bain, P. et al (2000)*: Focuses on examining the job content, working hours and work life balance, and managerial/supervisory style and strategies within two call centres in terms of their impact on the quality of CSOs working life.
- *Union Research Centre on Organization and Technology (2000)*: Demonstrated that call centre employees continue to have concerns about working in telephone-based environments. Also provides a useful framework for identifying gaps and for assisting researchers to explore the internal operations of centres. In the meantime, there are a number of useful implications of this research for unions to consider in planning recruitment and other associated activities.
- *Wallace,C. et al (2000)*: Outlines current debates, highlighting the importance of bringing together and marrying these two branches of research. A qualitative research agenda constituting case study analysis of two call centres is introduced. A framework grounded in a job characteristics approach, comprising 10 key job-quality elements is also proposed as a means of examining the quality of work life in this context.
- *Batt, R. et al (2002)*: Outlines three alternative production models and discuss their applicability to call centre management. These include the classic mass production model, the professional service model and the mass customization model. A theoretical framework is developed that identifies potential causal links between management practices, workers affective and cognitive reactions, and performance outcomes.
- *Campbell, I. (2002)*: States that a productivity orientation and employee focus are not a mutually exclusive phenomenon. Union presence and public-sector status do not guarantee better working conditions and higher QWL. Managerial styles and

strategies have a significant impact on QWL in the call center context.

- *Deery, S. et al (2002)*: Quality of Work Life (QWL) is both a goal and an on-going process for achieving it. As a goal, QWL is the commitment of any organization to work improvement - the creation of more involving, satisfying and effective jobs and work environment for people at all levels of the organization. As a process, QWL calls for efforts to realise this goal through the active involvement of people throughout the organization.
- *Deery, S. et al (2002)*: The purpose of this is to assess service quality of a call centre as perceived by its employees using the SERVQUAL model. It also aims to explore factors predicting front-line employee satisfaction and behavioural intentions in a call centre. Behavioural intentions are to be measured in terms of employees' willingness to recommend the call centre and their intentions to stay.
- *Mulholland, K. (2002)*: The aim is to determine whether and how the quality of work life varies between the two types of call centres in different sectors and the implications of HRM on these findings. Three quality of work life factors are reported: job content, working hours and work-life balance, and managerial/supervisory style and strategies.
- *Van den Broek, D. (2002)*: Outlines management's stance towards unions within the sample of Western Australian call centres, detailing the forms their co-operation and resistance take. It explores the link between management's control strategies and their attitudes towards unions and, finally, identifies several factors influencing management's stance towards unions which will further improves Quality of Work Life.
- *Cascio, W.F. (2003)*: Emphasized on how do one cope with stress in the workplace to achieve a more

balanced lifestyle? Stress is a part of everybody's life. Depending on the level of stress, it can control our lives, especially in the workplace. If one can control over stress then there is assured good quality of work life and success.

- *Zeffane, R. et al (2003)*: Seeks to determine whether and how the quality of working life (QWL) varies between call centres (CCs) in the in-house/ outsourced, public and private sectors and the implications of these findings on human resource management (HRM).
- *Australian Communications Association (2004)*: Implies that the call centre sector in particular has risen to the forefront of discussions about job quality because of the rapid growth and development of these new forms of work organization over the past two decades. However, despite there being an extensive quality of work life literature, and emerging research on call centre job quality, there is yet to be a study that systematically links the quality of work with employment in the call centre context.
- *Burgess, J. et al (2004)*: Describes that Call centre work, however, falls within a spectrum of service jobs requiring simultaneous and multifaceted work with people, information and technology, This activity, which is called as `articulation work', is often performed within tight timeframes and requires workers, first, to integrate their own tasks into an ongoing `line' of work, and second, to collaborate in maintaining the overall work-flow.
- *Connell, J. et al (2004)*: Describes public-sector Call Centres emerges as being inferior in terms of job content, working hours and managerial/supervisory style and strategies. Conversely, Sales plus features a management model that is more akin to what would be expected in a Call Center operating under a professional service model.
- *(Meneze, 2005)*: Implies that due to low quality of

work life, work force suffers from Job stress which is considered rising and has become challenge for the employer and because high level stress is results in low productivity, increased absenteeism and collection to other employee problems like alcoholism, drug abuse, hypertension and host of cardiovascular problems

- *Weinkopf, C. (2006)*: Described Call centres as'electronic sweatshops' and'slave galleons of the twenty first century' and, contrarily as progressive, team based and career fulfilling work environments. Quality of Work Life is the key to real success.

Thus far, quality of work life has been a traditionally under-researched area where call centres are concerned. The bulk of the call centre literature that touches on job quality has tended to adopt a Marxist labour process approach,where critical analysis has focused on the manifestation of the logic of capitalism in work organisation; the inherent power struggle between employers and workers; and worker response in these respects. Furthermore, much of the existing call centre research has centred primarily on isolated aspects of call centre work including stress, burnout and emotional labour, gender, monitoring and surveillance and team-work.

The present study is an attempt to investigate the quality of work life experienced by the employees of various call centres like and its impact on their efficiency. Lack of quality of work life is costly for employers, reflected in lower productivity, reduced motivation and job skills, and increased accidents. Because employees spend roughly one third of their lives working in an organizational goal setting, employee mental health is of particular importance which can be brought with the help of quality of work life.

RESEARCH HYPOTHESIS

- Do Call Centres provide their employees with accommodation Facility?
- Are the employees getting timely incentives?
- Do call centres have lengthy working hours?

- Do they suffer from physical or psychological problems like stress due to lengthy working hours?
- Are the employees satisfied with all the facilities they are getting?
- Whether the employees are well aware regarding all the facilities they are getting or not?
- Do the call center employees satisfied with their job?
- Are they able to maintain proper balance between their personal and professional life?
- Are they satisfied with the Quality of Work Life they are getting?

RESEARCH METHODOLOGY

The word research refers to finding the truth about something through a systematic study.

Research may be done to:

- Gain familiarity with a phenomenon or to achieve new insights into it.
- Portray accurately the characteristics of the particular individual, situation or a group.
- Determination the frequency with which phenomenon occurs or with which it is associated with another.
- Test a hypothesis of a casual relationship between variables.

Index